Dance and Dancers in the Victorian
and Edwardian Music Hall Ballet

For Simon

Dance and Dancers in the Victorian and Edwardian Music Hall Ballet

ALEXANDRA CARTER

LONDON AND NEW YORK

First published 2005 by Ashgate Publishing

Reissued 2018 by Routledge
2 Park Square, Milton Park, Abingdon, Oxon OX14 4RN
711 Third Avenue, New York, NY 10017, USA

Routledge is an imprint of the Taylor & Francis Group, an informa business

First issued in paperback 2018

© Alexandra Carter 2005

Alexandra Carter has asserted her moral right under the Copyright, Designs and Patents Act, 1988, to be identified as the author of this work.

All rights reserved. No part of this book may be reprinted or reproduced or utilised in any form or by any electronic, mechanical, or other means, now known or hereafter invented, including photocopying and recording, or in any information storage or retrieval system, without permission in writing from the publishers.

A Library of Congress record exists under LC control number: 2004025745

Notice:
Product or corporate names may be trademarks or registered trademarks, and are used only for identification and explanation without intent to infringe.

Publisher's Note
The publisher has gone to great lengths to ensure the quality of this reprint but points out that some imperfections in the original copies may be apparent.

Disclaimer
The publisher has made every effort to trace copyright holders and welcomes correspondence from those they have been unable to contact.

ISBN 13: 978-0-815-34627-2 (hbk)
ISBN 13: 978-1-138-61868-8 (pbk)
ISBN 13: 978-1-351-16364-4 (ebk)

Contents

List of Illustrations	vi
General Editor's Series Preface	vii
Preface	viii
Prologue	1
1. In Fit and Seemly Luxury: Ballet at the Alhambra and the Empire	7
The British music hall	8
Ballet at the Alhambra and the Empire	14
Promenades and the public: the moral context of the ballet	24
2. From the Principals to the *Passées*: Performers in the Music Hall Ballets	29
The hierarchical tradition	30
Training for the music hall ballet	38
The working conditions of the dancers	41
3. Dancing the Feminine: Gender and Sexuality on Stage	49
Utterly and obviously feminine: the *en travestie* performer	63
4. A Fairyland of Fair Women: Dancing the Narratives of the Age	81
5. Images and Imagination: Poetry, Fiction and the Eye of the Writer	95
6. Prejudicial to Public Morality: The Moral Image of the Dance and Dancer	107
The psyche of the era	121
7. Cara's Tale	129
Epilogue	137
Appendices	147
I Ballets at the Alhambra 1884-1912: artistic collaborators	150
II Ballets at the Empire 1884-1915: artistic collaborators	153
III Ballets at the Alhambra 1884-1912: subject matter	157
IV Ballets at the Empire 1884-1915: subject matter	160
Bibliography	163
Index	171

List of Illustrations

1. The Empire promenade, 1902 — 72
2. 'An undress rehearsal at the Alhambra', with Carlo Coppi — 73
3. 'The incomparable Lydia Kyasht' — 74
4. '*Titania*, the New Ballet at the Alhambra: A Group of Coryphées' — 75
5. Programme cover, the Alhambra 1896 — 76
6. Back programme cover, the Alhambra 1896 — 77
7. Programme cover, the Alhambra 1893 — 78
8. '*Titania*, The New Ballet at the Alhambra: Attendants on Hippolyta' — 79

General Editor's Series Preface

Music in nineteenth-century Britain has been studied as a topic of musicology for over two hundred years. It was explored widely in the nineteenth century itself, and in the twentieth century grew into research with strong methodological and theoretical import. Today, the topic has burgeoned into a broad, yet incisive, cultural study with critical potential for scholars in a wide range of disciplines. Indeed, it is largely because of its interdisciplinary qualities that music in nineteenth-century Britain has become such a prominent part of the modern musicological landscape.

This series aims to explore the wealth of music and musical culture of Britain in the nineteenth century and surrounding years. It does this by covering an extensive array of music-related topics and situating them within the most up-to-date interpretative frameworks. All books provide relevant contextual background and detailed source investigations, as well as considerable bibliographical material of use for further study. Areas included in the series reflect its widely interdisciplinary aims and, although principally designed for musicologists, the series is also intended to be accessible to scholars working outside of music, in areas such as history; literature; science; philosophy; poetry and performing arts. Topics include criticism and aesthetics; musical genres; music and the church; music education; composers and performers; analysis; concert venues, promoters and organisations; the reception of foreign music in Britain; instrumental repertoire, manufacture and pedagogy; music hall and dance; gender studies; and music in literature, poetry and letters.

Although the nineteenth century has often been viewed as a fallow period in British musical culture, it is clear from the vast extent of current scholarship that this view is entirely erroneous. Far from being a 'land without music', nineteenth-century Britain abounded with musical activity. All society was affected by it, and everyone in that society recognised its importance in some way or other. It remains for us today to trace the significance of music and musical culture in that period, and to bring it alive for scholars to study and interpret. This is the principal aim of the Music in Nineteenth-Century Britain series - to advance scholarship in the area and expand our understanding of its importance in the wider cultural context of the time.

Dr Bennett Zon
University of Durham, UK

Preface

The only other book that exists on this period of dance history is Ivor Guest's *Ballet in Leicester Square* (1992), an amalgam of two previous monographs, *The Alhambra ballet* (1959) and *The Empire ballet* (1962). I am indebted to Guest for inspiring my own interest in the period; those who are similarly attracted will find, in his text, richly descriptive accounts of the ballets, including some detailed scenarios which give a flavour of the works. Guest also provides accounts of the principal dancers and useful appendices on their appearances in the venues.

This text does not attempt to replicate Guest. Here, my concern is to place the ballets within the social context of Victorian and Edwardian London and to explore their relationship to the dominant beliefs and value systems of sexuality and morality. To this end, I am concerned with how the image of the dancer was constructed by the ballets, by primary and secondary sources, and by the dancers themselves. I also wish to place the period within the web of British dance history by claiming its significance not only in its time, but also for its contribution to the development of ballet in the twentieth century.

This text also differs from Guest in its concern with the status, background and working lives of the ballet girls. Missing from history, it is their story I wish to share.

Prologue

When Lottie Collins roared her song 'Ta-ra-ra-boom-de-ay' at the audiences of the late Victorian music hall, she punctuated it with back bends, pirouettes and notorious high kicks which hit the 'boom' of the refrain. Like many before her, Collins was aware of the enhanced entertainment value of combining song and dance.[1] Some performers in the halls just danced, offering attractions such as clog, step, skirt or Serpentine dancing. Salome danced, courtesy of Maud Allan, across the European halls and London's Alhambra palace of varieties parodied her performance in *Sal! Oh! My!* (1908). In the music hall and variety bills of Britain and Europe, in the vaudeville of America, wherever there was entertainment outside of the legitimate theatre, dance was a key component. Some forms, like the can-can, remain in public consciousness; some entertainers, such as Josephine Baker, retain their charisma down the ages. The music halls and similar venues also provided a home, for lack of any other, for those who have since acquired a respectable reputation in the history of the art of dance. In the first decade of the twentieth century, Loïe Fuller nurtured her experiments with lighting and costume in Parisian variety; Ruth St. Denis worked in music hall in New York, and the Russian dancers who preceded Diaghilev's Ballets Russes presented the art of ballet in the larger halls of London. The halls, the variety stage and vaudeville all presented popular entertainment which, in its diversity, its non-reliance on the spoken word, the brevity of its acts and the opportunities it offered for solo performance, was ideally suited to dance. Yet so much of the history of that dance has gone unrecorded. Dance historians, concerned with sustaining the respectability of the art, have tended to focus on its heritage from Imperial Russia and France; writers on theatre and popular entertainment perhaps have not felt equipped to tackle such a seemingly specialist activity as dance.[2] This falling between the gaps of history is nowhere more apparent than in the case of ballet in Britain's music hall.

Most historiography which traces the history of ballet in Britain in the nineteenth century delights in recording the period of the 1830s and 1840s, to which the term the Romantic era is ascribed. Reflecting, albeit a little belatedly, the Romantic dichotomies between flesh and spirit; human and supernatural; love and death; culture and nature, works such as *La Sylphide* (1832) and *Giselle* (1841) are still in repertoire today, in narrative and general choreographic design if not in 'original' choreographic form. The presence of ballet was sustained on the stages of respectable theatres such as the King's Theatre (later Her Majesty's) in London until the late 1850s, when the fashion for opera overtook ballet. Its history from the 1850s to 1880s is still shadowy but it is safe to say that, whilst retaining a place in opera productions, ballet as a discrete form lost favour. It did not disappear, however, but was sustained within the context of popular entertainment. Here, it reached an apogee of privileged programming and popularity on the stages of two of the large music halls in London's Leicester Square. Between 1884 and 1915 at least one, usually two and sometimes three ballets were presented nightly at the Alhambra and Empire.[3] A total of one hundred and forty one new works were produced. Although sandwiched between other acts, they were the main attraction on the programmes.

During this period, the ballet employed thousands of people. Although some works comprised small casts (even solo and duet work), the emphasis was on spectacle, largely achieved by the deployment of a *corps de ballet* of between one and two hundred performers. It played to packed houses nightly and was a vital part of London's entertainment scene. Its management was entirely male, but its executants were largely women. As such, not only has the period disappeared from dance history but so too have the working lives and achievements of thousands of women.

This book aims to redress this gap in dance and social history by identifying the importance of dance in general, and ballet in particular, as a cultural activity in which the body of the dancer and the symbolic constructs of the dance both produce and reflect the concerns - and the spirit - of the age. As Shires (1992: xi) claims,

> we need to examine Victorian culture through analysis of institutions and through close attention to symbolic forms and representations ... the public reception and manipulation of symbols, most of us would agree, is as important to social relations as the formulation of public policy.

Furthermore, whilst exploring the specificity of the work in relation to its age, the ballet of the late Victorian and Edwardian period is returned to the history of performance, and the contribution of the marginalised performers of that history, the 'unsung many' (Hutcheon 1989: 66), is privileged, for it is they who captured the artistic imagination of the period.

The book is structured as follows. The context of the British music hall is set briefly by outlining its history and comparing the nature of its entertainment with that of its European and American counterparts. Although the cultural context of the Victorian and Edwardian age will be woven throughout the book, the general relationship of the music hall to its age will be specifically identified. The focus will then turn to the ballets at the Alhambra and the Empire, not simply as case studies but because these venues were famed, first and foremost, for their ballet productions and for the moral controversies which arose from activity in their auditoria and on stage. The management of the venues, the artistic creators of the works and the audiences are characterised. So, too, are the performers, with an emphasis on their working lives off stage (an under-researched field) as well as their appearance on stage. The ballets themselves are explored, both through a description of their constituent parts and, significantly, for their relevance to the historical period. It is in the production and reception of these works that the thrust of this book resides. Produced under the auspices of a male management, playing to not solely but largely male audiences and, most significantly, recorded through the perceptions of male writers, poets and artists, it is argued that the ballets and their executants dance out the sexual psyche of the age. The moral image of the dancer, ascribed to her by others, is set against her own self image, and dancers' voices are used where possible to resist the notion that the body is passive, that sexuality is not just ascribed, but experienced. Penultimately, resisting the weight of traditional historiography, a dancer - not a star, but one of the *corps de ballet* - talks back.

Although claiming the importance of the ballet in its specific time and place, and justifying this history mainly on those grounds rather than for its overt contribution to a heritage, I cannot resist challenging the historical lineage of British ballet as traditionally recorded. I conclude, therefore, with an Epilogue which traces that lineage and, by doing so, disrupts conventional notions that 'British' ballet was 'born' with the efforts of Ninette de Valois and Marie Rambert in the 1930s. This book concludes with the claim that the recorded history of British ballet is flawed; that it is one based on value, on artistic standards, rather than on the prevalence and popularity of the activity itself.

Critical strategies

Any attempt to revisit history is necessarily coloured by the consciousness of the present day. That consciousness is formed by questions, debates and points of view which contribute to and feed upon the dominant theoretical perspectives of the time when research is undertaken, and written. This investigation is informed not by one critical perspective or disciplinary stance, but several intersecting fields of knowledge and a range of critical strategies. Debates about historiography and the role of the historian are implicit, but central. As claims are made about the cultural impact of ballet in a specific time and place, the reader may need to be persuaded about the links between dance and society. Furthermore, as a study of the artistic and cultural representations of women in the ballets, critical thinking about how dance embodies gender and sexuality is also key to the task of interpreting this history.

It is now axiomatic that the role of the historian is not one of retrieving facts, but is an interpretative act which requires imagination, inference and speculation. As Husbands (1996: 59) claims, if 'the argument is that the understanding of the past is itself a creative act which can be rendered differently by historians, novelists and poets', then 'the place of the imagination in the construction of historical accounts becomes central.' Nevertheless, historiography is not an arbitrary act, but one based on thorough research of the evidence of the past. As none of the ballets of the period are extant, the evidence is dependent on primary sources which record the productions of the ballets as written by their creators (and occasionally, executants) and those who received the ballet such as journalists, critics, poets, biographers and social commentators. This evidence is not, of course, a way of gaining 'second hand' access to the works themselves, for the meanings of these works, like all cultural activity, are ascribed to them and do not pre-exist either the interpretation of the time, or the interpretation of the historian. The historian, by giving form and shape to selected evidence, imposes a narrative structure on that evidence - a beginning, middle and end. When the evidence is not available, such as that which describes the subjective experience of the actor on the historical stage or, in our case, the dancer on the ballet stage, then the historian's imagination becomes even more active. In Chapter 7 the imagined voice of the dancer offers an alternative interpretation of the evidence in all the preceding chapters which comprise the conventional source material of history. Cara Tranders' testimony is rooted in this source material, and her recorded experience hovers on the cusp of history and fiction; of history as a creative act, of imagined phenomenology.[4] Such a strategy allows for the minor characters of history to be acknowledged as makers of their own meaning of their own experience. It also recognises that the interplay between institutions and individuals, between the structures of society and the agency of the subject, embraces not just the famous, not just the named, but everyone.[5]

In discourse on cultural representation the focus has tended to be on arts such as literature, theatre, music, film and the visual arts. Dance, in its social and theatre forms, tends to be absent and its contribution to the cultural life of society is neglected. Furthermore, as suggested, even in the histories of British theatre dance the period from the mid-nineteenth century to the early twentieth is also almost ignored. Dance writers have preferred to overlook what was described as a 'lamentable fall' (Haskell 1938: 30) in the artistic standards of the period. And yet, whatever the retrospective judgment of these standards (for it was certainly not the judgment of the time), and whether deemed popular entertainment or 'art', this historically specific dance practice was a vital part of London's popular culture. By exploring the institution of the music hall and the works presented there, the music hall ballet can be seen as embodying dominant ideological concerns of the age. In undertaking such an exposure, however, I am wary of offering a reductive account, for the ideologies of any period are diverse and contested both in their time and after. Shires (1992: 185) warns of the dangers of accepting the fixity of Victorian ideologies, arguing that 'the instability of any ideology in the period and even more radical instability of Victorian representations must count as a defining characteristics of the age'. Notwithstanding, whilst wary of 'Victorian' and 'Edwardian' archetypes, there are trends in the beliefs and customs of a particular age which become reified in the public domain. Generalisations they may be, but it is difficult, if not impossible, to proceed without them. What is offered here, therefore, is an example of the symbiotic relationship between dance and culture, revealed in the on-stage embodiment of ideologies of gender and sexuality.

One of the ideological constructs which appears to be so key to the age was the binary opposition ascribed to women's sexuality and, by overt association, their status. They were either the angel in the house or the whore in the street; the lily or the rose; the Madonna or the Magdalene. Close examination of the ballets and the images of their executants reveals how they were imbued with these oppositional images. And yet our post-feminist thinking warns us to be wary of these binaries, for they are categories that are monolithic and exclusive. When ascribed to the gendered constructs such as those above, this is undoubtedly the case, for these categories solidify sexuality and leave out all kinds of diverse personal identities. Furthermore, all research is imbued with a particular critical framework and the results of the research will bear its imprint; if looking for binaries, they will be found. When I commenced this research I had no such gender perspective in mind;

my project was, initially, a historical one centred on the ballets. It became more and more evident, however, that the performers in the ballets were symbols, on and off stage, of public sexual categories that were not new to the Victorian age but high in its consciousness. In identifying these categories: the untouchable and chaste ballerina; the accessible and immoral ballet girl and, in the case of the *en travestie* performer, the not-quite-sure, my intention is not to disguise the diversity of actual sexuality but to expose the contribution of ballet in the music halls to the public construction of women's sexuality and moral image. Central to this exposure is the tension described in Compton Mackenzie's novel (1929) between the public identity of the dancer as she appeared on stage, 'over the footlights' and her private self, in the street outside, 'under the moon' of London's night skies.

NOTES

1. See Koritz (1990) for a dance analysis of Collins' act.
2. The ballet writers of the 1930s-1960s were, in the main, initially responsible for the neglect of this period, though few of them had first hand experience of the actual performances. Haskell (1934: 188) speculates 'I imagine that the Empire ballet was choreographically, musically and artistically negligible' whilst Beaumont (1940: 3) was more fascinated by the promenade than by the stage performance. Lynham (1947) gives some attention to the period but focuses on the composers rather than the choreographers. Lawson (1964) makes a brief reference; Reyna (1964) and Kraus (1969) each give the period one sentence and Kirstein (1971) makes no acknowledgement at all. Clarke and Crisp (1978: 89) make the erroneous statement that it was Diaghilev who gave ballet 'to the people at large'; Sorell (1981) discuss the 'gay' nineties, Loïe Fuller and dance at the Moulin Rouge but ignores the vast amount of activity on the London stage.

    The theatre historian Short (1951) has a chapter on the palaces of varieties and acknowledges that the Alhambra and Empire were primarily renowned for ballet, but passes over these in a sentence or two. Leslie (1978) comments on an Alhambra programme cover of the *corps de ballet* that this image 'proves that the chorus line had arrived in Britain'. Such a mistaken nomenclature would have infuriated the ballet dancers. Most texts on the music hall ignore ballet completely, even in the face of evidence in their own books. For example, Kift (1996) acknowledges dance and ballet in her text and there is a skirt dancer on the book cover, but despite her claim that she will look at the hall programmes as a whole, she overlooks dance except for one brief paragraph about ballet in a regional music hall.
3. There is, as identified in Ch. 1, a distinction between the different kinds of music hall, their programmes and their clientele. Whilst the Alhambra and the Empire, like other larger venues, were each known by the more prestigious title of 'palace of varieties' the common perception of the period and later historiography includes them within the generic realm of 'music hall'.
4. Tranders' account is also an intertextual one, for she moved in the world of Compton Mackenzie's *Carnival* and *Figure of Eight*, and George Gissing's *The Odd Women*.
5. See Tomko in Carter (2004) for a discussion of these historiographic tensions in relation to dance history.

CHAPTER ONE

In Fit and Seemly Luxury: Ballet at the Alhambra and the Empire

The term 'music hall' is a generic one used to describe both the venues and the type of programme presented therein. This programme can be characterised as that which, in social class terms, grew from 'the bottom up'; that which, over the history of the halls from the mid-nineteenth century to the early twentieth, embraced diverse, unrelated acts such as song, dance, comedy sketches, music, acrobatics, animal acts and, in the larger venues, more spectacular treats such as trapeze and *tableaux vivants*. These were all linked by a master of ceremonies who managed the order of the acts as well as inciting, and keeping in check, the audience. The acts embraced almost anything, in fact, that was not legitimate theatre, though performers did cross from one to the other.[1] Evolving from entertainment by and for the people, its main characteristic, argues Leslie (1978: 14) was 'the interaction between artists and audience which was peculiar to them and their time'. This notion of peculiarity to time and place is key. Though the halls in different cultural locations may have had similar precursors, they catered for the indigenous tastes of their location. To take the French halls as an example, they developed from the *boîte*, the *bal musette* and the *guingette* - similar to the British taverns, dancing saloons and pleasure gardens. Although modelled on the British music hall (the Folies Bergère was based on Leicester Square's Alhambra), there was a more political, satiric edge to their acts. From the 1900s, the French (or rather Parisian) halls focussed on spectacle and revue, thus departing from the traditional programmes by separating the lived experience of the audience from the erotic and exotic fantasies on the stage. American vaudeville (possibly a corruption of *voix de ville*: 'voices of the town') was similar in its component acts but there were significant differences in the tastes of the public. Two of these key differences were, first, that vaudeville had a cleaner, more respectable flavour compared with the vulgarity of the British halls (even though, being the Victorian era, that vulgarity was disguised in the central performance strategies of its songs, repartee and body language - innuendo and *double entendre*). Second, the vaudeville acts were more detached from the experiences of the audience; there was not the same sense of complicity, of shared toils and tribulations, of parody of the habits of the middle and upper classes which only the class conscious British could produce. Neither did vaudeville attract the literary and artistic milieu, those who flirted with the sensations of the *fin de siècle* which the larger halls of Britain and north western Europe presented in abundance.

It would be erroneous to trace a linear development of the halls in any given location, for their development is a web of intersecting and culturally specific influences. If commonalities can be discerned, however, they would cohere around the expansion of entertainment from that offered by the working class to their own class, with a commonality of interest (assumed or otherwise), to an increasingly theatricalised and commercialised profession. Performers were separated from audiences, both in spatial terms and then with stage curtains; attention was paid to costume and lighting and there evolved a professional hierarchy of performers. Most significantly, from free entertainment within a small community, entry charges were introduced and the music hall became big business.

The British music hall

Although the above commonalities can be traced across different national forms of popular entertainment, the concern here is with the distinctly British phenomenon of music hall. Its history is well documented and reveals a diversity of size, programmes, clientele and atmosphere.[2] A key thread in their history can be traced back to the 1830s and 1840s; to the all-male song and supper rooms and amateur entertainment offered in public houses (or taverns). Enterprising publicans or 'caterers' began to formally manage and present this entertainment, thus distinguishing the start of the halls. Charles Moreton is credited with the opening of the most famous of the early halls which he built in 1852 adjacent to his public house, the Canterbury Arms in London. Moreton not only encouraged the attendance of women, but also funded the entertainment on offer by charging for a refreshment ticket, a system adopted by many of the burgeoning halls in London and in provincial cities. The sale of drink was therefore inextricably connected to the provision of entertainment, a connection which was largely responsible for the disreputable status of the music hall throughout the remainder of its history.[3] The halls developed apace, varying in size and atmosphere from the intimate concert rooms in the local tavern to large, purpose built or converted venues. From 1878, however, changes in safety laws for places of public entertainment, such as the statutory requirement for safety curtains and adequate exits, led to a decline in traditional venues and also in the spontaneity and informality nurtured by more basic facilities. A new class of entrepreneur evolved and both producers and performers drew apart from the social class whose experiences they appropriated but no longer shared. As Stuart and Park (1895: 190) observe,

> The opening of the new Pavilion in 1884 may be said to have inaugurated a fresh area in music hall history. It marked the final and complete severance of the variety stage from its old associations of the tavern and the concert salon ... hitherto the halls had borne unmistakable evidence of their origin, but the last vestiges of their old connections were now thrown aside, and they emerged in all the splendour of their new born glory.

This seemingly linear development was particular to London, however, for the regional halls did not suffer the constraints of competition and retained their special characteristics far longer.

By 1890 Anstey (p.190) was able to distinguish four types of London music hall as:

> the aristocratic variety theatres of the West End ... the smaller and less aristocratic West End halls ... the larger bourgeois halls of the less fashionable parts of London ... (and) ... the minor music halls of the poor and squalid districts.

By the outbreak of the First World War music hall in its conventional form had declined and by the Second World War even the variety theatres had lost to the competition of cinema and broadcasting.

Throughout the history of the British halls, programmes were diverse but there was an emphasis on song interspersed with dialogue.[4] Many artists adopted songs which become their trademark and these, together with a distinct use of spoken and body language, comprised the artists' stage identities or 'characters'. Some halls ran two shows a night, others a continuous evening of acts; a programme from the Tivoli in London, 1892, lists twenty eight different 'turns' (Disher 1938: 23). Whilst rooted in the lower strata of a highly inequitable class system, working class music hall was far from radical. The upper classes, or 'toffs' were depicted with fondness rather than resentment. In songs, character roles and in the topical ballets (see Ch. 4) the social classes were juxtaposed but the hierarchy was never questioned.

The rapid expansion of music hall gave rise to opportunities for a large number of amateur performers to achieve fame. A circuit of established artists developed and the new ease and speed of transport enabled the more popular ones to perform at several venues on the same night and also to tour the provinces, thus becoming national stars. Whilst actresses in legitimate theatre were fighting for recognition and status with actors (see, for example, Holledge 1981; Davis 1991) women, from the 1880s, had a well established and frequently starring role in music hall. Performers such as Marie Lloyd, Vesta Tilley, Jennie Hill and Lottie Collins became household names; music hall was a rare outlet for women to make public their creative talents and lead independent lives. Part of their acceptability, however, was their distancing from the audience by costume and stage persona. Stage clothes were exotic or ornate, bearing little resemblance to the working class apparel of the time. Women performers were often girlish or ingénue or, the ultimate in distancing, cross-dressed.

The popularity of the halls is indicated by the words of a song which included the lines:

> And I'd bring her to see the music halls
> Every Saturday night
> Pearsall 1983: 74

Although these lyrics are undated, they signal not only the frequency of attendance but also the fact that audiences were of mixed sex. In the halls of the industrial north of England, women would attend unaccompanied without detriment to their reputation, for it was recognised that the large number of female factory workers were entitled to leisure. In the differently constituted demography of London, however, it was more challenging for a woman to attend a place of entertainment alone without being viewed with suspicion. The high population of prostitutes on public display compounded this suspicion. Although it is impossible to ascertain accurate statistical data for the number of people who attended the halls, the rapid expansion in the number of venues; their increased seating capacity; their significance in popular folklore; the attention given to them in the popular press and contemporary testimony such as the above song, all bear witness to their popularity. Even those who would never have contemplated the idea of setting foot in a hall, such as Rose Macaulay's highly respectable, staid and staunchly middle class fictional Grandpapa, were aware of their product: 'Grandpapa was more stirred ... by the alarming increase of female bicyclists and by the prevalent nuisance of that popular song, 'Ta-ra-ra-boomdeay' (Macaulay [1923] 1986: 111).

The halls undoubtedly reached the peak of their popularity in the final decades of the nineteenth century. In order to see how the spirit of the *fin de siècle* (a French term, but one which resonates with the spirit of the 1880s and 1890s in Britain), it is to the cultural context of the age that I now turn.

The vibrations of life: the music hall and the fin de siècle

History does not, of course, separate itself into distinct decades; it is historians who achieve this by ascribing common phenomena to a period, albeit rather loosely. (For example, the Swingin' 'Sixties of the twentieth century actually happened in the 1970s.) Nevertheless, the end of the nineteenth century does appear to be a particular kind of age, the specificity of which lies in contrast to the preceding decades. Houghton, in his key text *The Victorian frame of mind* (1957) frames his investigation within the years 1830 - 1870, stopping when Queen Victoria herself had thirty more years to reign. His rationale for defining Victorianism thus is that

> After 1870, while many of the characteristics persist through the century ... their dominance and their peculiar coherence were breaking down. Victorianism was dying, and a new frame of mind was emerging, a *late* Victorian frame of mind, which pointed forward to the postwar temper of the 1920's.
>
> 1957: xv

It is this late Victorian 'frame of mind' with which we are concerned here. Queen Victoria had reigned since 1837 and although she had become more of a recluse than an active monarch her Golden (1887) and Diamond (1897) Jubilees were celebrated with due recognition for all the 'achievements' of her reign. There was a resurgence of her popularity - a phenomenon also seen with Queen Elizabeth II's Jubilees. Industrial development at home and colonisation abroad had made Britain a tremendously powerful nation, not only in economic and military terms but also through the dissemination of religious tenets and social systems. There was a sense of the old passing and the new beginning or, as Wilson, using the metaphor of advances in the photographic image, looking at the 1880s is 'both like watching the modern world beginning to rouse and like intruding into a world about to evaporate' (2002: 437). As Darwinism had exposed fundamental flaws in traditional notions of man's relationship with God and the research of social reformers such as Rowntree and Booth brought into question man's relationship with man (women were not considered to have had much of a relationship with anyone, except their families), religious, political and social ideologies began to crumble. The Boer War of 1899-1902 dented the nation's confidence and complacency was further disrupted by the psychological significance of the end of a millennium, the death of Queen Victoria in 1901 and the accession at long last of her son Edward VII.

The late Victorian and Edwardian age emerges as a time of tremendous change in beliefs, values and customs. The fact that the heyday of the music hall embraces this period from the 1880s to the outbreak of the First World War is no coincidence. For the working classes, there was an increase in leisure time and disposable income. Many of the aristocracy, freed from the constraints of mid-Victorian court life, made a pastime of pleasure. Those who had become wealthy through trade and commerce comprised a new plutocracy. For a golden sovereign, a man could 'dine well wherever he pleased and after his wine and cigar would still have enough to pass him in to the Empire or the Alhambra, or drive him to his club' (Booth, J.B. 1929: 22). (As discussed in Ch. 2 a 'golden sovereign', or approximately one old British pound sterling, would have been the weekly wage of a ballet girl.)

The relaxation of repressive social customs was manifest in the 'gay 'nineties'. Life was far from 'gay' for the masses and there was still appalling poverty, but the period did seem to represent a nation letting out its breath, having held it for so long. J. B. Booth, who took an active part in London life, chronicles it with fondness.

> The nineteenth century closed in national prosperity and its last decade had been one of fierce interest in literature, in art, in the theatre and in life. Life was extraordinarily vivid, it had a gusto, a savour; there was an intense craving for the new.
>
> 1929: 28

Paradoxically, serious theatre and music were at a low ebb, but there was plenty of music, song and drama of a kind being created in the music halls. It was 'the creative vitality of the music hall, in comparison with the legitimate theatre, which was its attraction' (Felsteiner in Green, ed. 1986: 47). Sorell (1981: 302) makes a similar observation:

> It was at the Alhambra in London or smaller dance halls in Vienna where ... the intellectual elite could find the fascination and vibrations of life that the commercial theatre did not offer.

It is within this context of moribund traditional art forms that Perugini could make the claim that the ballet in the music halls was 'among the few vital forms of art during the later years of the nineteenth and earlier years of the twentieth century' (1946: 261). Flitch (1912: 91) encapsulates the ambiance of the time and its manifestation in the dance. As the century came to a close,

> the older formal and unhasting rhythms tended to break up; the pace quickened; the tranquillity which the nineteenth century had carried over from the eighteenth had disappeared in the excitement of the *fin de siècle* spirit. Something of the change of the social spirit was reflected in the dance.

Ballet: a disappearing act

Dance, both as part of song or comedy routine and as an act in its own right, was a vital part of music hall programmes. Venues had to apply for a special licence for dancing, whether it was participatory by the public (a tradition from the older dancing saloons) or on stage. These licences might not be renewed if the local authorities were concerned about any perceived indecency in the performance, as was the case with the Empire in the mid-1880s (see Ch. 6). It is not always possible to discern exactly what kinds of dance were presented as artists were often billed, for example, as 'serio-comic and dancer'. Clog or step dancing, which derived from working class family tradition and was performed mainly by men, was often a feature. Other discernible forms included jigs and hornpipes, and later women engaged with Serpentine or skirt dancing. From the 1890s, John Tiller's girls presented precision dancing, particularly in northern venues before their popularity spread. As Barker (1987) suggests, despite the artistic aspirations of some acts, the music hall did not nurture the development of dance as an art, though this is no reason to ignore its significance in contemporary culture. It did, she argues, sustain male folk dancing and preserved both performing talent and audience taste for dance.

In western Europe, the art form of ballet had reached a height of popularity during the Romantic period of the 1830s and 1840s. In London, Jules Perrot produced a series of ballets and *divertissements* for Her Majesty's Theatre and all the renowned Romantic ballerinas performed in the city. Two revolutions, the French and the Industrial, had precipitated the change in subject matter of the ballets from mythology and allegory to more direct representations of humankind and human dilemmas. Changes in fashion enabled dancers to wear less restrictive costumes (see Chazin-Bennahum in Carter 2004) and this, in conjunction with technical developments such a *pointe* work and turnout, facilitated more mobility and an increasingly fleet style. Ballets tended either to reflect the developing interest in other countries and other peoples by offering 'national' dances which were more evocative of style than accurate of step, or they presented as metaphor the psyche of the artistic elite of a generation fascinated by its own soul and its own restless spirit. These ballets, now synonymous with the Romantic era, presented the natural and the supernatural; reality and dream; the commonplace and the ideal. The roles of women in the ballets included the stereotypes of the 'girl next door', the spirit/seductress and the malevolent avenger.[5] Off-stage, dancers were perceived with similar ambivalence and the ballet itself was regarded as both a high art form peopled by stars of impeccable virtue and a rather dubious activity for young women searching for a wealthy patron. This moral legacy, coloured by the concerns of the later part of the century, forms the focus of attention in Ch. 6.

By the 1850s, Victorian sensibilities, which reflected the attitudes of the Christian church in its suspicion of anything relating to human bodies and sexuality, shunned the ballet in favour of opera, and it disappeared as a discrete performance from the stages of Her Majesty's and Covent Garden. The epicentres of ballet moved to Denmark and Russia. Marius Petipa, a Frenchman, became ballet master at the Imperial theatres in Russia from 1862-1903 where he mounted works which had topical events as their subject matter and comprised sections of classical *divertissements*, *tableaux*, mime and folk dance. In their general subject matter, style and spectacle the ballets of Petipa were not dissimilar from those being presented concurrently in the British music halls.

Despite losing its place in British theatres from the mid nineteenth century onwards, the ballet was not completely lost to sight. A playbill of 1843 includes two dance acts, a hornpipe and a 'ballet of action' (Barker 1987: 33). Because performing spaces were small, these 'ballets of action' comprised a small cast of characters and tended to be mixed component performances rather than 'ballets' as we conceive them today. Nevertheless, as a description of a duet in a small hall in Bristol in 1866 suggests, the dance technique, though rudimentary, retained the basics of the classical school of ballet. The fact that in 1860 one Alfred Vance was offering burlesques of classical dancers such as Taglioni meant that she, and ballet itself, was still in public consciousness. A poster for the Prince of Wales venue in Birmingham in 1863 notifies the public that 'the performance to conclude each evening with a ballet divertissement, arr. by Miss Jenny White'. This starred the said Jenny White and 'ladies of the *corps de ballet*' (Theatre Museum, London). In 1866 Joseph Hansen advertised a *corps de ballet* in the Yorkshire Post, and advertisements for the People's Music Hall in Manchester in the mid 1870s feature ballet companies (Kift 1996: 59).

If the smaller halls presented the small-scale acts, ballet found a more privileged home, from the mid-nineteenth century onwards, on the stages of larger halls and variety theatres. Here, it was a significant component of that form of entertainment so loved by the Victorians - spectacle. Spectacle was especially manifest in pantomime and it was in this context that the larger scale ballet regained its popularity. Again, the term is used accurately but differently from today's usage, for the ballet provided large casts of women who were drilled in unison movement. Spectacle in pantomime 'was directed to the end of fantasy, a fantasy excessively pretty and ideally beautiful ... employing mass, colour and light for non-realistic purposes' (Booth, M.R. 1981: 60). Spectacle was also a feature of theatre and melodrama; that is, for more 'realistic' purposes.

From the 1880s the ballet re-emerged not just as a constituent part of musical spectacle or pantomime, but also as a fully-fledged act in its own right. It was in what Anstey characterised as the 'aristocratic variety theatres of the West End', most specifically the Alhambra and Empire palaces of varieties in Leicester Square, that the ballet recaptured the public imagination. But, although its lineage can be traced back to the Romantic period in terms of the training and experience of its key creators and principal performers, and to some extent the subject matter of the works, its public was different, and so too was its production style. Despite producing more works than, say, the Ballets Russes, and playing to far larger audiences over a longer period of time,[6] it is because of the very context of its production in popular entertainment that the ballets in the music halls have almost disappeared from mainstream history.[7] In order to contextualise the work of the executants and the ballets themselves, an account is now offered of the venues, their management and the artistic collaborators. A description then follows of the audiences for the ballet and, most significantly, of the moral context which impacted on the bodies of the performers the diverse ascriptions of sexual morality so specific to the period.

Ballet at the Alhambra and the Empire

The Alhambra, opened as the Royal Panopticon of Science and Art in 1854, was converted to a music hall with a stage and proscenium arch in 1860. When Frederick Strange took over the management in 1864 he announced that 'the Establishment has been adapted to Lyric and Terpsichorean Art' and 'one of the great attractions will be the production, upon a scale of unexampled magnificence, of a Grand Ballet, supported by artists from the chief Theatres (*sic*) at home and abroad' (anon. 1864: 16).

It was these ballets which caused trouble with the licensing authorities after claims that they contained 'pantomimic actions', thus contravening the music and dancing only laws. After a fire destroyed most of the building in 1882, it reopened as the Alhambra Theatre Royal and the following year, having regained its music and dancing licence, it reverted to a music hall. From 1884 onwards the two spectacular ballets which were presented each evening were the prominent attraction: 'the main and distinctive feature of the entertainment is the ballet *divertissement*, for which all else is scarcely more than padding' (Anstey 1890: 191). In total, eighty ballets were presented at the Alhambra between 1884 and 1912. Carlo Coppi, an ex-principal mime from La Scala and experienced ballet arranger, was responsible for nineteen works between 1891 and 1902. His predecessors were Joseph Hansen and Eugenio Casati; on Coppi's retirement Lucia Cormani, Alfredo Curti and Elise Clerc succeeded him. Georges Jacobi, the composer and music arranger who made the most substantial contribution, collaborated on thirty-five consecutive works between 1884 and 1896, plus several before and after that period. Unlike the Empire, which promoted Adeline Genée, the Alhambra never retained a permanent *première danseuse* but presented a variety of principal dancers.

After the first decade of the twentieth century public preference for revue and the growing popularity of the Russian dancers contributed to the decline of indigenous ballet at the Alhambra and its last 'in-house' work was presented in

1912. Its connection with ballet was not severed, however, for a Ballets Russes season was given in 1919 and again in 1921 when Diaghilev presented his production of *The Sleeping Princess* to British audiences. The venue continued to house the ballet sporadically with a highly successful Ballets Russes de Monte Carlo season in 1933, the National Ballet of Lithuania the following year and the René Blum company in 1936. Later that year the theatre closed its doors for the last time and the building was demolished to make way for the Odeon cinema which stands on its site today.

A second Leicester Square venue, the Empire, opened its doors to the public in April 1884 with a production of an operetta, *Chilperic*. Bertrand, an ex-ballet master from the Alhambra, arranged the three ballets incorporated in the operetta. A review of one of these succinctly captures both the production and the journalistic style of the period, describing 'an electric ballet of Amazons ... fifty beautiful ladies, arranged in armour of exquisite design and performing various brilliant evolutions with a precision and grace worthy of the utmost commendation' (anon. 1884a: 11). Reviews such as these were consistent, in style and content, throughout the period.

In 1884 Bertrand mounted productions of *Coppélia* and *Giselle* but without great acclaim; an indication, perhaps, of how public tastes had changed. Having tried these traditional ballets, burlesques, operetta and farce, the venue failed to find a formula for success and, with its applications for a music and dancing licence at first thwarted by the rival Alhambra, a new management team was brought in and from 1887 it reopened as a music hall under the name of the Empire Theatre of Varieties. The opening programme included two ballets, *Dilara* and *The Sports of England*, which presaged the Empire's commitment to ballet and to the presentation of works with traditional and topical themes. Katti Lanner was engaged to arrange these opening works and it was she, one of a creative triumvirate with Leopold Wenzel, the composer and music arranger, and C. Wilhelm, the designer, producer and librettist, who made by far the most substantial contribution to the venue's ballet history.

The Empire's greatest asset, from 1897 to 1907, was the *première danseuse* Adeline Genée. After Genée's retirement, the Empire had the foresight to look to Russia for its next ballerina, Lydia Kyasht. The fact that the management sent an agent to St. Petersburg signified not only their knowledge of the international dance world, but also a sense of their own importance within it.[8] The Empire also nurtured the first English *première danseuse*, Phyllis Bedells, and presented Malvina Cavallazzi, an ex-dancer turned mime, whose dramatic skills dictated the tone of a major part of the repertoire.

Ballet was undoubtedly the main attraction on the Empire programme. *The Era* noted that in comparison with the two ballets presented, 'the variety entertainment seemed to be regarded by the audience ... as subordinate to the spectacular portion of the evening's amusement' (anon. 1887a: 16). Also included in the review was the fact that the rest of the 'evening's amusement' (and typical of the acts on offer in the larger palaces) were a gentleman who imitated other music hall singers, a juggler who incorporated a trapeze-swinging poodle into his act, some aerial gymnasts and a contortionist. Such was the context of the ballet on the music hall programme.

From its first production in 1908, revue became a major part of the programme, eventually outdoing the ballet and variety acts in popularity. The last in-house ballet was presented in 1915; the promenade was finally closed down in 1916 due to concerns about the influence of prostitution on soldiers on leave from the Front (Kift 1996). The Empire maintained its dance connections with seasons by Russian dancers. In 1924, Balanchine appeared in a short *divertissement* and soon afterwards, Massine and Trefilova presented a programme. In 1927 the theatre closed and the building was demolished to make way for a cinema. It was not the end of ballet at the Empire, however, for it featured there in revue in the early 1950s. A different genre concluded the Empire's connection with dance when in 1963 half of the building was converted to the Empire Ballroom.

The makers of the ballets

Biographical information on the choreographers, designers and composers of the ballets is scarce; as the period itself has been written out of history, so too have the people.[9] As Janet Wolff argues, the premise that art is socially constructed does not mean that 'biographical, existential or motivational aspects' need not be taken into account, but that 'practical activity and creativity are in a mutual relation of interdependence with social structure' (1981: 9). In the case of the choreographers, musical directors and composers, designers and librettists of the music hall ballets, the following brief overview of their artistic pedigree does not imply their individual, conscious agency in the construction of the symbolic imagery of the works or in the construction of the dancers' image but further reveals the complex social and artistic structure which comprised the institution of the music hall.

Although I have slipped in to its usage here, the term 'choreographed by' was rarely used in the printed programmes; works were usually 'arranged', 'devised' or 'produced'. This indicates not only a change of terminology which evolved during the twentieth century but also an evolution of the role and status of the choreographer. In the music hall ballets, as in pre-twentieth ballet generally, the principals and solo character dancers would frequently arrange their own dances. The ballet master or mistress arranged the *corps* and small group dances, coordinated the relationships between these and the ballet soloists, and had a variable input into the dances of the latter. Printed programmes did not always clarify who was responsible for which aspects of the choreographic input and even when specific names were given, these could be misleading.[10]

The Alhambra and the Empire employed in-house ballet masters and mistresses who were responsible for all the works presented during their tenure. In total, nine choreographers made works for the Empire, of whom by far the most prolific was Lanner.[11] A renowned dancer and mime who had worked with choreographers such as Paul Taglioni and Bournonville, she was described by Wilson as 'an important figure in English ballet, forming a direct link between the Romantic era and Adeline Genée' (Wilson 1974: 297). Lanner arranged thirty-six ballets for the Empire alone, and her work received consistent critical acclaim.

Lanner's successor at the Empire was Fred Farren, a character and eccentric dancer who had made his career on the London stage.[12] Bedells' (1954: 35-36) description of her own professional relationship with Farren illustrates the nature of his role as arranger of the ballets.

> Farren himself had very little pure ballet technique, but he had a decided flair for making individual dance arrangements and fitting these together into a plan of work. I would plot out my own dances to the music I was given, and take what I had done to him for criticism. He would add a touch of his own here and there and incorporate my material into the whole.

Such an admission is a revealing insight in to how the creative contribution of so many dancers has been hidden behind the name of the ballet master.

Farren is worth mention for the fact that his lack of a ballet background was an exception; most of the other Empire choreographers such as Bertrand, Alexander and Adeline Genée, Kyasht, and Leon and Eduoard Espinoza had their professional training and performance careers in the *danse d'école*. A similar artistic pedigree belonged to the Alhambra ballet arrangers, some seventeen of whom made or contributed to work throughout the period. Most prolific of these was the Italian, Carlo Coppi. Others included his compatriots Casati, Pratesio and Curti. The debt to the Italian school is evident in Perugini's tribute to Curti, who 'studies the art of Ballet ... composition on the traditional lines laid down by the virtual founder of the Milan school, Carlo Blasis' (1946: 233).

A biographical examination of the great majority of the Alhambra and Empire choreographers reveals their shared artistic pedigree and the common denominator of a dance vocabulary based on their training in the Italian *danse d'école*.[13] It would appear that these London venues were a perfectly acceptable part of the international ballet circuit and employment in them did no harm to future careers.[14] Perugini, in a discussion of the importance of dramatic story in ballet, cites the work of, among others, Noverre, Blasis, Perrot, Taglioni, Mme. Lanner, Wilhelm, Curti, Fokine and Massine. In Perugini at least, the music hall choreographers take their place in the most illustrious company.

Both the Alhambra and the Empire employed in-house musical directors whose role was to compose the new music for ballets, to select and arrange existing scores and to rehearse and direct the theatre orchestra (see Appendices I and II). The use of pre-existing scores was not at all unusual in musical theatre or ballet. This, and the composition of 'formula' music comprising a series of social dance pieces such as waltzes, polkas, etc., was one of the traditions against which Fokine rebelled (Fokine 1914). Although the musical directors tended to come from respectable professional backgrounds and were highly regarded within their field, in the eyes of some contemporary observers, their status was not equal to the composers of concert music.[15] Again, the printed programme can mislead, in this case by obscuring the actual music used. For example, Georges Jacobi is credited with the music for *Don Juan* (Alhambra 1892) but an account of a rehearsal for this ballet mentions how he 'makes a mixture of Mozart and himself trickle from his melodious fingers' (Mayhew, A. 1892: 62).

Jacobi was the most prolific composer/arranger for the Alhambra (see Sorley Walker 1947) and Leopold Wenzel was for the Empire. As would be expected in the light of career opportunities for women, all of the musical input was made by men, with the exception of Dora Bright who created several works at the Empire and elsewhere for her friend Adeline Genée (Guest 1958: 88). It is almost certain, however, that unlike her male contemporaries, she never conducted the orchestra in public performances of the ballets.[16]

The role of designers for the ballets was crucial, and far more prominent than that awarded today. The success of the ballets was judged as much, if not more, on the spectacle created by colour, costume and effects as on the dancing itself. Sources are ambiguous on what the sets comprised; critics rarely mention this aspect of the works. It would seem that although the stage environment contributed to the spectacle, it was the dancers' bodies which caught the critical eye. Nevertheless, photographs of most of the ballets often show quite grand, specifically designed sets.

The most productive and admired designer, who worked for both the Alhambra and the Empire and also designed for pantomime, was William Pitcher, known professionally as C. Wilhelm.[17] It is not known why Pitcher changed his name but it can be speculated that, as the son of a shipbuilder and a self trained draughtsman, a foreign sounding name would have given him more credibility. Wilhelm was responsible for the design of most of the Empire ballets between 1889 and 1915. As a recognised artist, he was elected a member of the Royal Institute of Painters in Water Colours in 1919. The Alhambra used a variety of designers (see Appendix I) but it was Mons. and Mde. Alias, the long-standing executants of the costumes, who tended to receive critical praise. So well regarded were the Alias's, claimed as 'costumier to the principal London, Paris, American, Provincial and Colonial Theatres (programme, *Our Army and Navy*, Theatre Museum, London) that a benefit performance was given for them on 2 June 1885. Mayhew, in 1892, gives an evocative description of Mons. Alias's working methods, and also reveals some of the other main roles necessary for the large-scale, spectacular productions. These comprised, in addition to the costumier, a property man, a stage carpenter and a person in charge of special effects, called the 'machinist', plus, of course, all the semi- and unskilled technical support. Another essential role was that of wig maker(s).

A characteristic of the music hall ballet was that it was not unusual to have the narrative progression of the works devised by someone other than the arranger, for a detailed plan of action was prepared before the choreography was embarked upon. For most of the Empire's history, this overview of the work came from Wilhelm in his triple role of designer, scenarist and supervisor of the overall production. This creative overview gave the Empire ballets a unity and artistic integrity which was much admired. As Perugini claimed, 'the artistic influence of the late Mr. C. Wilhelm had already raised ballet from the desert of dead conventions to the plane of artistic achievement' (1925a: 1175). A detailed scenario might be conceived by the ballet arranger, by another in-house collaborator or sometimes by an external source (for example, the writer and critic S.L. Bensusan contributed the scenario for *In Japan*, Alhambra 1902). Before any work commenced, however, it had to be submitted for approval to those who made the final decisions. These decisions were the prerogative of the theatre management and it was they, or the board of directors, who commissioned the ballets and it was they who initiated or approved the subject matter.

The management of the ballets

The growth in the size and complexity of the music halls was due to a new breed of entrepreneurial manager who changed the economic basis of the system. By the 1890s, the music halls had become business ventures, owned by shareholders who were represented by a board of directors. Increasingly, these boards incorporated commercial interests and the overall management of the music hall evolved from the individual, very personal style of the 'mine host' or 'caterer' to that of the absent magnate. Although the economic organisation had changed, however, the 'hands-on' managers of the large halls had been nurtured in the entertainment world and they maintained a personal intervention in the programmes. They were powerful in two ways, for this intervention embraced artistic and well as general management decisions. It is only by acknowledging the theatrical pedigree of these powerful businessmen that the degree of their involvement in the actual ballets can be comprehended.[18]

Although some managers have been credited with a very specific artistic input into the ballets, the degree of their involvement has not been fully recognised. It is only comments such as the following, in which the contribution of the designer of the ballets is discussed, that the extent of the management's influence is revealed:

> He ... (the designer) ... is, of course, subject from the first to the fiat of the manager, or the directors of the theatre, not only in respect of the subject matter of the ballets but also, of course, in regard to those plans and arrangements which affect the general expense of the undertaking.
> 'S' 1898: 372

It might be expected that the 'general expense' would come within the management's remit but it is significant that the subject matter of the ballets was also initiated or approved by them. Similarly, the many duties of Hitchens, when manager of the Empire, included the facts that he 'listens to new ballet music' and 'studies the design of new costumes' (Belfort 1902: 236). What is crucial here is not only the influence of management on the themes of the ballets but also their conscious prioritising of the production value of spectacle. The large music halls, as commercial operations, had to consistently attract not a locally loyal audience but a far broader one. The Alhambra and the Empire were great rivals in their ballet productions and, as the theatre programmes demonstrate, both 'sold' their works on factors such as the size of the cast and the 'special effects'.

An example of the dominance of commercial interests is the presentation of ballets with topical themes (see Ch. 4). As Jacobi's comment that these works were 'inevitably vulgar' reveals ('A.S.' 1895: 77), they were not necessarily the result of any artistic choice made freely by the arrangers, composers, librettists or designers.

Katti Lanner's comment on the difficulty of recreating endless 'military' sequences and her own artistic pedigree would suggest that she, too, was not enamoured of these works. Her attitude is similarly expressed in her accusation to Will Bishop that 'his comic dance and red nose had ruined her ballet' (anon. 1932: 267). The arrangers of the ballets brought with them their artistic heritage but it was the management who decided how this tradition was to be presented to contemporary audiences. It is significant that a sketch of the curtain call after *Don Juan* (Alhambra 1892) depicts the ballet arranger Coppi, the composer/music arranger Jacobi, the costume designer Alias and the Alhambra manager Hollingshead (Mayhew, 1892: 69). Likewise, the success of *Britannia's Realm* (Alhambra 1902) was described as 'another great triumph for Mr. C. Dundas Slater' (Belfort 1902: 236). Dundas Slater was the theatre manager. Flitch (1912: 63) attributes the lack of an artistic imperative during this period to such control, for: 'there had been a time when the foremost men of letters and composers had shared in the production of the ballets. Now its direction was left to the music hall manager. The result was necessarily a vulgarisation of the ballet.'

Most visual images of the Victorian period, from the paintings of 'high' art to the advertisements of popular culture, were created by men. The ballets, too, were visual images created in effect, if not in detail, by men. They were also created for a predominantly male audience.

Audiences and the ballet

In dance literature the popularity of the music hall ballet with audiences is almost totally overlooked. Even Lynn Garafola, one of the first writers to make a serious study of the receivers rather than just the producers and creators of dance, mentions the music hall but ignores the popularity of the ballet within it. In relation to the Ballets Russes, she comments that

> not since the romantic era of the 1830s and 1840s had ballet attracted so huge a following ... before the advent of the Ballets Russes it was said that ballet was for children and old men.
>
> 1989: xii

Not only did the Alhambra and the Empire have huge audiences for their ballets but these audiences also comprised many others besides old men (and children did not appear to frequent the halls at all unless there was a programme especially arranged for them). Belfort, in 1902, observed that 'aristocrats, artists, bourgeois, students, provincials, foreigners and the "man in the street" form component parts of the Empire public'. It may be argued that ballet was only part of the programme and that the audience was a general rather than a specific ballet audience (though as the Ballets Russes' post-war London appearances were also on variety programmes the same argument could apply). Primary sources, however, are unanimous in suggesting that ballet was the main attraction in the programme, though it must be noted that the sale of 'rover' tickets enabled people to walk around the theatre and there were a large number who frequented the bars and the promenade who paid little attention to the entertainment on stage. Nevertheless, each ballet often played for two, three or four months in theatres which had official seating and standing capacities of 2336 at the Alhambra and 1726 at the Empire (in Howard 1970). A small number of ballets also reached audiences in other venues.[19] It was also not unusual for charity performances to be presented at both venues. For example, at the Empire in 1896 *La Danse* was on a special programme to raise money to provide 'Boots and Warm Clothing for the Poorer Classes of Children attending the London Board Schools' and in 1897, *Monte Cristo* was presented for the slightly less evocative but undoubtedly worthy Royal National Lifeboat Institution (both programme covers, Theatre Museum).

The place of the ballet as part of the cultural life of London was well recognised. A popular song published in 1895 about Maria, a deserter from the Salvation Army, included the lines:

> Sister 'Ria, Sister 'Ria of the Army soon began to tire
> So she sold her tambourine
> Now she's nightly to be seen
> Dancing in the ballet at the Empire.[20]

In W. Somerset Maugham's *Liza of Lambeth*, Liza entertains the street crowd with the challenge, 'talk of the ballet at the Canterbury and the South London. You just wite (*sic*) till you see the ballet at Vere Street, Lambeth - we'll knock 'em' (1934: 8). It is difficult to imagine the Royal Ballet at Covent Garden today being referred to with such familiarity, despite their outreach policies.

As Belfort (above) suggests, audiences for the ballets at the palaces, unlike the traditional halls, were not predominantly of working class origin. The contradictory elements of increased respectability yet still *risque* connotations of both the ballets and the famed promenades drew a new audience from a far broader social class background. Writing in 1895, Stuart and Park note that

> Hitherto, the halls had been almost exclusively patronised by a class composed mainly, if not exclusively, of the lower and middle grade of society, that huge section of the public comprehensively summed up in the term 'the people'. Now, however, wealth, fashion and *ton* became attracted to these handsome palaces of amusement, and in the grand saloon of the West End halls the most prominent and distinguished representatives of art, literature and the law mingled nightly with city financiers, lights of the sporting world, and a very liberal sprinkling of the 'upper crust', as represented by the golden youth of the period.
>
> 1895:191

In one of the most evocative descriptions of the Empire promenade, the biographer and social commentator J.B. Booth notes how this part of the venue served as a meeting place, 'the cosmopolitan club of Empire ... for the cognoscenti, the men of the world' (1929: 147). It can be noted that this analogy of a 'club' fits well with the high Victorian male psyche, for 'clubs' of all kinds and catering for all social classes were very much a part of men's social world. A rarely mentioned faction of these 'men of the world', however, appeared to be those of the homosexual milieu. The Empire promenade, and most likely the Alhambra, appeared to be a meeting place for homosexual men; in 1894, an anonymous letter to the London County Council Licensing Committee in support of withdrawing the Empire's licence, revealed that the writer had been informed by a theatre attendant that more than half the audience in the shilling promenade were 'sodomites' and that 'he often turned out half a dozen a night and gave them a good kicking' (LCC 15 October 1894). Allowing for a degree of exaggeration, it was probably the case that the promenades were meeting places for all kinds of liaisons.

Booth continues his reminiscences, reflecting that

> as one looks back, the soft ceaseless murmur of voices once again rises; the blend of cigar smoke and faint scents once more fills the nostrils; once more the duchesses trail back and forth with faint swishing of silk.

('Duchesses' was Booth's name for prostitutes.) Then, when 'weary of the soft, ceaseless movement and murmur of the promenade' the gentlemen could descend to the stalls, where: 'in vast peace and comfort, one can watch great dancing in fit and seemly luxury. One did not eat caviar out of a winkle saucer.'

A large number of patrons, part of the 'cosmopolitan club', were home from the colonies, for the Empire palace, particularly, was

> something more than a mere music hall ... it was ... an Englishman's club, an Empire club, famous wherever Englishmen fought, worked, adventured. Britishers prospecting in the Klondyke, shooting in jungles, tea-planting in Ceylon, wherever they fore-gathered in cities of Africa, Asia and America would bid one another goodbye with a 'See you at the Empire one day when we're back in town.'
>
> Booth 1929: 142

The apparent incongruity between the artistic pedigree of the arrangers of the ballets and the principal performers, and the presentation of ballets on jingoistic themes so popular around the turn of the century can be largely explained by the composition of this new audience. As suggested, the choice of themes for the ballets very often rested with the management of the venues whose main concern was to accommodate the interests of their patrons.

The ballet was popular with royalty and the aristocracy who not only invited ballerinas to perform in their private houses but who actually visited the halls. Kyasht (1978), Bedells (1954) and Genée (Guest 1958) all record their experiences in the private salons of the aristocracy; a six-month run of *Victoria and Merrie England* (Alhambra 1897) was 'honoured with nearly a score of royal visits' (Perugini 1946: 227). Anstey observed that at the Empire, 'most of the men are in evening dress and in the boxes some ladies, also in evening costume, many of them belonging to what is called good society' (1890: 190). Although women of 'good society' began to frequent the palaces, there was still a stigma attached to the outing. Lady St. Just remembers seeing Genée, 'I think at the Alhambra' (though it was much more likely to have been at the Empire): 'it was in those days a music hall, and my father disapproved of my going to an entertainment of that kind. I remember being smuggled in just as the short ballet started, and out again as the curtain fell' (St. Just in Haskell, ed. 1957: 62).

Most visual sources of the Alhambra and the Empire promenade audience (such as that in illus. 1) depict the men in full evening dress and top hats, an image confirmed by Booth who noted that anyone wearing a bowler hat would be relegated to the circle rather than the stalls (1929: 146). On Boat Race night the Empire theatre was very popular, particularly with undergraduates and the youth of the upper classes. These occasions became an excuse for celebration which verged on rowdyism, and as Guest (1958) notes, on one occasion Genée walked off the stage at the Empire in protest at the noisy behaviour of the audience.

Garafola (1989) attributes the growth of an intellectual and artistic audience for ballet to the appearances of the Ballets Russes in London from 1911 onwards, but the large music halls had been drawing such an audience before the Russians arrived. 'Poets and painters' says Sorell 'were caught by this music hall life as if it were a world apart, which in many ways it was' (1981: 302). This 'world apart' was particularly the world of the working classes; although inevitably glamorised, the programmes offered a voyeuristic look at a life fascinating in its unfamiliarity.

Although the ballet drew an audience varied in social class, occupation and, perhaps, motivation, most reviews of the works appear to demonstrate the lack of a knowledgeable public or body of critics. Flitch (1912) suggested that the indifference to artistic standards was largely the cause of indifferent productions. Perugini (1925a), however, noted the eventual growth of a more discriminating audience which was therefore better prepared for the Russian ballet. The fact that there was an audience attuned to seeing ballet is significantly overlooked in most dance literature. Haskell's (1934) comment that the Empire public was not Diaghilev's one is highly dubious; a partly new audience may have been drawn to the Russians but to suggest that the music hall audience was an uncultured one is misconceived. Instances such as the varied receptions given to different *premières danseuses*, the popularity of Genée for not just her technical skills but also her nuances of expression, and the appreciation of Cavallazzi's mime suggest that it was an audience more discerning and discriminating than is generally credited. This view is endorsed by Booth who claims that for the *aficionados* 'the whole attraction lay in the hope of the creation of an English ballet' (1929: 136).

It is probable that the audiences for the ballet were not dissimilar from an average commercial theatre audience throughout history, which comprises those who go to be entertained and are oblivious of the traditions and skills of theatre and those who are motivated by such matters. As Symons noted, lovers of the ballet became so for many reasons: 'from abstract interest in dancing, from concrete interest in dancers, from a general liking for gorgeous spectacle and from a real taste for the beauty of the picture in motion' ('A.S.' 1894a: 557). In general, audiences for the ballet in the music halls were not dissimilar from those in the

Imperial theatres in Russia during the same period: conservative, happy with what they recognised and seduced by spectacle.[21]

Although the prominence of ballet on the programmes eventually changed the male/female ratio of the audiences, it is the perceptions of male writers which are recorded. It is also the perceptions of an elite: of the writers, poets and critics of the time who were drawn to the 'world apart' produced by the exotic subject matter, colour, spectacle and erotic connotations. Rarely are the reactions of the general audience recorded though the non-attributed newspaper critics may come closest. With the exception of dancers like Bedells or Kyasht, who viewed the ballet from a professional stance, how the women in the audience received the ballet is neither documented nor speculated upon.[22] It is the response of men, therefore, which produced the images of the ballet and inscribed the image of the dancer on her moving body. It is an image charged with connotations of sexuality and sensuality. Such connotations were imbued in the institution of the music hall itself.

Promenades and the public: the moral context of the ballet

Traditional music hall had always suffered from a disreputable name, particularly in the perceptions of the middle classes. As discussed, the halls had their origins largely in the entertainment of the taverns, the epitome of a culture above which a whole social class of Victorians were, in their hierarchical terms, aspiring to rise. Respectability was a driving force of not only the middle class but the aspirant working class and the halls were associated with two entirely immoral activities: drinking and prostitution. (The fact that the aristocracy frequently engaged in both did not prohibit these 'evils' being attributed to the working classes and much Victorian reform was aimed at saving these lost souls.) The initial impetus for the halls was the increased sale of drink and many appeared to condone prostitution on their premises. One notorious claim to fame of the Alhambra and the Empire was their promenades, areas which were frequented, as claimed in many accounts, by prostitutes. Public responses to this prostitution ranged from simple acknowledgement, condonement or attack. The following accounts of four responses to this phenomenon demonstrates how the historian needs to disentangle the personal perspectives and vested interests of those who are witnesses to contemporary events: the unwitting testimony of historiography.

A famous case which typifies the attitude of one public faction to the halls was the Ormiston Chant campaign. Literature on this campaign leaves an image of Laura Ormiston Chant as a prudish, staid woman of so-called typical Victorian morality. This is contested, however, by her background, her social and political interests, and her own articulate and rational accounts of events.

Laura Ormiston Chant, a one-time teacher and nurse, was one of those stalwart Victorians who espoused the cause of women through a concern with 'saving' those who had fallen into disrepute. In her activities and her writing she demonstrates an awareness that society rather than the individual was to blame for their fate.[23] One of her major campaigns, aimed particularly at the Empire, was an attempt to 'civilise' the large music halls by accusing the management of condoning immorality off and on the stage (see Ch. 6 for a detailed account of the latter). In her testimony to the London County Council Theatres and Music Halls Committee in October 1894, which she made in opposition to the renewal of the Empire's licence, Ormiston Chant described her visit to the Empire where she noticed

> numbers of young women coming in alone, most of them very painted, all of them more or less gaudily dressed ... they either sat on the lounges or sofas, or took up their position at the foot of the stairs and watched particularly the men who came out of the stalls and walked up and down the promenade.
> Chant in Donahue 1987: 55[24]

Whether it was the popularity of the Empire and the publicity given to her campaign or whether she was the target of the ridicule accorded to strong women of independent means who spoke against the norm, Ormiston Chant 'found herself satirised in the form of grotesque pictorial sketches, rhyming lampoons, and in the following November had the distinction of figuring as one of the principal "guys" of the year' (Stuart & Park 1895: 195).

On the other hand, the dance historian, Perugini, chose to blithely ignore the connections of the ballet with prostitution, and merely notes that the Empire was closed for a week owing to the intervention of the County Council. Apart from mistaking the year of the closure (it was 1894 not 1893 as he suggests) he does not acknowledge that the cause of the closure was due to concerns about the immoral trafficking. Two other perceptions of the affair are found in the memoirs of the men who themselves frequented the palaces. Winston Churchill, who visited the Empire with his Sandhurst friends, made an indignant defence of the promenade in which he painted a more innocent, perhaps somewhat disingenuous, picture:

> This large space behind the dress circle was frequently crowded during the evening performance and especially on Saturdays, with young people of both sexes, who not only conversed together during the performance and its intervals, but also from time to time refreshed themselves with alcoholic liquors.
> 1930: 58-59

Churchill further documents his role in the demolition of the Empire barriers, which were erected by the management to separate the promenade from the auditorium, on which occasion, he claims, he made his maiden speech.

Similarly, in an account based on personal reminiscence, Booth presents an admiring image of the habitants of the promenade, where 'thrilling ladies in marvellous confections paced slowly with the air of duchesses' (1929: 146). Although we must be wary of making assumptions, the subject matter of illus. 1 does appear to present these 'duchesses' and their gentlemen admirers. Whether overtly attacked or condoned, or ignored by historians wishing to protect the reputation of their art form, the element of prostitution in the promenades coloured both contemporary and future perceptions of the palaces. It was within this moral context that the ballet was presented.

The neglect, cursory treatment or dismissal of the music hall ballet in literature can be attributed to various kinds of bias, the roots of which can be found in the institution of the music hall itself. It is clear that the literature reflects an artistic bias formed in hindsight, for whilst the great majority of primary sources have high praise for both the productions and the dancing, almost all secondary sources undermine the artistic standards of the works. But as Perugini warns his readers of the 1920s, the works should not be judged in a contemporary light, for

> it is as well for them to know that their immediate forebears were in a position to see examples of Ballet that were extraordinarily wide in range of subject matter and as artistic - though different in spirit from those we see today - as any that have been recorded in the history of the art.
>
> 1925a: 1177

Managed by businessmen and funded entirely by private shareholders and box office receipts, the ballet was firmly a commercial venture. Like the situation with Petipa during his later period at the Imperial theatres, acquiescence to audience taste may have hindered innovation. Nevertheless, it is doubtful if its popularity would have been sustained for approximately thirty years had it lacked credibility according to the artistic standards of the period. A further prejudice is a moral one. Dance makes direct use of the body as the prime mode of expression. Implicitly or explicitly, celebrated or feared, dance has been associated with sensuality and sexuality. In the context of a heightened consciousness of morality, a public display of the female body connoted more than artistry and the traditions of the art form. The long association of the music hall with vice compounded this connotation. It is not, however, only discrimination on artistic and moral grounds which has demoted this period in history, but also a social prejudice. The commercial context; the working class origins of the halls and of the *corps de ballet*; the place of ballet within a diverse programme and the fact that the cast was predominantly female are all characteristics of the music hall ballet which have impacted on its status in the historiography of dance and cultural studies. Furthermore, it was the social, moral and artistic values of the institution, embodied in the texts of the ballets themselves, which produced the image of the dancer: an image which resonated deeply with the psyche of the time.

NOTES

1. See Kift (1996) for an overview of the licensing laws which largely dictated the kinds of acts which could be presented in the halls and theatres. Although the venues were discrete, artists themselves often performed in both kinds of venue (see Stuart and Park 1895).
2. Texts on the British music hall vary between those in a popular, journalistic style which focus on the star acts to more scholarly accounts such as Bailey (ed. 1986), Bratton (ed. 1986) and Kift (1996). Green (ed. 1986) is a useful collection of primary source material.

3. From the 1960s onwards, British 'fringe' theatre was often housed in the entertainment rooms above the drinking spaces in local pubs.
4. Many of these songs have passed through the generations, though it remains to be seen whether they will continue to do so. As a child of the '60s who grew up with the Beatles and the Rolling Stones, I can happily sing the lyrics which start 'My old man said "follow the van"', regularly rendered by Marie Lloyd, but how I learned them is a mystery.
5. Works such as *La Sylphide* (Taglioni 1832), *Ondine* (Taglioni 1836) and *Giselle* (Coralli and Perrot 1841) share these characteristics.
6. The music hall ballet lasted, in all, for over thirty years and the Ballets Russes, under Diaghilev, for twenty years. One hundred and forty-one new works were presented from 1884 onwards by the Alhambra and Empire jointly; seventy-one works were made or restaged by the Ballets Russes. The latter performed in limited seasons to an elite audience; the music hall productions ran nightly for six months or more to houses of very mixed social background.
7. The only detailed account of the venues and their works can be found in Guest (1992) where the history of the venues, and descriptive accounts of the ballets, artistic collaborators and principal dancers can be found.
8. In 1911 the Alhambra also entered into negotiations to bring over a company headed by Fokine but these floundered due to the Russians' very high fees (Guest 1992: 76-77).
9. For example, in the great majority of dance history texts Katti Lanner, the most prolific of Empire choreographers, is either not mentioned at all or only briefly acknowledged. There is no description of her work or evaluation of her contribution. Wilson (1974), Fonteyn (1980) and Guest (1992) are notable exceptions to this neglect.
10. For example, Alexander Genée is credited with arranging his niece Adeline's dances in *The Bugle Call* (1905) but Guest notes it was she who created them. Similarly she created *The Dryad* (1908) though she 'thought it wise to efface herself ... for the sake of family peace' and Alexander is credited with the arrangement (Guest 1958: 100).
11. See 'S.L.B.' (1901: 318); Hibbert (1916: 108); Kyasht (1978: 164) and Bedells (1954: 20) for brief but evocative descriptions of Lanner. An interview with her is recorded in *The Sketch* (anon.1895a: 694).
12. Farren joined the Empire as a performer in 1904, having previously worked at the Alhambra and in pantomime. Guest (1992: 124) notes that Genée 'did not think him sufficiently competent to choreograph for her', a sentiment almost inevitably caused by his lack of ballet training. Nevertheless, he is credited with the choreography of eleven works and this absence of a ballet background indicates how the role of the ballet arranger has changed during the twentieth century. Another example was Will Bishop, an eccentric and clog dancer who went on to become ballet master and producer at the Coliseum. The direct involvement of Farren and other British artists, and the utilisation of their own theatrical expertise suggest that a British style of ballet was evolving as a precursor to the Vic-Wells and Ballet Rambert works of the 1920s and 1930s. See my Epilogue for further discussion.
13. Headlam's publication of Blasis in 1888 demonstrates the predominance of the Italian school.
14. For example, Joseph Hansen left the Alhambra to take up the post of *premier maitre de ballet* at the Paris Opera.
15. See Tillett (1982) for an indication of how some sectors of the musical world reacted to Arthur Sullivan composing for the Alhambra. However, as Williamson (1951: 400)

	suggests, the importance of the music hall ballet lay 'in the fact that a composer of Sullivan's status should have been commissioned ... to write a ballet at all'.
16.	Many middle class women were accomplished musicians, of course, but only played instruments which were perceived as suitable for them and their prime role was regarded as either teachers or musical dilettantes. However, a picture of a rehearsal at the Alhambra ballet shows a woman at the piano so it appears that they were used as rehearsal pianists (illus.2).
17.	See 'T.H.L.' 1893: 343-44 for 'A chat with a costumier'. A collection of Wilhelm's designs held at the Royal Academy of Dance, London, bears witness to the care and detail with which they were executed; each design is a painting in its own right.
18.	Stuart and Park (1895) discuss the music hall management and Kyasht (1978) gives an 'insider' account of her relationship with the Empire management.
19.	See Pritchard (1995) for an account of five ballets which were exported from the Empire to the Manchester Palace of Varieties during 1891-92. Alhambra works by Hansen and Curti were restaged in Belgium and Paris respectively; Coppi's were reworked for Milan, Monte Carlo and Naples; two of Lanner's works were presented in Berlin and Monte Carlo.
20.	Sister 'Ria, written by A.J. Mills, composed by Arthur Lennard, published by F.D.H. in 1895. The song suggests that from the Salvation Army 'Ria: 'was missing one fine day, and very sad to tell ... Not only she, but other things had walked away as well.'
21.	One element in the audience who cared little whether a performance was good or bad but who received it according to how much money had been received from the performers was the claque. It is difficult to know the extent of their influence for their activities are little documented, though Kyasht (1978: 168) describes how the penalty for non-payment was severe: 'if an artist took a firm stand and refused to pay, the Claque always avenged themselves by applauding in the wrong place'. Bedells (1954) notes the existence of a professional claque in the gallery but points out that it was never paid by her; she may have been too young for their attention.
22.	Arnold Bennett (1971: 56-57) offers a brief and speculative account of a barmaid's wistful reaction to a *première danseuse*.
23.	Ormiston Chant 'took up public advocacy of women's suffrage, Temperance, Purity and Liberal Politics' (*Who Was Who 1916 – 1928*, pub. 1967). She spoke before the Social Purity Alliance, an organisation which typified the late Victorian concern for social and moral reform.
24.	Ormiston Chant's original testimony can be seen in the London Metropolitan Archives (LCC 10 October 1894) but as the handwriting is, at times, almost illegible, references are given here for Donahue's transcription.

CHAPTER TWO

From the Principals to the *Passées:* Performers in the Music Hall Ballets

The nineteenth century saw the growth of a social structure in which the classes became increasingly more segregated geographically, socially and politically, and henceforth more self-conscious. Industrialisation and economic expansion had vastly increased employment opportunities and the move from country to town had taken many women out of agricultural labour and home-based work in to factories, domestic service and commerce. A new breed of clerical and shop assistants arose and by the 1870s work outside the home had become the norm for girls in their late 'teens and early twenties. While women were relegated to low status and low pay work, this demographic change resulted in increased freedom and independence. Marriage, however, was the goal for women of all classes, for it was only marriage which brought status and the potential for financial security. For the working class woman, however, it did not bring freedom from the work force; even pregnancy and child rearing gave no respite from having to earn a wage. The contribution of women to the family income, however small, was vital. Even those in the seemingly glamorous world of the ballet earned their money to partially or wholly maintain their family: 'and when the tired little worker at last leaves the theatre - her place of business - she is only too glad to fly off to the home which, in nine cases out of ten, she helps to support' (Booth 1929: 152).

The theatre in London provided considerable employment opportunities for women. Census records show that the number of those registered as actresses, a category which included dancers, rose from 2368 in 1881 to 6443 in 1901 and 9171 in 1911.[1] An overview of opportunities for women published in 1894 establishes even more clearly that 'the ballet, in London, employs thousands of women' (Bulley & Whitley 1894: 34-35). Nevertheless, the theatrical profession was a stigmatised profession, most particularly for women. Although in society generally and in the performing arts specifically it was actresses who were at the forefront of gaining acceptance for British women as independent and creative people, in the early Victorian theatre, acting as a profession was shunned as decadent by the bourgeoisie and 'performers were seen as rogues and vagabonds, especially actresses, who were seen as scarlet women soliciting from the stage rather than the streets' (Holledge 1981: 7).

That such a stigma still existed by the latter part of the century is evident in an analysis of *The Englishwomen's Review*, a monthly journal published from 1873 to 1909. Aimed at educated, middle class women it contained articles of broad interest such as women's suffrage, rather than just domestic affairs. A major section in each issue was on women's employment and this made reference to careers such as dentistry, wood carving and, surprisingly, stockbroking. Although women visual artists and musicians are referred to in the index there is no mention at all, throughout the whole of the period, of the theatrical careers of acting or dancing.

In the ballet, almost all of the *premières danseuses* were foreign and this, somehow, may have rendered them classless. Their nationality and their very evident display of skill accorded them some status. Paradoxically, however, in secondary source documentation they retain the stigma of their music hall performances.[2] A complex amalgam of tradition, lack of training opportunities and social disapproval militated against British women becoming *premières danseuses* though there were some small exceptions.[3] Some British dancers, such as Kate Seymour and Kate Vaughan, achieved fame through skirt dancing, a form initially based on a balletic vocabulary for the lower body. According to Perugini (1925c) it was not until the social and moral conventions of pre-war Britain had relaxed and the Ballets Russes had established its post-war popularity, that ballet dancing became an acceptable career for British women.

The hierarchical tradition

The dancers attached to the Alhambra and the Empire could be said to form a company in the sense that they were employed directly by the venues and were part of a clear internal structure. This structure, reflecting the hierarchical nature of the stratified society from whence ballet originated and in which it still existed, generally comprised principals, seconds, *coryphées*, *corps*, supernumeraries and children. The principals were the *danseuses*, *danseurs* and mimes. The far smaller number of *danseurs* (male dancers) was due to a prejudice in the West (with the exception of Denmark, with its Bournonville legacy) against male dancers which had originated in the Romantic era and lasted until the advent of the Russians during the first decade of the twentieth century. The ballerinas were partnered, though not in the current sense of the *pas de deux*, by women performers *en travestie*. These roles tended to be mime or dramatic action rather than dance but the skills of the executants were held in high esteem by critics of the period. Of secondary importance to the principals were other solo artists who also performed in the classical ballet genre and soloists or duettists who were character, eccentric or speciality dancers. The *coryphées*, as in all ballet companies, performed in small groups while the *corps de ballet* comprised the large groupings. Some sources refer to these as the chorus, but all programmes refer to the *corps* and there was a clear distinction between a ballet girl and a chorus girl. As would be expected with the *corps*, there was a big difference in experience and skill. Mayhew (1892: 64) notes that in an Alhambra rehearsal, 'with the *coryphées* very little trouble is necessary, but on the less efficient ladies of the *corps* unflagging pains and patience have to be expended.' It is not clear in illus. 2 whether these are *corps* or *coryphées*, but the sketch does show a lively demonstration from Carlo Coppi while the dancers watch, dressed in their rehearsal 'garibaldi' jackets, skirts and dark hose.

There were also various non-dancing supernumeraries or 'extras', including children, who made up the huge casts of one hundred and fifty to two hundred people which were common for the ballets in their heyday. Although not typical of the repertoire there were some ballets which incorporated singing (sometimes choral) and/or dialogue, such as *The Dryad* (Empire 1908) for one dancer and baritone singer. Performers with the appropriate skills were hired for these works.

The hierarchy of the ballet companies was rigid and, if it happened at all, it was rare for dancers to progress from *corps* to principal status. The *corps*, however, had a clearly defined internal structure based on 'rows' or lines. The dancers were placed in first, second and third rows depending not just on their talent but also on their age and looks. As Leppington (1891: 17) comments, 'a dancer's position in these rows is determined by her proficiency and by her personal appearance. The back rows are composed of the beginners, the *passées* and the unskilled.' The principals and the *corps* had little to do with each other. Kyasht, for example, was outraged at Farren's suggestion that she should dance with each member of the *corps*: 'I was furious with him for wishing me to do such a thing, because none of the chorus were experiences ballerinas and our steps did not fit properly' (1978: 155). Such was her tantrum at the incident that it is likely that her refusal was as much to do with the social barriers that existed between the top and bottom strata of the company hierarchy as on artistic grounds. If Anstey (1890: 191-92) is to be believed, the relationship between the principals and the *corps* during the performance could also be less than harmonious. In an account of a ballet at either the Alhambra or the Empire he interprets the attitude of the *corps* to the performance of the *première danseuse* as:

> some are severely critical and obviously of the opinion that they could do it infinitely better themselves; others whisper disparagement to sympathetic ears; others again study the signorina's every movement until she is opposite them, whereupon they assume an ostentatious abstraction as if she was really below their notice. And then she stops suddenly, amidst thunders of applause, the infantine smile giving place to a calm superiority as she haughtily makes her way to the wings through the ranks of the *coryphées*.

In the music hall ballet there was an inflexible hierarchy and resultant lack of opportunity for young dancers. The tradition of foreign principals, the inferior technical training of the *corps* and their working class origins all produced the strict demarcation lines within the companies which paralleled those in society generally.

The most important dancer to appear in the music hall ballets was, without doubt, Adeline Genée. Unusual in that she came from Denmark rather than Italy (or later, Russia), she had trained with her uncle, Alexander, in a style that appeared to be a fusion of the Italian and French schools.[4] Genée is significant not just for the longevity of her career at the Empire which lasted from 1897-1909 but for the quality of her work in both technical and expressive terms. She performed to consistent critical acclaim; in the view of an unknown contributor to the Green Room book (Hunt, ed. 1906: 141) she: 'has won the reputation of being the most graceful and accomplished dancer in the world.' Similarly, Flitch (1912: 179-80) suggested that: 'in proficiency in the strict, classical school of ballet dancing, it is possible that Madame Genée has never been surpassed and perhaps not even equalled.' In spite of this highest acclaim, however, Genée has never been mythologised in the same way as her contemporary, Anna Pavlova. Her name is now far less generally recognised; it would be interesting to speculate on how her fame might have spread or her image changed had she accepted Diaghilev's invitation to join the Ballets Russes (Haskell 1934: 192). Her performing skills, dedication and seemingly impeccable lifestyle enhanced the reputation of the dancer and helped to establish dancing as a respectable career. In these respects, together with her involvement with the founding of both the Association of Operatic Dancing in 1920 (from 1936, the Royal Academy of Dancing, now Royal Academy of Dance) and the Camargo Society (1930-33), Genée is a direct link between the music hall ballet and the resurgence of interest in 'British' ballet in the 1920s. This claim is expanded in the Epilogue.

London, like St. Petersburg, Moscow and major European cities, generally imported its *premières danseuses* from Italy. Among these were Emma Bessone (Alhambra 1885-86 and 1888-89) who was trained at La Scala and became prima ballerina for both the Maryinsky and Bolshoi companies in Russia. When Petipa revived *Giselle* in 1884 it was with Bessone in the title role. Carlotta Brianza (Empire 1888 and 1893-84) was a pupil of Blasis, principal in Milan and was chosen by Petipa as his first Aurora in *The Sleeping Beauty* (1890). Pierina Legnani (Alhambra intermittently between 1882 and 1897) studied with the famous teacher Caterina Beretta at la Scala and went on to receive the rare title of *prima ballerina assoluta* from the Russian Imperial Ballet. It was Legnani who first displayed the now ubiquitous thirty-two *fouettés* at the Alhambra in *Aladdin* (1892) before Petipa allowed her to insert them into the role of Odette-Odile which he created for her in his and Ivanov's production of *Swan Lake* (1895).[5] In an interview in *The Sketch* (E.F-S. 1893) Legnani admits that she can make thirty two turns on 'tiptoe' and attributes this skill to ballet shoes from Italy.

The era of the supremacy of the Italian ballerinas came to a close during the first decade of the twentieth century. Indicative of this was the Empire management's decision to send their agent to the Imperial Theatres in Russia to look for a successor to Genée. That successor was Lydia Kyasht who records that the Tsar had been horrified at the prospect of her dancing on the stage of a music hall, but was mollified when it was reported that she was maintaining the tradition of the Imperial Russian Ballet (Kyasht 1978: 150-51). Kyasht, who in her autobiography rather exaggerates her own contribution to the Empire's fame, remained there from 1908-1913 when she was succeeded by Phyllis Bedells, a dancer who is recorded but now commonly forgotten as the first English *première danseuse*.[6]

The principal female dancers at the Alhambra and the Empire did not always perform in the ballet genre. Evidence that both Genée and Legnani also demonstrated their skills in skirt dancing indicates that they were able to adapt to work with topical subject matter (see Ch. 4) and fashionable dances.[7] Such demonstrations were not, however, popular with critics for they undermined the traditional image of the ballerina. A few works did not deploy the ballet vocabulary even for the principals; for example, La Belle Leonora, a dancer of Spanish origin who generally performed her national dances, made her debut in the principal role of Maud Allan in the parody ballet *Sal! Oh! My!* (Alhambra 1908). This was exceptional, however, for the great majority of principal dancing roles were based on the classical vocabulary of the *danse d'école*.

This traditional element in their technical training and, with a few exceptions, their foreign nationalities and experiences in the major theatres of Europe, were common factors in the backgrounds and professional careers of the *premières danseuses*. It is clear that the creators and the principal performers of the ballets shared a common dance vocabulary and an understanding of a performance and production style which was part of an international ballet tradition. They also performed, whilst in London, at other venues such as Her Majesty's, the Lyceum, the Coliseum, Drury Lane and the Royal Opera House. Even though they practised their art in an unusual context, they were secure in their tradition and thought little of any dance which deviated from it. These 'deviations', presented by performers such as Isadora Duncan, Ruth St. Denis and Maud Allen, were also termed 'classic' dancing by their protagonists. Perugini (1925b: 1245) recalls an interview 'with a very cultured and distinguished *maitre de ballet*' (location and timing would suggest Carlo Coppi of the Alhambra) in which he asked the gentleman what he thought the new classic dancing. The reply from the Milan trained *maitre* was '*Ce n'est pas l'art, ce n'est pas classique, ce n'est pas la danse!*' ('It is not art, it is not classics; it is not dance!'). It is interesting that history had radically reassessed the status of these co-existing dance forms.

The tradition of the *danse d'école* privileged the formal, virtuosic aspects of dance performance and 'exalted technical proficiency at the expense of the display of personality' (Flitch 1912: 72). Furthermore, as Jacobi assessed, if the ballerina's work 'has appeared a trifle monotonous of late, it is because they are nearly all pupils of the same mistress in Milan, and may have adopted certain mannerisms' (in 'A.S.' 1895: 77). The skills of these performers were, therefore, perceived as technically adept but somewhat dehumanised. As such, the reality of the dancer as person did not intervene in the image of dancer as performer.

The performance vocabularies of the male dancers are far more difficult to discern. Although Guest (1992) lists a total of sixty-five names of principal male dancers at the Alhambra and Empire after 1884, many of these performed in character or dramatic roles. The fact that there were far fewer male than female dancers with ballet training reflects the situation generally. Such was the prejudice against male dancers that Grove (1895: 363) wrote,

> at present the idea of a male dancer has something ludicrous in it, and though men usually form part of the ballets they rarely now take a prominent role. The poet Southey declares that a male dancer should be hamstrung.

As Southey died in 1843, Grove is calling on much earlier evidence to support her case; nevertheless, she found all aspects of the music hall ballets unacceptable. Her sentiments on men dancing are echoed by *The Times* (reprinted in Empire

Theatrical Souvenirs, 1906) where the view was expressed that 'towards male dancers as a rule we have a feeling for which the word dislike is too mild a name'. A more pragmatic, but hardly enthusiastic, commentator was the Alhambra choreographer Jacobi, who declared that 'male dancers are not very interesting, but they are required to support the *première* or for groups, while a good comic male dancer helps a piece along considerably' (in 'A.S.' 1895: 77). As this comment indicates, the casting of a male 'dancer' was no guarantee of the nature or extent of his dancing role. One male performer who definitely did have a dancing role was Vittorio de Vincenti. Described as a 'wonderful pirouettist' (Hibbert 1916: 107) he was a success as the Evil Genie in the Alhambra's *The Sleeping Beauty* (1890) before moving across Leicester Square to dance at the Empire between 1891 and 1895. George Bernard Shaw, a frequent inhabiter of the halls, was inspired to attempt various balletic feats for himself in the street after seeing Vincenti perform, though his account of these is probably more fantasy than fact (Laurence, ed. 1981a: 932).

Another indication of the lack of partner work in the currently accepted form of the *pas de deux* is that Genée did not have a male partner at the Empire until 1901 when the Italian Amadeo Santini partnered her in an adage in *Old China*. Another partner of Genée's was Paul Sundberg whom the Empire hired for the ballet *The Duel in the Snow* (revived 1903). Sundberg had danced with the ballerina at Stettin and continued to do so in several works at the Empire until 1907. Other male dancers from the ballet tradition included Enrico Cecchetti, Edouard Espinoza and Adolphe Bolm. Cecchetti performed at the Empire periodically between 1888-1892. A sketch in the *Illustrated Sporting and Dramatic News* (anon. 1888: 198), captioned 'A Human Teetotum', shows Cecchetti in doublet, hose and a whirl of motion. It is a rare graphic illustration of a male ballet dancer in action, an indication, perhaps, of the lack of press and public interest in them. Espinoza, son of the renowned dancer and teacher, Leon, took on the title role of the Dancing Master in his own revival (1914) of Farren's 1910 production. As this role had originally been danced by the non-trained Farren himself it is unlikely, unless Espinoza changed the choreography, to have been balletically based. Adolphe Bolm, who had trained at the Imperial Ballet Academy, St. Petersburg, appeared on the Empire variety bill with Lydia Kyasht before she was engaged there as *première danseuse* and he returned in 1910 to partner her again in a series of dances produced by himself. However, he was never involved in the 'company' ballets at the Empire.

Information on male dancers who appeared in the music hall ballets is scarce; not only is it difficult to ascertain their background or training but, when it is known that a dancer had a ballet pedigree it is not clear the extent to which the vocabulary of the *danse d'école* was used. With the majority of male parts being played *en travestie* it is evident that the exact nature of the male 'dancing' role has to be treated with caution. The lack of male dancers was a significant characteristic of the music hall ballet and, as will be claimed in Ch. 3, this had a resonance more profound than its strategy as a mere casting device would suggest.

Since the Romantic period, the unpopularity of male dancers with audiences had resulted in the convention of male roles being played *en travestie*, as was also common in pantomime and burlesque. Although some visual sources depict an *en travestie* performer supporting a ballerina who is in *arabesque* or *en pointe* these were primarily non-dancing, mime roles. Mime was an important element in the Italian pedagogy and it was common, in Italian ballets, to separate the dance and mime roles.

Two of the most famous *en travestie* performers in the music hall ballets were Italian women who previously had prestigious careers as dancers. Malvina Cavallazzi had been *prima ballerina* at the New York Metropolitan Opera House; she made her first appearance at the Empire in *Diana* (1888) in a dancing role but, henceforth, all her parts were *en travestie* though on retirement she opened her own Academy of Dancing where she taught the Italian pedagogy (Bedells 1954: 21). The other renowned Italian artist was Francesca Zanfretta, a dancer who, according to de Valois (1959: 95), only appeared in mime roles after the birth of her daughter because neither she nor her husband 'considered that the shortened skirt and the low-cut bodice of a dancer's costume were seemly for a wife and mother'. Zanfretta was the leading mime at the Empire for twelve years from 1895 and it was she who taught the art to Ursula Moreton, who passed on the teaching in de Valois' school. Thus, as explored in the Epilogue, another connection can be made between the music hall ballets and the development of 'British' ballet.

Another famous mime with an Italian name was, in fact, British. Carlotta Mossetti was born in London of an Italian father and an Irish mother. She was apprenticed to the School of Dancing at the Alhambra when ten years old and made her first appearance in *Paquita* (1908) at the age of eighteen. She modelled her *travestie* style on de Vincenti and partnered Genée and Bedells. She was, according to the *Ballet Annual* (Haskell, ed. 1960: 139), 'probably the last of the British travesti (*sic*) dancers.' As well as performing, Mossetti, as Ballet Mistress at the Alhambra, arranged dances in several works. Although it is not always possible to ascertain the nationality of the lesser known artists it is probable that those such as Julia Searle, Flo Martell, Edith Slack, Dorothy Craske and 'Miss Matthews', all of whom appeared mainly but not solely *en travestie*, were British. The suspicion of British talent is revealed in the comment that Julia Searle, 'though British, has technique as a dancer and a gift for miming' (anon. 1898: 490). Important though these roles were, they did not demand the virtuosic dancing skills of the ballerinas and therefore offered career opportunities for the indigenous performers of the music hall ballets.

A key facet of the music hall ballets was the importance of character or speciality roles though it is not always possible to distinguish the female dancers who drew upon some kind of ballet training from those who were primarily character dancers; it is probable that most of them had a variety of skills. For example, Elise Clerc, part French and part British, receives mention for her eccentric dances (Perugini 1946: 248) and for the character role as an Ugly Sister in *Cinderella* (Empire 1906) but she also went on to become ballet mistress at the Alhambra for which she produced five works. (As the careers of Fred Farren and Will Bishop suggest, however, this role did not necessarily depend on a ballet training.) Beatrice Collier was a well-known character dancer and mime whose

Apache Dance with Fred Farren in *A Day in Paris* (Empire 1908) became mildly notorious for the brutal passions it presented.

If the training of the female dancers equipped them for a variety of styles it is clear that the majority of male performers in the ballets were either eccentric or character dancers or actor/mimes. Unlike the *premiers danseurs* they tended to be British and came from a general pantomime, stage or variety background. These performers included Fred Farren; Will Bishop, an eccentric and clog dancer who after his career at the Empire went on to become ballet master and producer at the Coliseum; Frank Lawton, eccentric dancer renowned for his whistling and Fred Storey, an actor and dancer who also painted the scenery for a number of Alhambra productions. Tom Walls, who generally played the villain or *roué* at the Empire, eventually became a well known actor, manager and producer in the London theatre and, from the late 1920s, acted in and directed films. An examination of the careers of these performers, together with descriptions of their roles in contemporary critical reviews, reveals the variety of genres and performing styles that the music hall ballets embraced, most especially in the later topical ballets. It is this feature of the ballets which perhaps made them distinctly 'British'.

Dancers who performed in small groups, usually of four or under, were named in the programmes and this information casts light on their identity in two respects: their nationality and their family connections. With a few exceptions, the names of the dancers suggest British nationality. As Cochran notes of the Alhambra and the Empire, 'each of these houses maintained a permanent *corps de ballet* of native birth - it used to be said of the Alhambra that the members were reared on the premises' (Cochran 1945: 208-209).

The printed names in the programmes also indicate the degree to which a career in the ballet was often a family tradition. At the Empire, for example, there were five Collier sisters: Beatrice, Elsie, Lily, Millicent and Daisy, the first four of whom were named in the cast for *Cinderella* (1906). Also in *Cinderella* were three Craskes and in *Les Papillons* (Empire 1902) three Vincents were cast. A common name does not, of course, necessarily indicate a family relationship but such was the nature of the theatrical community that these connections were more probable than not.

As might be expected within such a community, matrimonial relationships developed. Tom Walls, leading man in dramatic roles at the Empire, married one of its dancers, Hilda Edwardes; Frank Lawton, eccentric dancer, married Daisy Collier (Bedells 1954). There appeared to be no stigma attached to married women who continued working in the theatre generally. The census of 1901 records that, of the 1023 women aged between twenty-five and thirty-five who gave their profession as 'actors' (a category which included dancers, chorus girls and music hall artistes), 510 were single and 513 were married or widowed. The next category, aged thirty-five to forty-five years showed 84 single women and 207 married or widowed. As dancers very often either contributed to the family income or were the sole breadwinners it is likely that only those who married into a higher social class could afford to retire. Unity More, a colleague of Bedells at the Empire, retired on the occasion of her marriage to Captain Haigh, MC, RA. It could be speculated but not proven that, whilst performers like Zanfretta who married within the profession to actor Charles Lauri, remained in the theatre after marriage and children, in More's case the social censure attached to the profession in general might have prompted her retirement from it.

The members of the large groups of dancers, the *corps de ballet*, were referred to in common parlance as the 'ballet girls' or 'ladies of the ballet'. It is interesting how the ascription of 'girls', whatever their age, denies women maturity, and the term 'ladies', as used in 'charladies' or 'ladies of the street' was often used to describe women who were clearly not 'ladies' in the conventional sense. Both of these terms, however, were part of theatrical language. As always, it is difficult to discern the identity and background of these mainly unnamed dancers, but these are hinted at in artistic rather than social sources.[8] A poem by 'J.M.B.' (possibly J.M. Barrie) on the apotheosis scene of *Faust* (Empire 1895) refers to the *corps*, who were cast in this scene as angels. After the curtain had fallen,

> No more the angels deck the sky -
> Those angels hail from Peckham Rye
> From Bow or Kentish Town.
> 'J.M.B.' 1896: 524

An unreferenced quotation in Flitch (1912: 65) describes the *corps* as 'rank after rank and file after file of honest breadwinners from Camberwell and Peckham Rye.'

The incongruity between the individual identities of the *corps* and the fantasy world of the ballet which presents the dancers as a glamorous but homogeneous mass is the theme of a poem, *The Ballet*, by Thomas Hardy:

> Though all alike in their tinsel livery,
> And indistinguishable at a sweeping glance,
> They muster, maybe
> As lives wide in irrelevance
> A world of her own has each one underneath
> Detached as a sword from its sheath.
> Thomas Hardy 1917 in Gibson (ed.) 1976: 492

It is probable that part of the attraction felt by writers and artists for these ballet girls, as discussed in Ch. 5, was attributable to their fascination with women from a lower social class, particularly during an era when strict social etiquette rendered women of their own class sexually unobtainable.

The age at which the dancers joined the *corps* was young compared with current standards. By 1901, although there was no statutory school leaving age, the minimum age at which young people could undertake full-time employment was twelve. Bedells was thirteen when she joined the Empire and, although given solo roles, 'first dressed with the two youngest members of the *corps* because we were considered too young to be in the grown-ups dressing rooms' (Bedells 1954:

23). Unity More made her first appearance on the Empire stage around the age of fifteen (Bedells 1954: 39). The issue is complicated, however, by the fact that dancers, including children, who were apprenticed at the associated schools were hired to the theatres and therefore might have appeared from a very early age. It is unknown as to which age the *corps* retired from performing, but youth was not necessarily a prerequisite for employment, for 'so long as a dancer retains the necessary amount of agility, she can remain on the boards, in spite of advancing years, well on into middle life; mother and daughter have danced in the same ballet before now' (Leppington 1891: 251). Bedells confirms that 'many of the women had spent their whole lives on the stage - some were even grandmothers - and they were very proud of their tradition' (Borgnis 1982: 24).

As suggested above, children were cast in dancing or auxiliary roles, a feature of professional theatre which was not uncommon. Included in a bequest for the female performers and stage staff at the Alhambra were 'many of the underage girls' who, says Booth (1929: 154), 'danced on as robins, or swallows or other small birds'. Lanner took her pupils from the age of ten and these children would have appeared in the Empire ballets. Dancers who performed at other venues and joined the ballet at key points during the performance also enlarged the cast. The performer Cleo Collins explained how she did a 'turn' at the Royal every evening, 'and then I hurry up and get to the Empire in time to come in the procession' ('M.L.C.' 1893: 24).

In order to swell the numbers on stage, non-dancing roles were sometimes recruited from backstage staff, friends and families of the performers or creators of the ballets. For example, Guest (1992: 69) notes that a friend of the Alhambra choreographer, Alfredo Curti, was sometimes given a small role in the ballets as a reward for his help with Curti's research. Perugini (1915d: 274) mentions a cast list for the Alhambra's *Soldiers of the Queen* (1900) which included a *corps de ballet*, chorus and auxiliaries numbering over two hundred and fifty people in all. Other programmes advertising a *corps* of one hundred and fifty dancers were not uncommon. Such large casts, which ranged from the virtuoso principal dancers to the 'extras', served to create the spectacle which was the most significant feature of the music hall ballet.

Training for the music hall ballet

It is apparent that during this period there was an increase in both the provision and standards of training for the dancer. Whilst the principals brought their technical expertise with them, before the 1880s the indigenous British performers had little opportunity to undertake a systematic training in a permanent school. In 1888 the Reverend Stewart Headlam, a champion of the classical ballet tradition, blamed the apparently poor standards of dancing on this lack of opportunity.

> The absence of any regular school permanently connected with a Theatre or Opera, in which English Dancers can be trained ... naturally discourages and

often absolutely prevents the English Dancers from giving that energy and time to Practice, which is so entirely necessary for all who would be perfect in their art.

Headlam (ed.) 1888: xi

In another source in which the situation in Russia is compared with that in England, the author sees the problem in a far broader context. Acknowledging the view that 'it is said that English girls would make the finest dancers in the world', s/he bemoans the lack of a positive attitude to art generally and the absence of State nurture and support ('I', 1913).

Even when training opportunities were available there were other circumstances which militated against their effectiveness. In a comparison between European and Russian dancers, Flitch observed that

> In England ... it has been the custom for the *danseuse* to go to this or that teacher or learn a single dance necessary for a certain performance, but not to learn dancing. Indeed it is impossible as a general rule for the dancer out of her slender salary to pay one or two guineas an hour ... in order to attain an efficiency which even when acquired is rarely appreciated.
>
> Flitch 1912: 63

Dancing schools did exist though their *raison d'être* was not to train students for a professional career in the theatre. For example, Mrs. Wordsworth, through whose school passed Unity More and Ninette de Valois, taught fancy dancing and deportment. She was described by de Valois (1959: 36) as having 'a puritanical loathing of dancing as a profession'. Even those who taught dancing as a social skill did not necessarily support a career in the theatre.

One training opportunity which was open to aspiring young professional dancers was an apprenticeship at the schools attached to the Alhambra and the Empire. The school opened by Leon Espinoza in Kennington Road, South London in 1872 supplied most of the Alhambra *corps*, as did Coppi's school subsequently. The latter is an example of the practice where principal teachers at the schools were also ballet mistresses or masters at the theatres and rehearsal for the productions which involved apprentice dancers would start in the schools.

The National Training School of Dancing, established by Colonel Mapleson, at 73 Tottenham Court Road, had been directed by Lanner since its inception in 1876.[9] By 1906, over 1000 pupils had apparently passed through this school (Hunt, ed. 1906: 200). Lanner took pupils from the age of ten years, for 'if they come any younger there is no end of worry with the School Boards, the Cruelty Boards, and ever so many other boards' (anon. 1893a: 15). From her own words in a most revealing interview, it would appear that Lanner kept her pupils up to their early twenties by which age they would have been performing regularly in the ballets. Other sources, however, do not mention or are ambiguous as to whether the Empire dancers continued to take lessons at a school; took what in current terminology would be the equivalent of a 'company' class; had private lessons elsewhere; kept up their skills with their own private practice or simply maintained them by the activity of performing.[10] For example, in Compton Mackenzie's fictional account ([1912] 1929) based on the Alhambra, he makes no mention of any further formal training for the dancers of the *corps* once they had joined the house company. It is probable that the continuing training of the dancer varied according to both the opportunities that were available throughout the period and the place of the dancer in the company hierarchy. What is very unlikely, as Flitch (above) suggests, is that the dancers of the *corps* could afford the personal tuition available to the principals.

Other schools which existed in London included the International Academy of Dancing, established by Alexander Genée in 1900 and situated at 5 Lisle Street, opposite the stage door of the Empire. It was Genée who made a significant contribution to the increase in technical standards; in *Coppélia* (Empire 1906) he gave the *corps* their first stage experience of *pointe* work (Guest 1958: 79). Whilst this signifies that such an important feature had been missing hitherto, it also suggests that they must have been equipped to cope with the demands of this skill. It was Genée, also, who offered an alternative system of training to the Italian school. When the Empire management felt that Bedells was becoming too set in the Italian style they offered to pay for her to take classes with Alexander Genée instead of giving her a salary increase (Borgnis 1982: 26). The Empire's Cavallazzi ran another school; a most amusing description of these classes is given by Bedells in her autobiography (1954).

One disadvantageous result of the close connection between the schools and the theatres was that the dancers were only prepared for the technical demands of their envisaged roles and the training, even though it was based on traditional principles, tended to be mechanical. Perugini, in a comparison of training in the 1920s with that of the Victorian era, acknowledges that the latter 'was generally somewhat parrot-like; the names of the various steps and *enchainements* not always being correct; and reasons seldom given for their performance' (1925c: 39). Such a picture is corroborated in Mackenzie's fictional description of his heroine's pre-Orient training at Madame Aldavini's (Mackenzie 1929: Ch.VIII). A more sympathetic view of the demands of a dancer's technical training is given by Booth (1929: 152):

> The trained dancer lives in a world of her own. For one thing, she is ever in the most rigid training. Her most ordinary daily exercises would cause the pet professional footballer to scratch his head anxiously and think seriously of increased wages.

Whilst it is clear from their autobiographies (Kyasht 1978; Bedells 1954; Genée in Guest 1958) that the principal dancers continued their studies, usually with personal tuition, Booth's account is unusual in that it hints at the continuing training of the other ranks of dancers. However, these 'exercises' may have simply been their regular preparation before performance. Undoubtedly, the technical training of the dancers destined for ranks lower than principal was limited in scope. They were trained with a particular end in view, that of a permanent place in the *corps de ballet*, rather than with the aim of a progressive career in dance. Such a lack of opportunity was recognised by Hibbert who noted that 'as a matter of fact, the average is not one possible *première danseuse*, of any grade, in a thousand pupils. Say ten or more may aspire to some lesser distinction' (1916: 198).

It is, therefore, hardly surprising that British dancers were accused of a lack of ambition when their sights were so limited and their opportunities so curtailed. Nevertheless, the dancers took pride in their work and a consequent rivalry between the two venues is evident from the following statements from dancers themselves. An ex-Alhambra dancer recalls that she and her peers 'were expected to dance, unlike the *corps de ballet* of the Empire, who merely "held up the scenery" and were in attendance on the prima ballerina' (Hayman in Guest 1992: 55). The Empire dancers were equally dismissive of their rivals: 'I am afraid we at the Empire rather looked down on the Alhambra girls, I dare say this because their theatre had never had a ballerina of Genée's status' (Bedells 1954: 37). Evidence such as this not only demonstrates the dancers' pride in their art, but also counteracts the insouciance attributed to the ballet girls in relation to their profession.

The working conditions of the dancers

The working life of the dancer of any rank was one of practice, rehearsal and performance at unsocial hours. However, particularly if compared with the other main fields of town-based employment for the working class woman such as domestic service and clerical work, and the very limited opportunities for the middle class woman, at least in the large venues their tenure was stable and secure. It is difficult to ascertain their income because sources which mention figures rarely give the year, or period during which the income was earned. In relation to the principal dancers, Hibbert (1916: 209) is the most useful source as he illustrates how wages increased from the 1870s-1880s through to 1907.

> Some dancers now receive very large salaries. At the Alhambra in the old days £25 a week was considered a large fee. Genée came to the Empire for £15 a week and for a long time she was content with thirty; towards the end of her time there she had £70. Then came the boom. Not to be precise, the four most prominent dancers of the day range from 250-270 pounds a week.

According to Guest (1958: 22) Genée's first contract at the Empire was £20 per week and this figure is likely to be more accurate than Hibbert's as Guest's text was approved by Genée herself. Hibbert's estimate of £70 is likely to be accurate as Kyasht, who succeeded Genée in 1908, was given a contract after a month's employment of £75 per week, rising to £150 in 1911 (Kyasht 1978: 152). Compared with her income of the equivalent of £7 per month at the Imperial Theatres, it is not surprising that Kyasht accepted the Empire's contract. Nevertheless, the income of a *danseuse* was good but not excessive. (Marie Lloyd, for example, could command £600 a week at the height of her career in the 1890s.) The *premiers danseurs* appeared to command far less than the women. Paul Sundberg was paid £5 per week when he partnered Genée in *The Duel in the Snow*

(Empire, revived 1903). Whilst Sundberg would not have had such a major dancing role as the *danseuses* this disparity of earnings reflected the relative status and popularity of male and female performers.

The wages of the *coryphées*, house *corps* and hired apprentices are more difficult to determine. Sources tend not to give specific dates and the term 'dancer' may cover a variety of levels in the company hierarchy. Perugini clarifies the distinction between those who were hired and those who had completed their training.

> There was a time when a young dancer was glad enough to appear in ballet ... as unpaid, or practically unpaid, apprentice of a teacher who farmed out the talents of her school ... When out of her apprenticeship she was glad to earn one portion of her income in business during the day, and another by appearing in some production at night for a salary of a pound a week. Indeed, a pound or thirty shillings was a fairly usual salary for a dancer or chorus lady some thirty years ago.
>
> Perugini 1925c: 39

This estimate is corroborated by Hibbert who locates the wages of a trained dancer at between 18s.-30s. per week. A chart published in 1891 (Leppington 1891: 261) indicates the hierarchical nature of the *corps,* placing the front eight dancers as earning 35s.-38s, the middle rows 15s.-30s. and the back rows and extras 10s.-15s. per week. In the same chart, a scene painter earned approximately £3 per week.[11] High (1985: 20) says that the dancers had to provide their own tights and shoes which cost between 2s.6d. and 5s. and lasted for three to four weeks. However, Bedells (1954: 22) points out that satin shoes and silk tights were provided. This discrepancy can either be accounted for by a change in management practice over time or High may be referring to the *corps* and Bedells to the principals.

As Booth, C. (1903: 324) describes a small family income of 2ls.-22s. as 'on or about the line of poverty' it can be seen that the dancers' incomes were low. Hibbert (1916: 108) was of the view that 'dancers of the rank and file are shamefully ill-paid'. His comment is particularly pertinent in view of the fact that 'the ballet girls are sometimes married women with families of their own, though more often they are girls living at home and supporting their parents, or else lodging by themselves or with some of their companions' (Leppington 1891: 251). Whatever the case, their income was crucial, for 'the survival unit for most working class people was the family and women's labour, paid and unpaid, was absolutely vital to it' (Yeo in Colls, ed. 1988: 17-18).

According to Guest (1992: 131) the senior pupils at Lanner's school who were hired to the Empire received £4-£8 per month and children ls.-2s. a performance. Bedells received £4 per week at the age of thirteen but she was employed directly by the Empire and was undertaking solo roles.

The *premières danseuses* under contract at the Alhambra and Empire were able to earn a good but not immoderate wage. For the hundreds of women of the *corps,* trained or otherwise, the financial rewards were poor. Hibbert (1916: 193), in one of the few accounts to address the employment opportunities and rewards, summarises the general situation:

> There are in London some 3000 young women who probably describe themselves as actresses and who, in varying degrees, really depend upon the theatre for a livelihood. They provide the decorative background of the stage; but they are capable of many sub divisions - dancers, singers, extra ladies and show girls are some. Many of these girls have a definite and laudable ambition, industry and courage. Not more than two-thirds of them can command regular work. Their salaries range from 18s. a week - at which rate, I regret to say, it is possible to engage a trained dancer - to £5, which in rare cases is given to a 'show girl'.

A realistic view from inside the profession comes from an itinerant dancer, who noted,

> there are no fortunes to be made as a dancer unless you happen to be a Loie Fuller, a Genée, a Maud Allan or a La Belle Otero. But most dancers like the stage life, and prefer it to business. They are doing the work they like, and this is compensation for their small pay.
>
> anon. 1913: 78

Even though poorly paid, the dancers' income was, as discussed, essential for their survival. In rare documentation in which the voice of the ballet girls is heard directly, their panic at the threatened closure of the Empire is evident (see Ch. 6). For a dancer to write to the men of the London County Council would have taken courage indeed, and Emily Banbury's letter is full of apologies. She pleads, 'my engagement at the Empire theatre is of subordinate character ... but as my position is my livelihood I am emboldened to appeal to you, not only in my own name but also in that of my two sisters and other ladies' (LCC 13 October 1894). Having performed at the Empire for seven years, she points out the serious consequences of the loss of jobs 'in the present already overcrowded state of the labour market'.[12] Such an appeal is a reminder of the devastation that the closure of the Empire would have caused to the lives of hundreds of working women and men employed by the theatre.

As with wages, the working conditions in the theatre differed according to the dancer's place in the hierarchy. The principals had their own dressing rooms as was, and still is, the custom in all branches of the theatre. A sketch of Genée's dressing room (Royal Academy of Dance archives), with its dressing table, chairs, lamps and flowers depicts a room which could belong in a private home. Facilities for the *corps* were the obverse. Mackenzie's (1929: Ch.II) fictional description of backstage is corroborated by a letter of complaint written to the London County Council. William J. Butler drew the inspectors' attention to the small, dirty, gas-lit rooms, with their inadequate sanitary provision and rats: 'In each of these rooms ten to 12 (*sic*) girls all perspiring from strenuous dancing have to spend the evening to earn a living. These conditions are liable I should say to lead to consumption and other illnesses' (LCC 5 August 1911).[13] A further letter from

Butler, a tenacious campaigner whose link with the theatre is unknown (a search among cast lists for the period may reveal a family connection), complained that, by January 1912, as men were being hired for the ballet the women were even more crowded in a fewer number of rooms (LCC 6 January 1912). The complaints did elicit an inspection, reports and recommendations, though it is not known what action was taken.

For the house ballet, however, the management of both the Alhambra and the Empire provided material perquisites which perhaps made the working life of a dancer less harsh than her contemporaries in other fields of employment. Bedells (1954: 24) describes how, when the performers were working extra long hours during the latter stages of rehearsal for a new production, 'food was provided in the foyer at the back of the circle for the *corps de ballet* and the stage staff.' The principals: 'were given excellent meals at the Queen's Hotel next door where a large table was kept laid and ready for any of us who were able to slip out of the theatre for half an hour or so.' In his colourful account of an Alhambra ballet, Mayhew describes how during the rehearsal, which usually lasted from eleven a.m. to two p.m., 'somewhere about mid-day there is a ten minute interval for luncheon, when 'mother' is in great demand, with her bread-and-cheese basket and cans of beer' (1892: 64).

An illustration in Mayhew (1892: 66) accompanying the article depicts this 'mother', an elderly, aproned woman with a large basket full of bottles. Another sketch shows the dancers at rest around a makeshift trestle table, with a bottle by their side and a glass in their hands. In sources on the music-hall ballet, such evidence of the working environment of the dancers is rare and, although presented in words and in pictures as rather rosily cosy, it effectively reveals the human element behind the fantasy world.

Further evidence of the working day of the dancers is provided by an article in the *Westminster Budget* of 1893 on the provision of a Rehearsal Club for ballet girls. This club was the idea of a member of the Alhambra ballet, who 'confided her views on the subject to Lady Magenis'. A committee was formed, the honorary secretary of which did her best to make the club 'popular with the class for whom it was opened' ('M.L.C.' 1893: 26). It was intended for use by the ballet girls between their daytime rehearsal (or matinee) and the evening performance. The journalist who visited the club found that 'there is a cheerful, independent spirit abroad ... Opinions are given freely on all subjects and good natured chaff rattles around like hail ... On the whole, a visit to the Rehearsal Club leaves a charming impression of jolly, unaffected girlhood (pp.24-25). Even allowing for a pert and rather patronising journalistic style, the matter-of-fact attitudes of the dancers to their daily job is evident, and makes an interesting contrast to the romantic perceptions of some writers of the period (see Ch.5).

The workload of the dancers during the evening performances differed according to whether there were one, two or three ballets on the programme and the scale of these works. Unlike the Imperial Theatres in Russia, for example, where ballets were cast from a number of principals, the Alhambra and Empire engaged only one or two *premières danseuses* at a time and they were therefore expected to dance at every performance. Kyasht felt overworked but recognised that her increase in salary was compensation: '(I) ... had to make two changes at every performance and dance three numbers in the space of fifteen minutes. At the Imperial Ballet I had been accustomed to dancing only two numbers and then resting for an hour' (Kyasht 1978: 154). Guest (1992: 132) records that dancers 'were not allowed out of their dressing rooms between the two ballets and unpunctuality and negligence were punished by fines'. This small detail reveals the disciplined environment in which the dancers worked and is a further strand of evidence to undermine the loose-living, dilettantish image of the dancer explored in Ch. 6.

The contrast between the glamour of the ballets and the working lives of their executants is highlighted by sympathetic writers of the period. Booth (1929: 152) admonishes his readers,

> it has perhaps been a cherished notion of yours that the life of the ballet-girl is one delirious round of champagne suppers and attendant admirers. It does not now surprise you in the least to hear that she is one of the hardest workers in the theatrical family. Her life is one unvarying, stereotyped routine of practice, rehearsal and performance. In the ballets there is no place for the frivolous butterfly of popular imagination; the discipline is merciless, and the physical demands exacting.

Booth describes the dancer's daily routine:

> In the theatre itself she lives amongst her own people; together they perform their highly specialised share of the evening's entertainment and, that over, home she scurries, for the belated meal and the rest before the next day's round of practice, rehearsal, theatre.

Hibbert (1916: 197-98) similarly stresses the hard working, mundane nature of the life of the working class dancer.

> She must devote herself each day to practice. At night she must report herself sober and competent. Shortly after eleven you may see her at Charing Cross waiting for the Brixton bus. To her, the Savoy is a shadow, and Romano's a romance. She is the sedate, painstaking artisan of the stage, with her sick clubs, and her boot clubs, and all the petty prudences of the working class.

Again, another writer was

> astonished at the amount of hard work the *corps de ballet* had to get through. Rehearsals were strenuous and frequent, and the girls appeared each morning with the regularity of factory workers. Their life seemed one incessant hurrying backwards and forwards from home to theatre.
>
> Willis in Green (ed.) 1986: 180

Symons, in a poem entitled 'Behind the Scenes: Empire' (in *London Nights* 1895: 21), encapsulates the incongruity between the identity, individuality and mortal world of the ballet girls and the fantasy world of their art:

> Blonde, and bewigged, and winged with gold,
> The shining creatures of the air
> Troop sadly, shivering with cold.
>
> All wigs and paint, they hurry in
> Then bid their radiant moment be
> The footlights' immortality!

Examination of the identity, background and training of the principal dancers reveals shared characteristics. Like the choreographers, they were either Italian in origin or studied the Italian system of training and this technical and performing tradition linked the music hall ballet to its forbears. Such a shared tradition, however, could also result in a bland uniformity of style. In Ch. 3 it is suggested that both the emphasis on technical virtuosity at the expense of personality, and the dehumanisation inherent in the genre, were not only responsible for inscribing the image of the ballerina but also for differentiating her from other performers.

The continuing importation of not only a tradition but also the executants of that tradition gave little opportunity for a 'national' performing style to develop or for indigenous dancers to achieve principal status, or, indeed, any status at all. For the British *corps de ballet* at the Alhambra and Empire, career prospects were almost non-existent, wages minimal and the daily life one of monotonous hard work. However, employment was regular and comparatively secure and, although they saw the obverse backstage, the ballet offered all the charm and excitement of the theatre. Such a world would have been enticing compared with other opportunities open to working class women of the time. Furthermore, disciplined though their lives were, the ballet must have given a sense, if not the reality, of independence. The world backstage was also a woman's world, offering friendship and *camaraderie,* where women could relate not just to men but also to each other. The working class dancer from the *corps de ballet*, able to earn an income of her own, however minimal, and achieve a degree of independence and eventual respect for her skills, exemplified the move towards emancipation and the change in social attitudes towards women.

Nevertheless, an examination of the ballet girls' working lives reveals the reality of their existence behind the glamour of the ballets. Backstage, as people, they trooped 'sadly, shivering with cold'. On stage, as performers, they were 'blonde, and bewigged, and winged with gold'. How this fantasy world of the ballet embodied not just the traditions of the genre but also the social and ideological consciousness of the period, and how the image of the dancer was formed by that consciousness, is now explored.

NOTES

1. Office of Population Census and Surveys Census records 1881, 1901 and 1911. There is no separate category for dancers but notes to the 1921 statistics clarify that the category for 'actors - female' includes 'dancers', 'ballet dancers', *danseuses* and 'chorus girls'. See, however, Davis (1991: 41-46) for discussion of the anomalies in census records in relation to the employment category of 'actress'.
2. For example, the music hall appearances of Emma Bessone (Alhambra 1885-86 and 1888-89); Carlotta Brianza (Empire 1888; 1893-94) and Enrico Cecchetti (Empire 1888; 1891 - are not mentioned in Wilson's (1974) or Koegler's (1987) dictionaries. Perhaps more significantly, general historical texts written during the mid twentieth century, reflecting on the development of so-called British ballet, omit either the performers or their music halls pasts. Noble (undated, circa 1949) on Bedells, leaps from her first appearance in 1906 to 1920, passing over her Empire performances from 1907 - 1915 during which she acquired the status of *première danseuse*.
3. Some British dancers achieved principal roles such as Louise Loveday, a protégée of Lanner's, who appeared as *première danseuse* in *Around the Town* (Empire 1893) and Minnie Tight, a soloist at the Empire and elsewhere. Topsy Sinden, primarily a skirt dancer, succeeded Genée as principal in *The Belle of the Ball* (Empire 1911) and Marjorie Skelley was Genée's understudy at the Empire and took on the Russian Yekaterina Geltzer's leading role in *The Dance Dream* (Alhambra 1911). Unity More, an Irish woman who learned with the famed Mrs. Wordsworth, took principal roles at the Empire from 1909 to 1913.
4. There was at least one other Danish dancer, Mlle. Britta (real name Petersen) who performed at the Alhambra from 1908-10. Alexander Genée trained in Russia as a pupil of Johannson, who himself was a pupil of Bournonville who studied with Vestris at the school of the Paris Opera. It is possible that the lauded expressive qualities of Adeline Genée's dancing were in part due to this French influence on her training.
5. A full list of principals can be found in Guest (1992) and further biographic details in dance encyclopaedias or dictionaries such as Haskell and Richardson (eds. 1932); Wilson (1974) or Koegler (1987).
6. Among other sources, it is indicated that Bedells was the first English ballerina in Gadan and Maillard (eds. 1959) and Clarke and Vaughan (eds. 1977). Haskell (1972: 71) refers to her as 'the first English dancer the English public had accepted'.
7. Skirt dancing did originally utilise a balletic vocabulary for the lower body which was elaborated upon with the manipulation of a long skirt around the legs. In time, the latter became the more important element and the technical skills were lost. (See Flitch 1912 Ch. 5.)
8. One dancer who achieved fame after allegedly auditioning for the Empire and being turned down was Isadora Duncan. Guest (1992: 121) cites an interview with an Empire dancer who remembers Duncan though it is not clear whether she was auditioning for a place in the ballet or as a speciality act. MacDonald (1977: 54) also states that Duncan 'had an audition at the Empire theatre with Katti Lanner, but she was not accepted' but the source of this information is not revealed. It would appear that Duncan did take ballet classes with Lanner and this may have promoted the connection with the Empire (see Daly 1995).
9. Col. Mapleson's son, the opera impresario Charles Mapleson, married the Empire performer, Cavallazzi.
10. Bedells notes that 'there were, eventually, a few company classes, but they weren't very satisfactory, so most dancers and company members found their own teachers to help them' (Borgnis 1982: 26).

11. By 1899, Rose Batchelor, who as leader of the *coryphées* would have been senior in rank, earned £4.10 for one week's work. (Alhambra artists engagement book, May 1898-December 1900. Theatre Museum, London.)
12. Another letter, the writer of whom is probably a dancer though this cannot be proven, is equally heartfelt. The loss of the Empire's licence 'will throw most of us out of engagement without being able to procure another ... most of us are the mainstay of our families - some having as many as five or six dependents on them - so you can imagine what hardships there will be' (LCC 16 October 1894).
13. Working conditions do seem to have improved from previous decades. In 1864, dancers of the *corps* who combined their performing work with that of seamstress, described their dancing life as 'laborious, unpleasant, comfortless, wet, sloppy and sorefooted' ('T.W.R.' 1864: 43).

CHAPTER THREE

Dancing the Feminine: Gender and Sexuality on Stage

The image of the dancer was produced, in different but complementary ways, by the constituent parts of the ballets and by the unifying characteristic of spectacle. In its emphasis on this production value, the music hall ballet paralleled the continental music hall, the mainstream theatre of the period and the fashionable design aesthetic. The flowing lines, decoration, colour and exuberance of *Art Nouveau* found their theatrical equivalence in the vitality of the can-can, the swirling draperies of Loïe Fuller and the clashing sabres and violent colours of Fokine's dances from *Prince Igor* (1909). In a discussion of the formalistic concerns of Nijinsky's ballets, Garafola (1989: 317) notes that his works 'made up but a fraction of the repertory. In the larger context of pre-war Ballets Russes, sensory thrill, not structure, was the pivot on which the company's aesthetic turned'. It was, she further suggests, this commonality of 'sensory thrill' which, in the eyes of Bloomsbury, vulgarised Bakst's designs and 'demoted them to the level of the music hall' (1989: 320).[1]

As argued earlier, images are constructed not only in cultural artefacts but also by their public reception. In the case of the music hall ballet, as with dance of any period, writers repeatedly chose certain characteristics of the dance for attention. It is these characteristics which were the most significant features of the ballets and which constitute their 'meanings' for the audiences of the period. The lack of any 'objective' critical writing and the very obvious personal engagement of the commentators on the ballets are not obstructive, for the historian cannot read 'through' the records to retrieve some unsullied 'fact'. It is the very bias or subjectivity embedded in the records which constitutes our knowledge and understanding of the past. The same idea applies to visual sources. These, in the main, comprise sketches and photographs which are posed either in the studio or in *tableaux* on stage. Their significance lies in *how* the artist or photographer chooses to present the dance and dancers. The choice of what to write about and how to present the visual image is revealing of the attitudes and perceptions of the time and it is these choices which contribute to the production of the image of the dancer.

Differentiated dancing

As with most classical ballets, the narrative was told primarily through mime or dramatic action; it was not advanced substantially by the actual dancing. The tenuous relationship between the dance and the plot was one of the conventions of the ballet against which Fokine (1914) rebelled so this was not a particular characteristic of the music hall. Because the movement vocabulary was based on the *danse d'école* for the *premières danseuses* and a much simplified version of this for the *corps*, together with what would appear to be stereotyped character dances and social dance steps, sources rarely state what the movement entailed. A description such as Espinoza's of Palladino in *Diana* (Empire 1888) is rare:

> she commenced at the top left corner of the Empire stage, placed in perfect *arabesque ouverte*, the back leg at hip level, the heel clearly visible below her instep. She executed a series of *relevé, arabesque, cabriole derrière*, sixteen times, travelling down to the lower right corner. No arm waving up and down - the back leg never lowering - a clear cut beat by the lower leg, rising to beat the top leg and sending it higher - perfect placement throughout - *and on one leg all the time!*
>
> Espinoza 1947: 17 [2]

Sources on the movement vocabulary of soloists other than the principals are also scarce though photographs of them in ballet shoes suggest that they too used the classical ballet vocabulary. Information on the *corps* is rarer still and tends to focus not on the movement but on the spatial patterns made by the *corps*.

Due to its adherence to the *danse d'école*, the formal elements of the movement vocabulary of the *premières danseuses* were more important than the expressive content, and pattern and spectacle were the most important features of the works overall. However, these characteristics of the genre do not negate the significance of the formal elements of the ballets in the construction of the image of the dancer. Although some of the following comments could apply to the ballet in other periods and other places, there are significant differences. For example, the music hall had no *pas de deux* as currently presented in ballet where the male dancer is active in dance movement terms.

The premières danseuses

Not all principals were classical ballet dancers and, as suggested, many of those who were also performed character and the social dances of the time.[3] However, as Shaw's comment (Laurence 1981b: 596) that Guiri in *By the Sea* (Empire 1891) 'condescended to frank step dancing' suggests, it was the *danse d'école* that was their *raison d'être* and the device by which they were differentiated from the rest of the cast.[4]

As Bensusan (in Flitch 1912: 66) admits, the vocabulary of the ballerina, when adequately executed, was admired although audiences did not appear to be too demanding of her technical skills.

> Several great dancers have told me that it is not worth their while to take trouble about very difficult steps, because unfortunately they are not understood, while something that is obvious and childlike in its simplicity, like a *pas de bourrée* is safe to meet with a measure of applause.

George Bernard Shaw was often extremely critical of this aspect of the choreography. The following extract is typical of Shaw's observations on the work of the *premières danseuses* who, he says,

> were still trying to give some freshness to the half-dozen *pas* of which every possible combination and permutation has been worn to death these hundred years, still calling each hopeless attempt a variation and still finishing up with a teetotum spin.
>
> Shaw in Laurence 1981c: 97

Shaw, who approached the ballet from a very particular critical perspective, often highlighted the 'teetotum spin' (that is, like a spinning top) which can be assumed to be a *pirouette* or possibly a *fouetté*, one of the recent extensions to the vocabulary of the Italian dancers.[5] Regardless of his preoccupation, however, the dances comprised more than *pirouettes*. Although there is not one contemporary description found to date (Espinoza's being published nearly thirty years after the performance), a composite picture culled from many written and visual sources indicates the use of *arabesque, attitude, retiré, batterie, tours, brisés, pas de bourrée* and other basic positions and movements which constitute the classical ballet vocabulary. Flitch, like Shaw, complained that the performers 'never seek to go outside the narrow circle of conventional gestures, which the Empire ballet has received as a sacred tradition from the Italian' (Flitch 1912: 175).

Even the non-technical description by Anstey reveals *pointe* work, fifth position *port de bras* and *pirouettes:*

> She advances ... on the points of her toes, her arms curved symmetrically above her head ... her high stepping prance around the stage, her little impulsive runs and bashful retreats ... her final teetotum whirl.
>
> Anstey 1890: 191

Sketches and photographs often show dancers *en pointe* on the tips of their toes, either in *retiré* or fifth position. The use of *pointe* work by the principal was one of the devices by which the demarcation between her and the *corps* was maintained. As Hanna suggests, a dancer *en pointe* not only achieves physical elevation but implies social and moral elevation as well, for 'in a sense, the toe shoe raised women above the herd and out of the house' (Hanna 1988: 125). The use of the *pointe* was a central characteristic of the classical ballet genre from the Romantic period onwards, though the development of the boxed shoe (from the 1860s) from the simply darned toe meant its significance changed from depicting the aerial, ephemeral feminine to enabling *terre-à-terre* (steps that barely leave the ground) displays of technical bravura, a key feature of the Italian school. The fact that the *première danseuse* was usually the only performer to utilise that convention, however, raised her above the heads, metaphorically if not totally literally, of all the other dancers on stage.

The great majority of visual sources depict the ballerina facing front, looking directly out at the viewer, a presentational stance which is, again, characteristic of the genre. It is important to distinguish, however, between posed photographic sources which almost always present the ballerina with her body and focus facing out to the viewer, and sketches of the dancer in action. These are more vital in their depiction of the movement and sometimes show a sideways stance. In contrast with the other performers, who are often facing the diagonal, gesturing towards the ballerina or in a more spatially confined pose, her whole body is exposed most fully to the viewer and their gaze engages her directly. As Berger (1972: 56) says, 'almost all post-Renaissance European sexual imagery is frontal - either literally or metaphorically - because the sexual protagonist is the spectator-owner looking on'.

Whilst Berger is discussing the nude in painting, his observation could also be applied to the ballerina on stage and in sketches and photographs. Even taking into account the fact that *ensemble* photographs were posed in *tableaux*, the frontal stance and centrality of the principal in comparison with every other person on stage, is clearly evident. She is not only central, but on display. The fact that the ballerina in the great majority of ballets either lacked a partner, or was partnered by an *en travestie* performer, meant that she was a comparatively independent figure on stage. She relied, physically, on no one.[6]

Despite her technical bravura and independent status on stage, the very frequent description of her personal and dancing qualities as 'charming' or 'graceful' and such comments as her 'smile of innocent childlike delight' or 'infantine smile' (both Anstey 1890: 190 and 191), gave the ballerina an image that was child-like in its (apparent) innocence. Similarly, Bensusan's observation (Flitch 1912: 66) that movement was chosen which was 'childlike in its simplicity' may be as indicative of the image of the dancer as it was descriptive of her movement. Anstey's choice of terminology in describing the dancer's 'impulsive runs ... bashful retreats ... and astonishing complacency' with which she is supported by her partner is such as may describe the actions of a child or young girl. However, many studio portraits of principal dancers depict them with a slight incline of the head to one side and the skirt lifted to show one leg in *tendu*. These present an image which is innocent but also coy. A picture of Kyasht (illus. 3) shows her *en pointe* with one arm extended *en seconde*. The classical position is subverted, however, for the other arm is bent at the elbow and closely frames a tilted head. The effect is bashful yet flirtatious. Photographs of Palladino, Genée and Bedells each one with her head thrown back and her arms raised and bent to the back of her head, are typical of the 'pin up' or glamour pose which raises and accentuates the breasts.[7]

In terms of how her dance vocabulary was described, the *première danseuse* appeared to display movements that were refined; simple to the point of cliché; graceful and charming rather than, as with today's dancers, powerfully virtuosic. Care must be taken, however, for the descriptions in primary sources reflect a dearth of critical knowledge and language. They may also be related to the notion that for women, it is appearance rather than action which is observed, and which defines their identity, for it is what the ballerinas look like rather than what they do which forms the bulk of critical comment. In reviews and writing on the ballets, the personal qualities of the ballerinas in action are repetitive: the girl-like qualities of gaiety and vivacity, and the lady-like ones of charm and grace were noticed more than any other attributes. Even when her skill was evidently missing, these qualities redeemed the ballerina: 'Mdlle. Mari is an attractive little dancer who, if she cannot equal some of her predecessors in skill, yields to none of them in charm and grace' (anon. 1903: 478).

Passion was admired in Spanish dancers such as Guerrero (Perugini 1946: 230) but the term was rarely, if ever, used to describe the dancing of the principals of the classical ballet school.

The corps de ballet

The dance vocabulary of the *premières danseuses* was so codified that the absence of description in contemporary criticism can be understood. As far as the *corps de ballet* is concerned there is an even greater dearth of information but this cannot be attributed to the same reason. The Alhambra and Empire *corps* did receive some training (see Ch.2) but it would appear, from lack of any comment otherwise, that they used the *danse d'école* at its simplest level of shape, gesture and travelling. As Flitch (1912: 174) describes, 'frequently, the *corps de ballet* have no room for any more elaborate step than an artless hop and a right-about turn, a kind of convalescent pirouette'. In a supposed compliment to Katti Lanner's work, it was said that she 'can always manage to show us something fresh in the way of ballet drill' (Jack-in-the-Box 1895).

The actions of the *corps* may have been more complex than those which Flitch rather unkindly suggests and, later in the period, the skills of the *coryphées* were used more extensively. The number of character and 'national' dances performed by the *corps* would call for a broader range of movement even if these dances were not authentic.[8] For example, the programme for *Enchantment* (Alhambra 1888) included Bell, Slave, Demon's and Rustic dances. Slightly more informative of the content of this work is the Looking Glass Polka and the Grand Valse. Many ballets finished with a galop, a stirring ending guaranteed to elicit applause. This social dance terminology is indicative of the tempo of the music but what is not clear is the extent to which actual social dance steps, rather than just the rhythms, were used. A description of 'a polka, danced by a little company of Japanese' (anon. 1904a) suggests that, in whatever manner social dances were presented, there was little regard for their appropriateness to the subject matter.

Visual sources are not helpful for they tend to show the *corps* in lines of static poses or, the sketches particularly, in an abandoned kind of movement which suggests travelling but little else. Posed, off-stage photographs can be misleading and more indicative of a certain image than of the actual choreography. For example, five *coryphées* from the ballet *Titania* (Alhambra 1895) are shown (*The Sketch* 14 August 1895) albeit looking rather ill at ease, standing with a hand or hands raised to the nape of the neck in a coquettish gesture, whilst one other dancer reclines on the floor in front of them.[9] No images of any actual ballets depict such a group formation or such a seductive pose. It is possible, though not certain, that this image is as likely to have come from the imagination of the photographer as from the ballet itself.

The shoes which were worn by the *corps* comprised, in the main, short-heeled character shoes or soft, calf-length boots. It was not until *Coppélia* (Empire 1906) that Alexander Genée gave the house *corps* some *pointe* work and various photos of *Roberto il Diavolo* (Empire 1909) and *The Dancing Master* (Empire 1910) also show them wearing ballet slippers. Although it is unclear whether these are soft or hard toe shoes it does suggest that, by this stage, the range of their dance vocabulary may have broadened.

The lack of a vocabulary from the *danse d'école* is further indicated by a comment of de Valois' and by many other visual sources. Referring to Madame Rosa, an ex-Alhambra dancer who was choreographing at the Lyceum in 1919, de Valois (1959: 42) says the *corps* 'always carried some implement for, as Rosa would imply, they had no *port de bras*'. Visual sources substantiate that this was also the case with the Alhambra and Empire *corps*. For example, in twenty-one of Wilhelm's designs for the ballet *Round the Town* (Empire 1892; displayed at the Royal Academy of Dance, London) all the dancers are holding a property in their hands or arms. The great majority of other visual sources depict the same device. Whilst the implements held by the *corps* would have contributed to the total visual display, they would have greatly hindered the dancers' movement potential. As illus. 4 demonstrates, the complexity of their costumes and headdresses would also have restricted freedom of movement.

Although some distinction must be made between the *coryphées*, who were often cast in groups of four, six or eight and the large mass of the general *corps*, it would appear that the dance vocabulary of both was simple and undemanding. Whatever they actually did, there was no question of any comparison between them and the ballerinas either in content or in execution.

Critical comment on the *corps* is almost always of a different order from that on the *premières danseuses*. Bensusan's description is typical of the elusive nature of what the former actually did and also the distinction between them and the ballerina: 'from the *première danseuse* you get at times the most delightful movement; the long rows of dancing girls who give effect to some exquisite colour scheme may move with ... grace' ('S.L.B.' 1899a: 173). Some commentators did see an improvement in the performance of the *corps*: 'it is noteworthy that during the past few years the standard of dancing of the rank and file has wonderfully improved' (anon. 1896a: 71), though this type of comment appeared to be related to their ability to march, drill or stay in straight lines. What is evident is that there was no expressive, dramatic or individual element to their dancing.

> The groupings and mass dances are done with great spirit and unfailing precision ... but I am bound to say, that once or twice when the 200 or 300 young ladies bobbed their heads and pointed their hands in unison, I should have liked them better had I grasped what they might mean.[10]
>
> anon. 1888:198

Further evidence of this lack of an interpretative imperative is Symon's observation on attending a rehearsal at the Alhambra that, as far as the 'ladies of the ballet' were concerned, 'no one knew anything about the plot of the ballet which was being rehearsed, and ... many were uncertain whether it was their fate to be a boy or a girl' (Symons 1896: 79).

What is clear is that whatever the *corps* did, they did *en masse*. Even though many of the ballets created scenes of bustle and employed large crowds it appeared to be the placing and dramatic actions of the supernumeraries or auxiliaries which created these scenes.[11]

> The stage was encumbered with gorgeous properties and with the crowd of those who did not dance but merely took their place in the pageant ... at the same time the ballet dancers, whose business it was to dance, were transformed into a chorus whose chief function it was to look pretty.
> Flitch 1912: 65

Flitch's general description of the *corps* was that they 'marched and counter-marched across the stage, performing a number of evolutions with a kind of military precision' (Flitch 1912: 65). Such a description is often echoed in reviews of the ballets, even to the extent that 'the precision, the almost military efficiency, of the *corps de ballet* will earn the praise of those most competent to award it - the officers of the Services' ('S.L.B.' 1899b: 348).

Such descriptions would certainly seem to be in accord with the military or patriotic ballets but the spatial configurations implied appeared to be common in works with a wide range of subject matter.[12] Even 'daintily clad geishas' performed 'evolutions' (anon. 1902a) and the programme for *Cleopatra* (Empire 1890) included 'evolutions of Romans and Eygptians'. The allocation of dancers to 'rows' in the *corps* suggests that, even if marching was not always incorporated, lines and rows of dancers were. Shaw describes the Alhambra and Empire *corps* as 'consisting of rows of commonplace dancers, individually uninteresting (from the artistic point of view) but useful for the production of lines and masses of colour in rhythmic motion' (Shaw in Laurence 1981b: 804).

The programme cover for the Alhambra which was used during the mid-1890s shows two long, perfect lines of dancers receding into the distance (illus. 5). The dancer at the front of the line is in a whirl of motion; the *corps* behind her each has one leg raised and the ones behind them simply stand holding a staff. The choice of such an image for the cover not only highlights the importance of ballet on the music hall programme but also suggests that a large cast arranged in long lines of identical movement or positions was a significant image associated with the Alhambra ballets at this point in their history.

Anstey offers one of the most evocative descriptions of the *corps* in action: 'company after company of girls, in costumes of delicately contrasted tints, march, trip or galop down the boards ... at each fresh stroke from the stage manager's gong they group themselves anew or perform some complicated figure except when they fall back in a circle and leave the stage clear for the *première danseuse*' (Anstey 1890: 190).[13] This description indicates the size of the cast, their movements, group formations and, interestingly, the off-stage prompting. It also reveals a common device used in classical ballet choreography until the twentieth century, that of signifying the pre-eminence of the ballerina through the use of spatial patterning on stage. In almost every visual source examined which depicts the *première danseuse* and *corps* together, the former is placed centre stage and the latter provides a frame, not just with their bodies but also with their gestures. The direction of their focus and their arms, often enhanced by the use of a property, constitute a network of patterning which draws attention to the central figure of the ballerina. The frequency of such an image, plus written evidence and the conventions of the ballet genre confirm that the hierarchy of the music hall ballet was as strictly delineated on stage as well as off.[14] One of the most important functions of the *corps* was, therefore, to highlight, accentuate and maintain the prominence of the *première danseuse*.

The lack of any individual choreographic identity for those other than the principals is evidenced by the fact that, in reviews of the ballets, these members of the cast are rarely named unless they are soloists in character roles, in which case the quality of their acting is observed rather than their dancing. It would be expected that members of the *corps* should remain anonymous when the casts were so large and the choreography called for conformity rather than individuality. However, even the small groups of *coryphées* were rarely singled out by name. Most critical comment on the *corps* emphasised their regulated, almost mechanistic role, their earnestness and collective ordinariness. They possessed 'well trained movement' (anon. 1896b: 87); 'the ensemble was in every way worthy' (anon. 1897b: 730). They were 'a battalion' who performed their task 'with as much grace as zeal' (anon. 1904b: 4). Grove (1895: 380) also describes 'battalions of girls' and Shaw (Laurence 1981b: 804-805) refers to 'successive squads of girls'. Such nomenclature was applied not just to military ballets but also to a wide variety of subject matter. It served to emphasise the automated nature of their dancing and, as such, their depersonalisation. However, as discussed in Ch. 5, it is interesting to note that, amongst all this conformity, some members of the audience were able to discern individual faces, though interest was in the dancers as people rather than as performers.

The lack of a skilled movement vocabulary, the uniformity in content and patterning and their spatial formations, particularly in relation to the principals, indicates that the prime function of the *corps* was to be decorative. Thus depersonalised, it was they who constituted one of the main devices on which the music hall ballets depended for their popularity: colour and spectacle.

The dancer as spectacle

The one characteristic feature of ballet in pantomime, in the larger music halls and at the Alhambra and the Empire especially was their spectacle, achieved through the mass use of people, colour, costume and the new technical device of electricity. In this respect, as in others, the ballet in London particularly was part of an international production aesthetic which reflected the cultural climate of the times. The decorative flamboyance of architecture and of interior design, and a taste for luxury which became increasingly affordable, was reflected on the stage.[15] Apart from certain periods when a dramatic plot was just as important as staging (see Guest 1992) the emphasis in music hall works, like most nineteenth century ballet, was on visual effect and 'in the colouring, the costuming, the lighting, in short, the stage presentation in the completest sense - an artistic design, an impulse towards brilliancy and grace of effect, is always dominant' (Shaw in Laurence, 1981b: 713).

In reviews of specific ballets it is the stage presentation which tends to receive the most complimentary attention. Some critics, however, found that although the staging was successful in itself it was detrimental to the dancing:

> That fine effect is gained by all this wealth of colour and display of dazzling dresses cannot be denied, but it is effect gained at the expense of dancing ... it is in reality the destruction of a high form of one art for an inferior form of another.
> St. Johnston 1906: 111-121[16]

As Grove (1895: 380) describes, one major device by which spectacle was achieved was 'whole battalions of girls ... made to pass before the public in a kaleidoscopic way'. In a discussion of how he used colour schemes as central organising ideas for the ballets, Wilhelm himself admits that 'the members of the *corps de ballet* ... became convenient units in the development of the scheme' ('T.H.L.' 1893: 344). The women of the *corps*, thus depersonalised as 'convenient units', function as moving pictures of colour and costume.

Although the *corps* lacked identity as people, criticism of the period reveals one respect in which they were identified, though again corporately rather than individually. Moving kaleidoscopes were an attraction of the ballets but it would appear that the bodies of the dancers were even more so. The question of the physical image of the dancer is later considered in detail but an examination of how costumes for the ballets were described in primary sources reveals the critical preoccupation of the time and the main aspects of their performance by which the dancers were identified.

The costumes of very many ballets were undoubtedly decorous, apt and seriously conceived. They were rarely seriously described, however, except in very generalised statements regarding their colour or luxury. It is probable that so many changes of costume within each ballet prohibited detailed description. For example, the costumes for *Round the Town Again* (Empire, 1899) comprised the 'fashionable, military, classical, rustic ...(and)... carnavalesque' (anon. 1899a: 808). However, as the following examples of descriptions of the ballets which span the whole period demonstrate, critical comment points to a more spurious perception of what, at least on many occasions, was functional design: 'the Hall of Stalactites ... scantily attired in costumes of brilliant colours' (anon. 1887b: 266); 'a squadron of Life Guards in undress ... trip it merrily to the tune of The British Grenadiers' (anon. 1889: 3); 'the nearest approach to shocking which an observance of the Lord Chamberlain's rules allows' (anon. 1891a: 6); 'pretty girls, very scantily attired' (anon. 1893b: 575); 'Amazon figures ... in burning flesh-tight armour' (anon. 1902b) and 'costumes which half conceal, half reveal the rose coloured fleshings beneath' (Perugini 1915a: 280).

As discussed in Ch. 6, Ormiston Chant, with a different motivation from that of the critics, was shocked at the supposed indecency of the ballets. Her concern, in relation to the two works she saw at the Empire in 1894 (*La Frolique* and *The Girl I Left Behind Me*), was about tights which imitated the colour of flesh so realistically that it looked as though none were being worn and 'cavaliers' with 'tights up to the waist and very little apology for extra clothing' (in Donahue 1987: 58). Whatever the motivations of the writers, these descriptions cannot be taken at face value. 'Lightly' or 'scantily' clad women would obviously have been perceived as such in relation to contemporary standards of fashion and, no matter how brief and flimsy the costume, the dancers would always have worn 'fleshings' or tights underneath. Sometimes the subject matter of the ballets necessitated such costumes. An exotic or Eastern scene called for diaphanous harem trousers such as those sketched in the programme for *Algeria* (Alhambra 1887); the Bathing Ballet in *By the Sea* (Empire 1891) which almost contravened the Lord Chamberlain's rules (as above) could be performed in little other than 'bathing costumes'. The potential of such costumes for titillation, however, would have been enhanced by the fact that not only were women displayed in such attire but also that they were actually moving in it.

Comments such as the above may have been valid in relation to specific works but it is how the collective image of the dancers in their costumes was presented which is of interest. The Alhambra's programme cover for 1893 (illus. 6) includes a sketch of a long row of dancers in vigorous travelling movement and seemingly semi-naked attire. What appears to be bare midriffs and legs are covered by the most transparent of gauze. The programme cover for the same theatre in 1908 shows a dancer with breasts barely concealed by a small bolero. This was how the management wished to present the dancers of the *corps to ballet* to their public.[17]

Another programme cover for the Empire 1897 referred not to a dancer in action but to a static representation of the Britannia personification which appeared in the ballet *Under One Flag*, the source of the new programme's design. The large figure of Britannia is presented with conventional regalia of helmet, shield and trident. She is barefoot and clothed in transparent robes which clearly reveal a naked body underneath. Thus, even Britannia was eroticised.

Even if the costume worn on stage was less provocative than the enticements on the printed programme suggested, they reflected the silhouette of fashion and thus enhanced certain features of the body. Costumes of the *en travestie* dancers or 'boys' were most interesting in this respect but even the 'girls', whatever the subject matter, tended to have their breasts or hips accentuated with decoration or by tightened waists. The traditional belle skirt of the classical ballet dancer, often worn with a tight 'V' shaped bodice, also accentuated the hip and pelvic areas of the body. Again, artistic licence prevailed in that the same Alhambra cover of 1893 (illus.7) depicts a dancer in balletic pose and what appears to be a ballet skirt which flares out just below her hips. All photographs show that ballet skirts were actually worn on or just above the knee. The presentation of this dancer in mid-air, with her skirt apparently blown by the wind, would seem an excuse for exposing an amount of leg which would never have been revealed by the dancer on stage.

In a number of works the ballerina adopted character costume for part or all of the ballet but, in the main, she wore the traditional belle skirt or tutu with an aptly decorated bodice. Such attire was often incongruous, particularly in the topical or 'national' ballets.[18] It did, however, set her apart from the other dancers. Unlike earlier ballets of the nineteenth century, in the great majority of works the *première danseuse* was the only dancer on stage in such a costume. With a few exceptions, such as *The Dancing Master* (Empire 1910) where the subject matter demanded this traditional style of costume, not even the *coryphées* were similarly attired. Whatever the nature of her role, such a distinctive costume contributed to the idealisation of the ballerina. This ideal image had to be protected and when she did don 'ordinary' dress and perform modern social dances there was critical consternation.

> It seems a mistake ... after showing Miss Bedells grace and skill in a conventional gauze skirt, to bring her on again in ordinary costume to do tango or ragtime steps or whatever they are. A *première danseuse* should surely be hedged around with more ceremony than is possible in this sort of frolic, or else we are in danger of mistaking her for an ordinary member of the cast.
>
> anon. in Bedells 1954: 67

Although this passage refers to a revue at the Empire in which Bedells danced a ballet solo as Pavlova, followed by a modern duet, her image as a ballerina was clearly at stake.

The other distinguishing feature relating to the *première danseuse* was that, if she was exempt from provocative attire on stage, she was also exempt from salacious comment in the press. Although remarks were made on her looks, her body was perceived quite differently from the bodies of other dancers. She did not contribute to what Clarke & Crisp (1981: 234) call: 'the naughtiness of any such entertainment.' The classical ballet vocabulary and its conventional costume protected the ballerinas from more overt 'naughtiness'. Neither device protected the *corps*.

The feminisation of the dancer

As would be expected, the actual body shape of the dancers reflected that of the fashion of the times. The ample figure of the mid-Victorian period is seen in photographs of Pitteri (Guest 1992: fig.8) and Pertoldi (fig.9), who performed at the Alhambra during the early years of the music hall ballet. By the standards of the late twentieth century, these dancers were large in stature. Pertoldi was described by Morton & Newton (1905: 157) as 'magnificently formed' and this, plus terms such as 'buxom' and 'statuesque' reflected the admiration of the mid-Victorian man for large women.[19] Over time, attitudes changed and by 1892 Shaw remarked on Palladino that she reminded him of the approaching opera season, an allusion to the shared buxomness of the dancer and female opera singer (Laurence 1981b: 596).[20] By the Edwardian period, the silhouette, rearranged by corsets, had changed to one which drew attention to the slimness of the waist by accentuating the curves of the bust and buttocks. The 'S' shape is the most common image of the Edwardian woman and it was certainly reflected in the ballet. Although a ballet skirt or tutu usually delineates the waist, during the music hall period the smallness of this part of the body was even more emphasised. As discussed later in this chapter, the 'S' silhouette was further exaggerated when the dancers were dressed as boys or men, thus removing any ambiguity as to their sex.

The body shape of the dancer was, therefore, as much to do with fashion as with natural physique. Booth, in a discussion of chorus girls, points out that 'it is a delusion of the post war school to imagine that the show girls of the early days of the century were over-plump, heavy and dull. So-called statuesque beauty was largely a matter of clothes and feminine fashion' (Booth 1929: 76). In an effort to remain in fashion and please their audiences, dancers in the ballets sometimes resorted to artifice. As Bedells reminisces, 'the fashion was for dancers to be rounder ... I remember two dancers with whom I shared a dressing room, who used to pad their behinds and busts to make them more curvaceous' (Bedells in Borgnis 1982: 24).

One of these dancers may have been Lizzie Osmond, a soloist at the Empire who tied a bustle under her dance skirt to give herself more shape (Bedells 1954: 35). Bedells herself was encouraged by Cavallazzi to pad out her calves because her legs were too thin. Thus, even the dancers conformed, by artifice if not naturally, to the desired body shape of women from the middle and upper classes of society. It was not until the advent of the Russian dancers such as Kyasht and Pavlova that the bodily appearance of the dancer began to change, as did that of post-war women in general.

As in fashionable society, the boning and corsetting of the dancer's body drew attention to erogenous zones. These zones, however, were acceptable and part of a legitimised socio-sexual code. The constriction of women's bodies highlighted potential sexuality but also contained it; the corsetted woman was a respectable woman. (Much of the fascination with, and censure for Isadora Duncan was that she rejected the corset, the symbol of Victorian 'straight lacing' in every sense.) The body shape of the *premières danseuses*, whether in traditional or in character costume, was nearly always confined by corsets and boning. Photographs of the *corps* suggest that they, too, were usually equally confined; Bensusan ('S.L.B.' 1896a: 523) wondered why it should be that dancers dressed as 'boys' were wearing girls' corsets.

Whatever their actual body shape the one important requirement for all dancers was that they be physically attractive. Descriptions of the dancers, both on and off stage, emphasised certain looks and personality traits as much as, if not more than skill. As Bensusan notes of the ballerina in general, 'so long as there are good looks, talent goes for nothing' ('S.L.B.' 1896b: 336). The Empire management's reaction on meeting the previously unseen Kyasht was one of relief when 'it was seen that so far as beauty was concerned the new dancer was everything that was hoped for' (Booth 1929: 139). Perugini (1946) has a marked paucity of vocabulary when describing the principals and soloists; adjectives such as 'attractive'; 'vivacious'; 'charming'; 'graceful' and 'handsome' abound. The fact that many writers, including Shaw and Fitch, deprecated this emphasis on the dancers' looks supports the prevalence of such practice.

So idealised was the physical image of the ballerina in particular that anything which distorted such an ideal met with disapproval. Beerbohm makes a scathing attack on the disproportion between a ballerina's arms and legs, the outcome of a long 'unnatural' training.

> This structure ... (of the dancer's body) ... jars my aesthetic sense, as being an obvious deviation from what is natural ... it is unnatural that dancing should be the business of her life. And Nature takes revenge by destroying her symmetry, by making her ridiculous. Poor ballerina!
>
> Beerbohm 1906: 614-15

Thus, the price paid for the achievement of the dancer's skill, muscular legs, was an offence against men's eyes. Beerbohm goes on to reveal another perception of the dancer in performance. It was extremely rare for any dancer to be credited with intelligence.

> Such power of thought she may once have had was long since absorbed into her toes ... she really fancies that she is admirable, admired. And so she is, in the way that a performing dog is admirable, admired.

(Beerbohm made an except for Genée, however, who was not a 'monstrous automaton' but had retained her personality.) A comment from twelve years earlier that a Spanish dancer, Candida (in *La Frolique,* Empire 1894) 'scorns the inane smile of the ordinary ballerina' ('Monocle' 1894: 258) supports the view that ballerinas in general were perceived as pretty, graceful and charming, but rather vacuous and vain. Displayed, in every respect, to the audience she is conscious of that display and her 'inane smile' is recognition of her function to please. She watches herself being watched. It is interesting that at least two photographic images of ballerinas depict them looking into mirrors.[21] This gesture most likely was conceived in the studio rather than on stage, though one complete ballet, (*Femina,* Alhambra 1910) was a moral tale based on the evils of feminine vanity. In European art, the depiction of women watching themselves was not uncommon and the mirror was one device used to compound the image of woman as 'sight'.

A clearly prized attribute of the dancers was their youth. One critic bemoaned that

> the only thing against a long run for a ballet ... is that it interferes with the pleasing illusion of youth that we associate with the ladies of the ballet. When a lady has played a prominent part throughout a production of this kind it is impossible to overlook the fact that she must be at least as old as the ballet. And I understand that the ladies are not always prepared to admit even that much.
>
> Golsworthy 1902: 410

This comment is clearly nonsensical if taken literally, for the ballets rarely ran for more than six months. However, it does stress the illusion of youth and implies the complicity of the dancers in the maintenance of that illusion.

Not only the ballerinas but also the *corps de ballet* was perceived as a 'sight'.[22] The one term which constantly recurs in description of the *corps* is 'pretty' and, as the following comment of Symons' epitomises, this appeared to be their main claim to fame. The Empire's *corps* was, he says, 'in some respects the choicest in Europe, not, certainly, for its skill in dancing, but as certainly for its youth, its juvenile grace, its actual physical charm' ('A.S.' 1894b: 624).

Symons was referring to the large groupings of dancers. The small group photographs which exist are probably of the *coryphées* who, being more experienced, would be older women. Nevertheless, despite the conformity demanded by the subject matter; the uniformity of movement imposed by the choreography; the facelessness implied by terms such as 'battalions' or 'squads' of dancers; the association of youth with the term 'girls' and the connotations of superficiality in the description of 'pretty' looks, actual photographs of the *corps* and *coryphées* present, literally, a different picture. They reveal women of a considerable variety of ages, heights and, whilst still conforming to the silhouette, body shapes. Also, whilst it is difficult to evaluate the physical appearances of one era by the standards of another, the significant feature of these photographs is the clear, often striking individuality of each dancer's looks. Unlike many images of the *premières danseuses* they look at the camera in an artless, open manner which lacks any hint of coy or overt seduction. Even when wearing near-identical wigs, their faces and bodies are far more disparate and full of character than written and other visual sources on the ballets lead one to expect.

So far, this Chapter has examined how the dancer was presented in the ballets, in iconographic representation of the works and in critical comment. Since, in many of its components, the music hall ballet was part of an established genre, some of the observations made could be applied to the image of the dancer in other periods and places. An image is made, however, by the circumstances of time and place and these circumstances may, or may not, be altered in different contexts. For example, the 'display' of the ballerina and the basic elements of her movement vocabulary are two central characteristics of the genre but these need to be interpreted not only in relation to the special nature of the music hall ballets and their audiences but also in terms of their contribution to the composite image of the dancer. The music hall ballet had enough distinguishing features to constitute a style of its own and it is in these respects that the image of the dancer can be particularised to the period. For example, a historical feature of the classical ballet is that the ballerina is presented and perceived differently from other members of the cast. Her movement vocabulary, her costume and her occupation of the stage space single her out. During this period the *corps*, lacking *pointe* work and restricted to the simplest of movements, were no competition and served to highlight and display the relative complexity of the ballerina's dancing. The isolation of the ballerina in the music halls was even more marked by the high degree of contrast between her and the rest of the performers. The ballerina's foreign 'otherness' and the *corps*' British-ness, compounded by the fixity of the class structure, were played out as rigidly on stage as it was in society.

The one respect in which the performers were treated alike was that their identity was defined as much by what they looked like, as by what they did. Even when the skill of a ballerina was remarked upon, so were her looks. Definition by physical appearance is not, of course, confined to the critics of the music hall ballet; it appears to be a response endemic to the genre. Three features of this era, however, make it particularly pervasive. Firstly, the lack of status of the music hall ballet resulted in a dearth of dance knowledge and related critical language about the choreography or the performance, but writers were on sure ground when describing the physical appearance of the dancers. Secondly, the difficulty of acquiring or demonstrating a knowledgeable critical perspective was compounded by the predominant and eventually stereotyped production value of spectacle which meant that visual effect was all-important. It eclipsed both plot and dancing. Lastly, and perhaps most significantly, women (except for those in the lower classes of society) in Victorian and Edwardian England were expected, above all else, to be decorative.[23]

Both ballerinas and *corps* shared this function of visual spectacle but were differentiated in the meanings embodied in the ballets and ascribed to their performance. If the ballerina on stage was distinguished from the rest of the cast, her classical ballet vocabulary also separated her from the subject matter itself. Her solos and variations did little, if anything, to advance the plot. She was, therefore, a remote figure on stage, occupying a different world by virtue of a dance vocabulary and costume particular to her alone. It was a vocabulary which lifted her out of the realm of the ordinary, even within 'ordinary' plots such as those which the topical ballets addressed. Paradoxically, it was also a vocabulary and style of presentation which exposed her body most fully to the audience. Such a distancing, yet accessibility is evident in many of the visual images of the ballerina. *En pointe*, she is not of this earth but her look and the stance of her upper body make her unquestionably female.[24] Her exposed foot in *tendu* emphasises the symbol of her art, the ballet shoe. It also draws attention to her foot and ankle which were erogenous areas of a woman's body. Woman as dancer merges with woman as erotic being in a composite image. The ballerina, idealised, otherworldly, hinted at accessibility but not attainability. She belonged, nevertheless, to the eye of the spectator. Such an image was made more potent, both in performance and in the iconography of the dancer, by the absence of a male partner.

Utterly and obviously feminine: the *en travestie* performer

The demise of the male dancer and the convention of women playing men's roles in men's attire dates from the Romantic period in the first half of the nineteenth century. Garafola notes the contributory factors which affected the production and consumption of the ballet itself. Cross-dressing on stage,

> coming into vogue at a time of major social, economic and aesthetic changes ... reflected a shift of the ballet from a courtly, aristocratic art to an entertainment geared to the marketplace and the tastes of the new bourgeois public.[25]
>
> Garafola 1985-86: 35

When commercial managers had to appease the 'market place' which comprised a predominantly male audience, the male dancer lost his appeal and only kept his place, if not his status, in the theatres of Russia and Denmark which retained their royal or imperial subsidy. By the 1870s in Western Europe, the male dancer had become such a maligned figure that he was virtually absent from the stage. The male role was undertaken by women *en travestie*, a convention matched in the music hall programmes by other performers whose act was based on cross-dressing. Some, like Vesta Tilley, evolved her entire stage persona around this device. A programme for the Alhambra in 1885 itemises Tilley's appearance on the bill together with two ballets, *Melusine* and *The Swans*. Likewise, in 1888, the programme included Tilley, *Antiope* and *Enchantment*. Although the nature of these performances was obviously very different, music hall audiences were attuned to seeing women dressed as men on stage. It was not until 1901 at the Empire when Santini partnered Genée and 1903 at the Alhambra when Volbert played Don Jose in *Carmen* that this travesty tradition for principal roles began to wane, though it was by no means lost altogether. Established performers such as Cavallazzi and Zanfretta were frequently praised for their dramatic skills. Although it cannot be established for certain in relation to all performers, it would appear that most had previously trained as ballet dancers; this was undoubtedly the case with the afore-mentioned two performers and British artists such as Flo Martell and Julia Searle are also named in programmes in non-travesty roles. It was extremely rare for the *première danseuse* to appear in travesty; Geneé's role in *The Bugle Call* (Empire 1905) was an exception. By presenting a more ambiguous image, however, the role lacked appeal for her admirers (Guest 1992: 124).

There were two main types of role played by the travesty performer. She was either the 'male' principal or she was one of the small groupings or lines of 'boys' in the *corps*.[26] As discussed below, the former acted, albeit non-verbally, and the latter danced.

The roles played by the travesty principals were those of heroes, usually benign, though they were also cast as more malevolent protagonists; any personification of human vice tended to be *en travestie*. There is irony in such militarist personifications as, for example, 'Demon of War' (*Entente Cordiale*, Alhambra 1904) being played by a woman, but these roles were exceptions rather than the norm. Whatever the nature of their roles, the travesty performers were active in the sense that, as 'men', the characters they played were agents of the narrative. Whether they captured or rescued the female lead, captained the army, initiated the romance or arranged the seduction, they were able to 'do' rather than just to 'be'; to act rather than simply react. They tended, however, not to be cast just in any male role. Women did not normally play elderly men, unattractive men or men who were fools or idiots. Since these tended to be comic and/or character parts they were taken by less 'serious' character actors or dancers. It was as if women could only take on a male persona if the idealised masculine attributes of strength, virility and good looks were not undermined.

A line of 'boys' was an inevitable feature in the composition of the *corps* and these roles often went to older members of the company. This was not always the case, though sketches which show undoubtedly youthful 'boys' must be treated with circumspection. It would appear that all ages, including children, were cast in travesty roles and, as indicated by Symons' (1896) comment that some members of the cast did not know if they were to be boys or girls, there were no consistent rules on the casting of travesty roles in the *corps*. In both topical and traditional works the most common types of role were soldiers or fighting men of one kind or another. They also danced various ethnic groups to suit the subject matter of the exotic ballets and represented all kinds of young men in the topical works, from cricketers (*The Sports of England*, Empire 1887) to costerboys (*Round the Town*, Empire 1892).

Although both principals and *corps* dressed as males the nature of their respective roles was very different due to their movement vocabularies. Visual sources which show the principal with the ballerina tend to depict the former either in some kind of dramatic gesture or acting as a supporting pillar. As Bedells says, the ballerina's work 'was always solo, with the exception of an occasional poised arabesque holding her lover's hand or shoulder; there were no lifts in the *pas de deux*' (undated mss., My dancing years).

The non-dancing travesty lead employed the mime of the Italian school. Her potency as a figure on stage not only came from her capacity to be active in her role but also from the nature of that activity. As suggested, by 'acting', albeit without words, the mime artist forwarded the narrative. Although the *premières danseuses* also used mime, for the travesty principal it was her only vocabulary. She did not dance, so all her gestures had almost literal meaning. Other devices, such as character dances and costume, indicated the story but it was the travesty performer who told it. The movement vocabulary of the 'boys' in the *corps* was the same as the *corps* generally and they fulfilled the same function: to provide a frame for the ballerina and to contribute to the kaleidoscopic spectacle.

There is a paradox in that, because of their costume and general appearance, the travesty performers were equally as feminised as the women of the ballets. Such a conclusion can be drawn not from overt statements in written sources but from an imaginative placing of the travesty costume in its broader social context and by the way in which these performers were presented in visual sources. The costumes of the 'boys' comprised variations on a theme of boots, tights and short tunics, and doublets or jerkins which were decorated to suit the roles. The principals wore the same but often with a longer tunic and/or the addition of a cloak. (For mature performers such as Cavallazzi, such a strategy may have added a little more dignity to her appearance.) The most obvious feature of this costume was that it allowed the display of the full length of the female leg not only up to the top of the thighs but, if sketches can be believed, up to the hip joint. In addition, the waist was drawn in tightly, thus accentuating, even more so than with the costumes of the female performers, the hips, breasts and buttocks. Not only was more of the female body revealed but its silhouette was uncluttered. Tillett's reading of the patriotic ballets at the Alhambra was that, among other functions, they served to allow the dancers to parade in 'bare essentials' of military costume which enabled them to reveal a 'substantial acreage' of their legs. Furthermore, according to Tillett, because of these 'bare essentials',

> popularity was assured, and decorum more or less preserved but the sale of opera glasses, in the front row of the stalls as much as the back row of the gallery, received an extraordinary stimulus.
>
> Tillett 1982: 7

Such an observation in a secondary source needs to be treated with caution as it is as much a reflection of Tillett's writing style as of fact. However, it does demonstrate very clearly how secondary sources perpetuate the eroticised image of the performer.

Clarke and Crisp's comment that 'the ladies of the *corps* dressed as soldiers - the combination of busby and silk tights was irresistibly funny' (1981: 235) is difficult to comprehend. No primary sources found to date indicate that this costuming was thought to be 'irresistibly funny'. It may have brought a smile to the faces of the male members of the audience, but this was likely to be for reasons other than its comic aspect.

Although Tillett's and Clarke and Crisp's comments probably reflect present day perceptions on past events, primary visual sources present an undoubtedly eroticised image of the travesty performer. In programmes such as that used for the Alhambra in 1886, the bodies of the dancers, particularly their thighs, are drawn with relish. Photographs of travesty performers are rare but even these, although they cannot match the slender lines and accentuated curves of the artists' imaginations, are posed to draw attention to the female body. Whether as principal mime or one of the dancing *corps*, any ambiguity in the femaleness of the image was also dispelled by other elements of the performer's attire. Visual sources show feminine hairstyles and wigs. One example is a Christmas card of Wilhelm's design for a *Mousquetaire* (musketeer) who wears a tunic which reaches the top of her legs, red tights and carries a musket. Her hair is long, ending in plaits which are tied with ribbons (Theatre Museum archives). The one fault Bensusan found with *On Brighton Pier* (Empire 1894) prompted his question, 'now, why will girls who dress as boys always wear girls' corsets and put on bracelets and rings ad nauseum? ('S.L.B.' 1896a: 523).[27]

As Davis claims in relation to actresses,

> in the Victorian theatre, adult female performers were never sexless: sex was always apparent in gendered costume, whether through tights, breeches, skirts, corsetted silhouettes or headgear.
>
> Davis 1991: 114

Likewise, the travesty performer in the ballets, far from being sexless, was presented and perceived as quite the opposite. The following comment from a review of Zanfretta as Mephistopheles in *Faust* (Empire 1895) reveals this most clearly.

> With her great, gleaming eyes and her insinuating movements ... (she) ... looks calculated to 'play the Devil' not only with 'Faust' but with every male who allowed his eyes to dwell upon her dangerous charms even for a dozen seconds.
>
> Jack-in-the-Box 1895

However, reviews of the principal travesty performers more commonly note the strength and power of their performance and photographs do not show the slender, youthful silhouette of the *corps* but far larger, sturdy women. For example, the 'male' attendants on Hippolyta (*Titania*, Alhambra 1895) are posed by the photographer with a solid, upright stance and their hands are on their waists or clasped in a suitable masculine pose (illus. 8). Two sit on chairs rather than recline on the floor, as the *coryphées* do in a companion photograph. This photograph makes a fascinating contrast with one of the female *coryphées* on the same page in which the lines of the grouping are far more sinuous and the gestures more overtly 'feminine' (illus. 4).

As Bratton suggests in relation to male impersonators in the legitimate theatre, 'a big voice and a commanding stage presence were at least as important as the twinkling legs and rounded backside. Maybe they were equally desirable' (1987: 13). It would not be far-fetched to suggest that an older, larger woman playing comparatively powerful roles could also be as evocative of sexual fantasy as any more conventional feminised image.

The logic of an overtly female body and the attribution of female characteristics to a 'male' role, as in the review of *Faust* cited above, was not questioned in critical response to the ballets and no writers point to the incongruity of a 'romance' between two women. As Davis (1991: 114) says, 'the offence to dramatic logic was substantial but inconsequential, for sexuality has its own dramatic logic.' Beerbohm completely missed the point of the inherent logic unrelated to role or narrative but contingent on the audiences' perception of the essential female. Asserting that the failure of women to succeed in art was because 'creative power, the power to achieve ideas and execute them is an attribute of virility: women are denied it', he attempts to prove his point.

> Never does one understand so well the failure of women in art as when one sees them deliberately impersonating men upon the stage and, despite all their efforts, remaining, as they always do, utterly and obviously feminine.
> 'Max' 1898: 498

Beerbohm suggests, with some complex reasoning, that it is easier for men to adopt women's qualities than *vice versa*. However, in the music hall ballets as on the legitimate stage, such a 'failure' was not to do with women's incapacity to act or look like men, but was a deliberate exposure and accentuation of the feminine.

Another perspective is offered by Garafola (1985-86: 39) who 'cannot help thinking that the buxom travesty heroes of the Second Empire and subsequent decades flaunted an outrageous femininity to ward off the sapphism inherent in their roles'.

The significance of placing two women in both a narrative and a movement relationship is interesting to contemplate. As indicated, a female 'hero' proved no barrier to dramatic logic but

> dancing by its very nature is a physical as much as a symbolic activity. In the formalised mating game of the travesty *pas de deux*, two women touching and moving in harmony conveyed an eroticism perhaps even more compelling than their individual physical charm.

In the music hall ballets, however, it would appear that there was little touching and even less moving in harmony than during the Romantic period which is the focus of Garafola's exposition. The travesty hero was a non-dancing role and any physical contact that existed between her and the ballerina appeared to be in the former's capacity as a pillar of support. There was not the physical intimacy of the traditional male-female *pas de deux* so Garafola's conclusion that

> the fantasy of females at play for the male eye is a staple of erotic literature ... Ballet's travesty *pas de deux* gave public form to this private fantasy, whetting audience desire, while keeping safely within the bounds of decorum.

needs to be treated with caution in relation to the music hall ballet, for erotic interplay between the travesty hero and the heroine was minimal.[28]

The travesty dancer in the ballets not only presented a persona of her own but also contributed to the stage image of the ballerina. In her role as principal male in the ballets, like the actress in the theatre, she 'impersonated young, vital and often heroic men in the prime of life. Unlike straight female roles, this permitted an actress to do things' (Davis 1991: 114). In the ballet, such a casting device also allowed ex-dancers to continue their stage careers, offered British women opportunities to take on principal roles and gave the performers the chance to develop and extend their dramatic skills.

Whether as principal or *corps* there was no question at all that the men and boys of the ballets were female. Yet, paradoxically, their roles were 'straight'; they offered no critique of masculinity but rather, in their guise as heroes, soldiers, pirates, aristocrats or men-about-town, they endorsed the idealised image of masculinity. Nevertheless, though their roles were male, the physical image was female. Unlike the stage actress, she had no voice to give her away but her hair, costume and silhouette dispelled any ambiguity. Her movement vocabulary, whether the stylised marching in complex formations or the asexual mime of the Italian school, did nothing to subvert this femininity. In the *corps*, she offered a display of legs and hips, an exposure of the female body totally at variance with social conventions. In her common guise as the military, some elements of sado-masochistic fantasy may have been enacted.[29] As principal, her non-dancing role was not in competition with the skills of the ballerina. As female partner to the ballerina, she also presented no threat to the males in the audience. They could place themselves in the position of the 'hero' not only as a man of action but also as romantic partner of the heroine. No real man came between them and the ballerina. The *en travestie* performer, eroticised herself, contributed to the image of the ballerina as sexually accessible to her audience, in private fantasy if not in public declaration, for her public image remained romanticised, coquettish yet ultimately chaste. This image did not belong to the *corps*. Unidealised by their movement vocabulary, their image is one of collective ordinariness and, as further argued in Ch. 6, they were perceived as sexually accessible and attainable.[30] These dichotomous images were also inscribed by the nature of the roles danced by these performers and by the very subject matter of the ballets themselves.

NOTES

1. Garafola (1989: 47) notes that, in pre-war productions, 'the emphasis on material luxury, a major production value up to 1914, indicates imperatives of a quasi-commercial order.' In other words, even Diaghilev's Ballets Russes was not exempt from having to cater for the love of spectacle endemic to the period.
2. Although the article is signed simply 'Espinoza' this would have been Edouard, who worked in the music halls (see Espinoza c.1946). As a dancer, teacher and choreographer writing for a specialist magazine, he would have been able to use more technical language than that utilised by the general critics of the period.
3. As a reviewer pointed out when discussing a *Pas de Fascination (The Handy Man* Alhambra 1900), a dance 'founded partly on dances that the Moors left in Spain ... (which) ... proves for the hundreth time that the Continental schools make every style of dance possible to the pupil who has mastered the severe training' (anon. 1900: 439).
4. The *danse d'école* also defined their self-perception in relation to dancers who practised other forms. An interview with Palladino on the relative merits of these and ballet records:

   'Then you assent to the assertion that the prima ballerina is the exponent of the higher art of dancing?'

   'Yes, certainly. It is very pretty indeed to see the Gaiety dances, but there is none of the *technique* in them of which the real ballet dancer is so proud.'
   anon. 1891a: 5

5. George Bernard Shaw's critical stance was one of a social realist who believed that the theatre had a moral role. Jowitt (1984: 28) suggests, 'I suspect that he mistrusted the body and thought that dancing looked more artistic and dancers more intelligent if the work involved acting though gesture.' It is hardly surprising that Shaw deplored the formal aspects of the ballet.
6. Genée's first male partner at the Empire was Santini in *Old China* (1901) but neither here, nor in later works, did the partnering appear to involve lifts.
7. A tilted head could be said to be a characteristic stance of the Romantic ballet and later, a feature of *epaulement*. However, its use with so many different gestures of the rest of the body is suggestive of more than just an element of the dance vocabulary. Sketches of dancers in action rarely reflect this pose; the ballerina's stance in these is nearly always upright. Similarly, a *tendu* is a gesture of the *danse d'école* but, when an ankle is exposed from under a lifted skirt, it takes on other meanings. A photograph of Edith Slack as a Greek dancer in a long embroidered dress and ballet shoes, lifting her dress to expose her outstretched foot, is an example of this common image (*The Sketch* 17 January 1900: 504).
8. The titles of many dances also indicate the use of 'national' or character dance steps or gestures. For example *Our Army and Navy* (Alhambra 1888) included Sailors', Irish, Grenadiers' and Highland dances. It is likely that these dances were distinguished as

much by costume and properties as by movement. In general, programmes named dances by character, nationality, social dance or dramatic event but the actual content of these is difficult to discern.
9. The reclining woman who, when nude, is described by Dijkstra (1986: 99) as 'the nymph with the broken back', was a very common image in Victorian painting.
10. The writer is exaggerating here, for the programme of *Dilara*, the work under discussion, specifies a *corps* of one hundred and fifty dancers.
11. Later, Fokine pleaded for the *corps* to contribute to the dramatic action of the ballets. *Petrushka* (1911) is an example of his intent.
12. In an interview she gave to *The Sketch* (anon. 1895a: 694) Lanner discussed her preparations for the military *tableau* in *Faust* (Empire 1895). One of her greatest difficulties, she says, is arranging these military scenes so that they do not look the same in every ballet.
13. Anstey does not give enough clues as to which ballet he is describing. His account of the *corps* as wearing 'burnished armour' suggests that it might be either *Astraea* (Alhambra 1889) or, perhaps more likely as the scenario included marches of Amazons, *Antiope* (Alhambra 1888).
14. In the visual and performing arts, the concept of space as hierarchical was central to Western European art. On the canvas and on the stage, the most important feature or figure was placed centrally. The democratisation of space began, or re-emerged, at the beginning of the twentieth century in the visual arts and Merce Cunningham, from the 1950s, was the first choreographer to question the relative significance of points in space.
15. Booth, M.R. (1981) examines the manifestations of, and reasons for, spectacle in Victorian theatre. He considers the legitimate theatre and pantomime but not the theatrical form which was the most spectacular of all, the ballet.
16. Grove (1895: 380); Bensusan ('S.L.B.' 1899a: 173); Image (1901: 465) and Flitch (1912: 63) were all concerned about the predominance of spectacle.
17. A series of photographs for *The Red Shoes* (Alhambra 1899) shows d'Alencon as the Avenging Angel dressed in semi-transparent drapes which reveal the outline of the body (Theatre Museum, London). This is the only photographic evidence found to date, however, which hints at nudity underneath an outer garment.
18. In reply to critics who found that not just the costume but also the balletic steps of the ballerina incongruous with certain subject matter, Palladino wrote a letter the *Daily Telegraph* (20 April 1891) in defence of her art, stating that 'the steps, being conventional, cannot be modified, whether the action takes place in China or America'. As the source of contention was the mythological ballet *Orfeo* (Empire 1891) she also pointed out that no one could know what the 'choreographic entertainment' of the Elysian fields were anyway.
19. In a society of 'conspicuous consumption', the ability to display wealth through the consumption of food as well as material goods was important. Throughout the Victorian and Edwardian period women were living examples of men's capacity to provide and, amongst the upper classes, the eating of vast quantities of food was common. Whilst the silhouette changed, women who displayed the physical results of such consumption were much admired.
20. Shaw's comment is supported by a revelation of Legnani's diet on a typical day. It is recorded that she had a good breakfast, including fillet of beef, and left home about 11.00a.m. for the theatre. Then, 'after practice for two hours, she lunched on five or six dishes and Chianti' ('E.F-S.' 1893: 761).

21. Two sketches, both of which are based on photographs by different photographic studios, appear in the *Daily Graphic* (anon. 1891a: 5). They show Palladino and de Sortis *en pointe*, each looking into a hand mirror.
22. The writer of a postcard (dated 5 May 1906, Mander and Mitchenson Collection) of *Parisiana* (Alhambra 1905) asks his correspondent 'have you been to the Alhambra lately, what price the legs ...?' This rare source supports the argument presented in this Chapter of how the ballet was perceived by an 'ordinary' member of the audience, as well as by writers and critics.
23. For a fascinating biographical account of the psychological distress and possible long-lasting damage caused by this aspect of women's prescribed role in late Victorian and Edwardian society, see Dunn (1990: Ch.3).
24. Many photographs, some of which have already been discussed, present this 'double image' of the ballerina. Kyasht (post-card advertising the Empire programme 1909) perches *en pointe* in *attitude* on a globe with her forefinger touching her lips. As Sylvia (anon. 1911: 4) she is again *en pointe* but, whilst her body faces to the side, her head turns and bends to face the camera in a coy gesture.
25. Although Garafola's article is entitled 'The travesty dancer in nineteenth century ballet', like many commentators on the ballet of this century she focuses, with one minor exception, on the period before the 1860s. Her concluding paragraph leaps to 1909 and the advent of the Ballets Russes. Again, a whole era of ballet history is overlooked. See also Daly, 1987-88: 59-60 for a feminist perspective on the reasons for and result of the absence of men from the ballet stage during the Romantic period.
26. Women who played men's roles tended to be known as 'boys' as in, for example, the 'principal boys' of pantomime. This could be attributed to their youthful appearance or, as with the terminology 'girls', reflect on their status.
27. It would be unusual for Wilhelm, who designed his costumes down to the last detail, to have allowed such incongruity of effect. However, historically it was not unusual for dancers to wear personal jewellery on stage for such public display of these possessions often denoted male patronage. For the *corps* of the music hall, it may have been an attempt to retain their individuality in the face of such collective homogeneity.
28. A rare photograph of a romantic relationship between principals is from *Soldiers of the Queen* (Alhambra 1900, in *The Sketch* 17 January 1900: 504). In it, Julia Searle is dressed as a Scottish Highlander in kilt and sporran. 'He' stands in a very masculine pose, with one hand on his waist holding a ceremonial sword and the other resting on a raised knee. 'He' stares directly out to the camera. Sitting by 'his' side the heroine is dressed in a long skirt, flounces and a large hat. She rests her arms on Searle's knee and gazes up to 'his' face. In dress and in posture they are stereotypically male and female. But any erotic, or even vaguely sensual, image is dispelled by the innocent urbanity of the pose. So conventional are the gestures, the photograph becomes almost caricature.
29. Bratton (1987: 13) suggests, with respect to male impersonators in the music halls that: 'by the 1900s the sexual fantasies played out in these acts were extensive and varied. One of the favourite roles of the male impersonator was the soldier. In an elaborate uniform ... sadomasochistic overtones echoed the glittering dominance of the principal boy.'
30. Such ordinariness is perpetuated in articles such as those by 'S.L.B.' (1896a), Symons (1896) and Booth's reminiscences (1929).

Illustration 1. The Empire promenade, 1902 (Mander and Mitchenson Theatre Collection, London)

Illustration 2. 'An undress rehearsal at the Alhambra', with Carlo Coppi (*The Sketch* 17 May 1893: 150).

Illustration 3. 'The Incomparable Lydia Kyasht' (Inside programme cover, the Empire c. 20 January 1912. Theatre Museum, London)

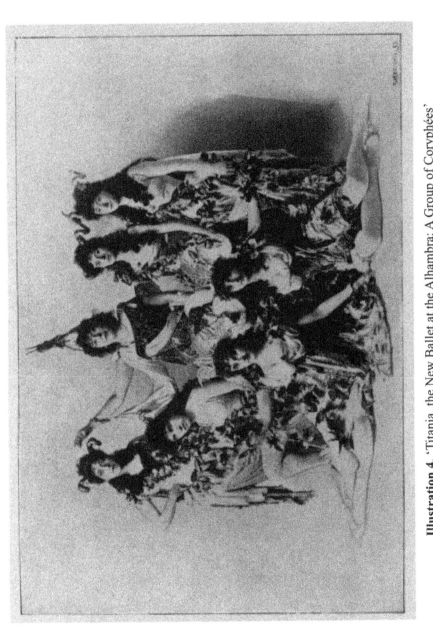

Illustration 4. 'Titania, the New Ballet at the Alhambra: A Group of Coryphées' (*The Sketch* 14 August 1895: 153)

Illustration 5. Programme cover, the Alhambra 1896 (Theatre Museum, London)

Illustration 6. Back programme cover, the Alhambra 1896 (Theatre Museum, London)

Illustration 7. Programme cover, the Alhambra 1893 (Theatre Museum, London)

Illustration 8. '*Titania*, The New Ballet at the Alhambra: Attendants on Hippolyta' (*The Sketch* 14 August 1895: 153)

CHAPTER FOUR

A Fairyland of Fair Women: Dancing the Narratives of the Age

During the thirty year history of the ballets at the Alhambra and the Empire there were changes in both the thematic material of the works and also in the treatment of that material (see Guest 1992), for the subject matter of the ballets mirrored the political and social concerns of the age. For example, many ballets dealt with imperialist themes which reflected the working class audience's familiarity with such ideology, if not any actual colonial experience. For the more affluent male patrons, many of whom travelled and worked in the colonies, the overt jingoism of the ballets would have had considerable meaning and relevance.

As Britain's sea power began to be threatened with the building of the German fleet, the ballets reinforced stirring images of the British military services both past and present. It could be surmised, however, that these themes were popular because they leant themselves to spectacular formations of dancers rather than for their potential to incite patriotic fervour. Other international occasions were celebrated in the ballets such as the signing of the *Entente Cordiale* with France in 1904 (*Entente Cordiale*, Alhambra 1904). Nevertheless, whilst the ballet acknowledged contemporary political events it neither addressed the issues nor questioned the ideologies. In its passive acknowledgement of social class differentiation, rigid gender roles and imperialist ideology, the ballet endorsed rather than challenged the *status quo*.[1]

Except for the large but hidden sub-class of those existing in abject poverty, living standards improved as new inventions and discoveries eased work, transport and domestic life. Electricity was brought into the home and the theatre, providing greatly increased opportunities in the latter for set and costume designers, as did the invention of the sewing machine. Ease of transport facilitated the annual seaside holiday, a theme addressed in several of the topical ballets. The bicycle became fashionable in the 1890s and appeared on stage as, later, did the motor car. The establishment of the *Daily Mail* in 1896 signified the growth of a popular press and a ballet was devoted to the topic (*The Press*, Empire 1898).

In broad terms, the subject matter of the ballets can be categorised into traditional themes that dealt with aspects of nature and the supernatural as contained in mythology, fairy tales and legend, and the topical works that were based on current events or interests. Historical times and foreign locations, particularly exotic ones, were common to both traditional and topical works as were sub-themes such as romance, the tussle between good and evil and the moral dilemma. (See Appendices III and IV for an indication of the general subject matter of the ballets.) Similarly, many roles shared common characteristics whatever the context of the narrative.

It can be argued that the subject matter of the works was the dancing itself, enshrined in spectacle. As *The Times* asserted, the plot 'is a matter of supreme indifference to an audience who only requires that the stage shall be filled with brightly dressed groups of pretty and graceful dancers (anon. 1884b: 4). This comment is, in itself, significant in its foregrounding of the looks and personal qualities of the dancers. Whilst the narrative may have been of secondary or of no importance, however, we are concerned here primarily with how it contributed to the construction of the image of the dancer rather than the story or plot *per se*.[2] Furthermore, whilst the audience may have been interested in 'pretty and graceful dancers', *how* those dancers were portrayed and the subliminal effects of that portrayal are of crucial importance. In other words, the ballets presented not just pretty girls in static isolation but women who moved in certain ways, with particular spatial configurations and in characteristic visual environments. They also adopted specific identities in named roles and 'acted' according to the framework of the narrative.

Fantastic, unreal and impossible: the supernatural world

The presentation of the supernatural is a significant characteristic of ballet's historical repertoire. For many people, the two are synonymous and the association of fairies and sylphs with dance has possibly done much to undermine its status as a serious art form. The music hall ballet reflected this tradition but the incongruity of, for example, the ballet *Rose d'Amour* appearing on the same programme as Jenny Hill ('The Vital Spark'), Dan Leno and Marie Loftus appears to have been accepted by contemporary audiences (Empire programme, 1888). During the late Victorian period there was an interest in the supernatural, in spiritualism and ghost hunting; fairies were even (allegedly) photographed. Within the broad social and cultural climate, the incongruity of presenting traditional fairy stories such as *Aladdin* (Alhambra 1892), *Ali Baba and the Forty Thieves* (Alhambra 1894) and *Cinderella* (Empire 1906) was not particular to the ballet, for

> the acceptance and rapid growth of fairyland as fit subject matter for literature, painting and the stage from the 1820s to the 1840s and its survival at least until the First World War is one of the most remarkable phenomena of nineteenth century culture.
>
> Booth, M.R. 1981: 36

Many of the topical ballets did not neglect the crucial role of a fairy. Even the Klondyke gold fields (*Alaska*, Empire 1898) had a Fairy Good Fortune. As with other personifications she would act as an agent of morality, revealing to the 'hero' the faults of his ways or guiding him to his destiny. Such revelations provided the excuse for yet more fairies in the vision scenes.

Aspects of the supernatural infiltrated the ballets in many ways, from the obvious to, by current perceptions, the almost ridiculous. Mythology and fairy story were common sources, though characters from the former tended to be minor rather than the all-powerful inhabitants of Mount Olympus. Artemis, goddess of the chase, made an appearance (leading two live borzoi dogs in *Sylvia*, Empire 1911), as did Hymen, goddess of marriage, and various other gods and goddesses of love. Goddesses, of mythological accuracy or otherwise, were far more common than their male counterparts, though the one authentic goddess from the Greek pantheon who was missing was Athene, goddess of wisdom. (Although it is possible to overstate the significance of this omission, it is, perhaps, an unsurprising one in the light of the perceived intelligence of the ballerina.) With their sylvan settings of the stories and the human involvement of the characters, these mythological ballets had a somewhat domestic air. Legend, ostensibly about the activities of humankind, also provided a supernatural element though it is difficult to distinguish between myth, fairy tale and legend. For example, in *The Faun* (Empire 1895) a mythological character of a faun appears in a 'blending of legend and mystery' (Perugini 1946: 257). The legend of *Faust* (Empire 1895) incorporated both spirits and angels.

Within the context of the ballets the appearance of the supernatural was part of the traditional excuse for colour, spectacle and fantastical costumes. It also served a purpose as escapism, as Symons so tellingly reveals in his review of *Titania* (Alhambra 1895).

> It is as fantastic and unreal and impossible as even I could wish for; and I like a ballet to have as much of the fantastic, unreal and impossible as it can be got to contain. I go to see a ballet in order to get as far as possible from the intolerable reality of the world around me.
>
> 'A.S.' 1895: 77

The world of the supernatural also served another purpose in terms of how the ballerina was presented. Although she may have led a *corps* of lesser luminaries, it was she who danced the significant supernatural role and it was a role of moral agency. She was thus distinguished by her quite literal other-worldliness and also by her goodness. Out of the entire supernatural repertoire there were few, if any, witches, demons, imps or other malevolent creatures played by the *corps* and certainly none by the *première danseuse*. In *Rose d'Amour*, for example, the malignant elf was danced by Cecchetti. Women in the ballets remained, even in their supernatural roles, generally untroublesome.

A flower herself: the natural world

One of the most common themes which provided either the substance and/or the setting of the ballets was that of nature. Mythological stories were chosen which gave the opportunity for a rural setting, as evidenced in Empire works such as *Diana* (1888); *Sylvia* (1911) and *The Water Nymph* (1912) and the Alhambra's *Narcisse* (1908) and *Psyche* (1909). Similarly, historical ballets such as *Versailles* (Empire 1892), *Sir Roger de Coverley* (Alhambra 1907) and *Fête Galante* (Empire 1906) were set, mainly or partly, in gardens. Works in which the pastoral theme was central included the Empire's *Rose d'Amour* (1888), *Les Papillons* (1901) and *The Reaper's Dream* (1913).

Such thematic material may be said to be part of the ballet tradition, particularly that which stemmed from the Romantic era, and this accorded with a resurgence of interest in Romanticism in the other arts. The neo-romantic themes of the arts in the 1890s revealed the fascination of an idealised country life, a fascination which stemmed from the mid-nineteenth century when the migration of agricultural workers to towns severed them from a harsh, but nevertheless a country life. The arts of the second half of the century appeared concerned with re-establishing that contact, but it was a 'nature' that was idealised and mythologised. As the century progressed and produced 'urban slums and vice ... how much healthier, it might seem, to turn instead to rural life' (Hennegan in Teich & Porter 1990: 198).

In a period which saw so many inventions, discoveries and developments which were to revolutionise social life and attitudes, the presentation of ballets concerned with fairies, flowers and fauna was not, therefore, so out of touch with the times as it may first appear. An example of how subject matter reflected contemporary interests is that the only Shakespeare text which was used as source material for an Alhambra or Empire ballet was *Midsummer Night's Dream* (*Titania*, Empire 1913). Whilst there may have been other influential factors such as the vogue or otherwise for Shakespearian productions, it seems that this work accommodated the pastoral, romantic and fairy themes which reflected not just the conventions of the ballet genre but also the psychological concerns of the period. The themes are even less incongruous when the roles of the dancers in these ballets are examined.

The significant feature of how dancers were presented in the pastoral ballets was their depiction not just as people populating country or garden scenes but the fact that they constituted the 'scenery' itself. In so many works, not only those with a pastoral subject matter, dancers were presented as flowers or other aspects of nature. Such 'roles' gave great opportunities to the costume designer and the arrangers of the ballets to present spectacular colour combinations and groupings of the *corps* as bouquets of flowers. However, the image of dancer-as-flower in the ballets and in painting signified more than just opportunities for colour and spectacle. Dijkstra (1986: 16) suggests that

> the 'pure' woman, the woman who, with her passive, submissive, imitative, tractable qualities, seemed to share with the flowers all the features characteristic of the plant life of the domestic garden, thus came very generally to be seen as a flower herself ...

One central motif of *Art Nouveau* design was the representation of women and flowers or fauna in a symbiotic relationship. In the ballets, women represented not only the natural phenomenon of flowers but also insects, butterflies and birds. Although there were few male dancers in the music hall ballets none appeared to be cast in these kinds of roles, neither were the male actors nor supernumeraries.

The impossibility of conceiving a male member of the cast as a flower or a butterfly reveals the gender specificity of such images.[3]

Links between ballet, the other arts and the period are more evident when consideration is given not just to which subject matter was chosen for the ballets, but which was ignored. As discussed, stories drawn from mythology were not generally the epic ones of major gods and goddesses, but those which were set in a pastoral landscape and included humans as principal characters. As Hennegan (in Teich & Porter 1990: 200) suggests, by the 1890s the countryside itself had so changed with depopulation and mechanisation, had become so tamed out of accord with poetic sensibility, that 'with tremendous thoroughness, the Decadents set about repopulating the English landscape' with nymphs, satyrs and 'Pan and his entourage dominate the rural scene'. In title roles such as the Dryad (Alhambra 1908) and the Water Nymph (Empire 1912) the principal dancers presented a complex image of the natural world to which men had access. As figures who were available for seduction or agents of seduction but who were never seduced, even their embodiments of the natural world had erotic connotations. It was 'the eroticised body of woman ... (which) ... became the late nineteenth century male's universal symbol of nature and all natural phenomenon' (Dijkstra 1986: 86).

Other places, other times: the international and historical worlds

A theme or a location which provided the excuse for the ballet and spanned both traditional and topical works was that of the internationally exotic. These works were set in or incorporated substantial scenes of distant places. Contrary to what might be expected, they tended not to be set in the countries of the British Empire. Among others, *Dilara* (Empire 1887) and *In Japan* (Alhambra 1902) had Eastern themes; Nisita (Empire 1891) was set in Albania and many works, including *Salandra* (Alhambra 1890) and *Tzigane* (Alhambra 1896) depicted the Magyar gipsy tribe, the Tzigane. The British Empire was not 'visited' in the ballets but, as might be deemed appropriate, its representatives came to Britain to pay homage. Many topical ballets included a dance of nations in which countries of the colonies, and the produce of those countries, were paraded in mass spectacle. Less exotic but equally evocative were the images offered by works set in France, of which there were a seemingly disproportionate number. This Francophilia reflected the political and cultural alliance of the two countries and the whole *fin de siècle* spirit was mutually fed. Fascination with the paintings of Watteau and Fragonard was one stimulus for Empire works such as *Versailles* (1892), *Fête Galante* (1906) and *The Dancing Master* (1910), all of which were located in a romanticised, historical France. All the *gaieté* of contemporary Paris was given full vent in ballets such as *The Gay City* (Alhambra 1900) and *A Day in Paris* (Empire 1908). Also closer to home, Spain not only provided opportunities for authentic Spanish dancers such as Maria la Bella to display their art but also for less authentic but highly colourful 'Spanish' dancing and costumes.

With world communication and travel becoming easier and knowledge of distant lands more accessible, these international ballets reflected contemporary interests. Many of the audience would have been well-travelled and to others the world had become a smaller place, in mind if not in their experience. What these ballets did offer was the opportunity to present spectacular and, by the standards of the time, *risqué* costumes.

> Every endeavour was made for the action of the ballets to shift from one country to another with each successive scene, since this afforded occasion for a complete change of costume and the introduction of character or speciality dances.
>
> Beaumont 1937: 758

However, the authenticity of either costume or dances was unlikely, for although Wilhelm at the Empire and Alias at the Alhambra were both renowned for their meticulous research and attention to detail, it is likely that the demands of an artistic colour scheme and the cohesion of *tableaux* would have been more influential than the imperative of authenticity. The imaginative approach to 'national' dances is exemplified in a critic's comment that 'a bevy of Indian beauties ... dance what is called a Nautch dance ... and it is not a bit like one - and end up with a peg-top twirling to furious pseudo-oriental music' (anon. 1893b: 575). Later, Ruth St. Denis presented her pseudo-oriental dances, including *Nautch* which she premiered in London in 1908.

The individual or collective roles of the dancers were varied but they usually represented national characters who were exotic, other-worldly and very far removed in both appearance and in movement from the reality of Victorian or Edwardian womanhood. Nautch girls, Eygptian slaves, Spanish dancers, odalisques and gipsies all contributed to the world of fantasy.

Historical ballets fulfilled the same function, being as much concerned with fantasy as with reality. They offered similar opportunities for imaginative sets and costumes based on a very selective history. Of ten 'historical' works produced at the Empire, at least six told tales specifically of the aristocracy and seven were set in France. Although supposedly dealing with a more 'real' world than that of mythology and the supernatural, ballets located in different times and different places were similarly based on a romanticised and idealised view of the world and its inhabitants.

Escape into reality: the contemporary world

One of the most common, though seemingly contrary, themes of the ballets was that of the up-to-date or topical subject. These themes were not particular to the British ballet during this period; Manzotti's famed *Excelsior* (La Scala 1881) referred to the building of the Suez Canal and the invention of the electric telegraph. In the music halls, however, these works became a staple feature on the programme which, when there were two productions nightly, would often include one traditional and one topical ballet. The artists who worked on them did not necessarily favour the latter. The Alhambra composer Jacobi, when asked what kind of ballet he preferred, replied 'the pastoral and mythological are certainly the best styles of ballet ... the sort called "up to date" is inevitably vulgar' ('A.S.' 1895: 77). Although Jones (in Waites *et al* (eds) 1982: 108) is referring to the smaller music halls rather than the larger palaces of varieties, his comment that 'music hall appealed to the London working class because it was both escapist and yet strongly rooted in the realities of working class life' is apt in relation to the programming of these two types of ballet which embraced both 'escape' and a version of 'reality'.

The topical works can be divided into three general sub-categories: those which reflected contemporary interests, those which referred to important events and, a combination of these, the patriotic or military ballet. Ballets in the first category included *The Sports of England* (Empire 1887); *The Press* (Empire 1898); works which reflected the new fashion for sea-side holidays exemplified in *By the Sea* (Empire 1891) and *On Brighton Pier* (Empire 1894) and those which dealt with travel and tourism such as *Chicago* (Alhambra 1893) and *Round the World* (Empire 1909, based on the Jules Verne novel *Around the World in Eighty Days*). The theatre dance of the time was not ignored: not only did *Sal! Oh! My!* (Alhambra 1908) parody Maud Allan's famous role, but *On the Sands* (Alhambra 1910) included a burlesque of Pavlova and Mordkin who were appearing at the Palace theatre. Special events were marked with ballets such as the aforementioned *Chicago* which coincided with the World Fair in that city; *Alaska* (Empire 1898) about the Klondyke Gold Rush; *Under One Flag* (Empire 1897), a commemoration of Victoria's Jubilee, and a work which marked the Coronation of Edward VII, entitled *Our Crown* (Empire 1902). The latter was also an example of a very popular theme for the ballets, that of the military and the patriotic. Between 1885 and 1914, thirteen works of this ilk were presented at the Alhambra and the Empire. Titles such as *Our Army and Navy* (Alhambra 1889); *Soldiers of the Queen* (Alhambra 1900, neatly becoming *Soldiers of the King* in 1901) and *Our Flag* (Alhambra 1909) evoke the spirit of these works. It is not difficult to source their popularity. The middle and upper classes who frequented the Alhambra and the Empire were often either service or ex-servicemen, colonial administrators or traders and the working classes at large, even if not directly involved, acquiesced to jingoism. The palaces, because of the nature of their audiences, positively embraced the British Empire.

> In these early years of the century ... (the Empire palace) ... was the dream of thousands of Empire-builders in tropic heat and yawning loneliness ... (and when) ... the lights of London at last shone for the exile ... it was to the Empire in Leicester Square that he winged.
>
> Booth 1929: 145

What is of interest in the topical ballets is what they ignore as well as what they address. One of the most topical social-political issues, particularly during the 1890s, was the question of the emancipation of women and the resultant disturbance of the sexual *status quo*. Despite the ideological shifts this entailed, only one work out of a total of over one hundred and forty ballets has been found which explicitly acknowledged the public fight for women's suffrage. This was

Elise Clerc's *On the Heath* (Alhambra 1909) which had a suffragette in the cast, though it is not possible to ascertain how that role was treated. That such issues were avoided in the ballets is demonstrated in a review of *Bluebeard* (Alhambra 1895) which suggested with apparent relief that

> elsewhere, 'Bluebeard' might be converted into a story of a woman's perilous search for knowledge, and the ultimate emancipation of the submerged sex. At the famous house in Leicester Square ... the famous story is treated with respect.
>
> anon. 1895b: 440

Such a statement reveals that there was a consciousness of women's search for and achievement of new roles in life but such roles were not enacted on stage. Or, if they could be interpreted as such, critics chose not to do so.

As the ballet did not offer any direct critique of political issues, except in its general Tory support of Tory values, it would be expected that the contentious topic of the place of women in society would similarly not be seen as suitable subject matter. What was also avoided was any representation of the New Woman. This phenomenon, the term for which was created in the 1890s, is reflected in novels such as George Gissing's *The Odd Women* but 'in paintings the New Woman is remarkably rare, if not conspicuous by her absence' (Casteras 1982: 146).[4] In the ballets, too, she is absent and even those works which dealt with events that affected the lives of women directly did not depict that effect. For example, *The Sports of England* (Empire 1887) neglected to show the new athletic prowess of women but celebrated male sports such as cricket, football and boxing even though, ironically, the roles were played by women dressed as men. Exceptions were in leisure pursuits which were reasonably acceptable for women; lady cyclists appeared in *On Brighton Pier* (Empire 1894) and hunting was shown in *High Jinks* (Empire 1904).

In the ballets concerned with world travel, it was generally not the women who travelled but the 'male' characters. Even if the New Woman took on the persona of the Amazon in painting, for 'she was in real life and art ... perceived as Amazonian in many ways' (Casteras 1982: 173) the ballets which presented Amazons, as a surprisingly large number did, negated their traditional warrior-like qualities.[5] No *première danseuse* appeared to be cast in such a potentially powerful role and for the *corps* who were, it provided an opportunity for shining costumes and spectacular stage formations. It is also interesting that, of over twenty works which had a female name as the title, only one (*Cleopatra*, Empire 1889) appeared to deal with a real woman, either contemporary or historical. Most were concerned with fictional or mythological women; not even the up-to-date ballets gave a real woman the prominent title role.

The Alhambra and the Empire presented topical issues but in such an anodyne way that any threatening, disturbing or critical element was absent. Unlike in the legitimate theatre where the plays of Ibsen, Shaw and Pinero were beginning to present new images of women, but like the painting of the period, the ballets in their essential conservatism made little reference to the changing roles, status or even the reality of women in society. On the contrary, the dancers' roles in these topical ballets, particularly in the patriotic works, reinforced traditional concepts such as peace, victory and nationhood as female. Whether the dancers were dressed as the military, who appeared in the patriotic works on parade rather than actually fighting, or were representing the countries of the Empire or patriotic imagery such as the Union Jack, they were symbolic. They symbolised the Empire; Britain's power in the Empire and internationally; her military glory and her role as keeper of the peace.[6] One of the main constructs by which the dancers presented these ideals was through a device as common in the ballets as in the visual arts, that of personification.

Embodiments of virtue: the world personified

The casting of 'spirit of', 'goddess of' or 'fairy of' was given to principal dancers in all kinds of music hall ballets. These roles were personifications of nature, artefacts, human virtues and achievements. The Spirit of the Wheatsheaf (*The Reaper's Dream*, Empire 1913), Spirit of Happiness (*All the Year Round*, Alhambra 1904) and Goddess of Genius (*Inspiration*, Alhambra 1901) were a few of many examples. Modern ideas or developments were embodied in roles such as the Spirit of Mechanism (*Sita*, Alhambra 1894) and the Goddess of Progress (*Entente Cordiale*, Alhambra 1904). Warner (1985: 85) discusses how the Victorian mind was able to give female personifications to technological developments for, by the mid-nineteenth century, 'allegorical convention had set so hard that it provided a solid foundation for some wondrously newfangled superstructures.' Therefore, the incongruity of such a concept as, for example, a 'Spirit of Mechanism' was not particular to the ballet.

Again, a personified image was common in painting, where there was

> a category of enigmatic female personifications endowed with a deliberate sense of abstraction and removal from everyday life ... (who) ... live in a static world of beauty where passion, rage and sensuality do not enter.
> Casteras 1982: 171

Unlike other female protagonists, these spirits did not relate to 'male' characters in the story but were independent entities. As they presented abstract qualities or ideas they were agents rather than recipients of events, immune from human passions and foibles. As such, they were part of the long tradition of allegorical womanhood which, particularly in the idealisation of womankind, reached a peak in the late Victorian and Edwardian period and became one of the characteristics of its culture (see Warner 1985).

> The expulsion of the middle-class woman from participation in practical life had become a fact; women had never been placed on a more lofty pedestal. An apparently insuperable plateau had been reached in her canonization as a priestess of virtuous inanity.
> Dijkstra 1986: 4

The role of women in society as the 'moral centre' can be perceived in novels of the period. In the ballets, the spirit or goddess role was also the moral centre of the narrative and it was a role which was given, almost always, to the principal dancer.[7]

This abstraction was not limited to concepts of the 'good' but also embraced the opposite. Human vices were portrayed in roles such as the Spirit of Gambling (*The Girl I Left Behind Me*, Empire 1893) and the Spirit of Vanity (*Femina*, Alhambra 1910). Even the topical work *Entente Cordiale* (Alhambra 1904) included in its cast list the Demon of War. What is of interest, however, is that with only a few exceptions, human vices were portrayed by men or by travesty performers. For example, a production photograph (Theatre Museum, London) of *Britannia's Realm* (Alhambra 1902) shows Justice, in a long dress, as conventionally and undoubtedly female. Malice and Envy are played by *en travestie* performers Edith Slack and Julia Reeve, who wear tunics, thonged boots and have covered hair. If they are not unequivocally 'male' they are certainly not female. As Warner points out,

> the predominance of feminine gender in words for virtue seems to have given virtue a monopoly on the feminine category: this, by contrast, has generated masculine gender imagery for its opposite.
> Warner 1985: 153

In relation to the ballet, this meant that the image of the female dancer remained untainted and her idealisation was uncorrupted.

These contrary roles of evil and adversity do not appear to have been presented with great seriousness, however, and almost all the ballets which dealt with conflict between good and evil resulted in unequivocal victory for the former.[8] It is in this respect that images in the visual arts, according to Casteras (1982) and Dijkstra's (1986) analyses, differ from those in the ballets. There are, in the ballets, no 'idols of perversity' (Dijkstra's title), and no obvious misogyny. The images appear to reflect woman-loving rather than woman-hating attitudes. However, representations of women as not corruptible, morally virtuous and essentially 'good' in character can be as negative and confining in their idealisation as any more malevolent representation.

Every man in the audience: the romantic world

One facet of misogynist imagery in the arts of the period was the casting of women as seductresses, or *femme fatale*.[9] If the ballet ignored changes in the status of women it also ignored the potent *femme fatale* image. Although seductions were a part of the scenario in some works, these appeared to be low-key events and the seductress was not an overt sexual being, at least not in relation to the other characters on stage. Even when Genée played the odalisque in *The Debutante* (Empire 1906), a 'good' temptress who uses her body to please the sultan in order to save her lover, the authenticity and potential allure of the character was undermined by the wearing of a long ballet skirt. It is interesting to note that one of the most popular stories depicted in the arts of the period, that of Salome, was never used as serious subject matter for any of the ballets presented at the Alhambra or the Empire. Tellingly, it was burlesqued in the aforementioned *Sal! Oh! My!* (Alhambra 1908). It was as though the depiction of such a woman, so powerful in her knowledge of her own sexuality, could not be accommodated on the music hall stage.

Although romance was a sub-theme in many works and in several it constituted the main plot, the ballerinas were not, in the main, sexual nor even overtly romantic characters. They were rarely, if at all, presented within the narrative as passionate women, and there was certainly no question of romantic liaisons in their personified roles. The actual living-or-dying fate of these heroines was not dependent on the men in their lives.[10] Few, if any, music hall ballet heroines ever died for love. When a heroine's fate did depend on a man it tended to be in the far more mundane respect of marriage (see Banes 1998, for her analyses of 'the marriage plot' in the 'traditional' ballet repertoire). Nearly every ballet which involved an element of romance ended happily.

The reason why love and romance played a common but subdued role in the music hall ballet is obvious. It was, and still is, a key theme in the human story but in the ballets of this period there were very few male dancers to complete the partnership. The fact that the 'male' lead was played *en travestie* meant that, although the convention was accepted, there could be no significant love relationship. Even when there was a romantic hero he tended to be played by an actor such as Lytton Grey. In neither case were there possibilities for romantic and certainly not passionate dance duets. Other male roles were played by character dancers who tended not to be cast as partners of the ballerina, for to do so would have undermined her status. Ballets which did include a male dancer such as de Vincenti, Sundberg or Santini could have presented a far more significant portrayal of a relationship. It is interesting that, to date, no visual sources have been found which present the ballerina in any kind of romantic involvement with a male character and no written sources comment, except superficially in a general outline of the plot, on the ballerina's role as a loved or loving character.[11]

Whilst there may have been a hint of romance between character dancers or other soloists as a tangential aspect of the plot, it would appear that in very few works were the *corps* or *coryphées* allowed to participate in any significant romantic role.[12] Even though most ballets presented lines of female *corps* dressed as 'boys' they did not appear to relate romantically to the 'girls'.

In the majority of works there was a lack of any significant portrayal of a love affair on stage. Those ballets in which it was a serious element tended to be based on pre-existing tales such as *Orfeo* (Empire 1891), *Don Juan* (Alhambra 1892) and *Carmen* (Alhambra 1903 and 1912). Whilst there was romance in many works, it was rare for the *première danseuse* to be seriously depicted as a woman in love. No love relationship on stage interfered with the love affair between the dancer and the audience. When George Edwards, the Empire manager, was asked why Genée never had a partner, his reply was, 'don't you see, dear boy, that every man in the audience is her partner?' (Guest 1958: 50).

Although many of the ballets had a dramatic content and a rare few such as *Don Juan* (Alhambra 1892) ended tragically, the works in general reflected their music hall context. They addressed no issues, appealed to the senses rather than to the mind or to the emotions and had not just happy but exhilarating endings. It may be the case that, if any of these works had survived, a different kind of perception would be brought to bear on them.[13] For example, the story of *The Faun* (Empire 1910) in which a sleeping girl loses her 'girdle' to a marble faun who has come to life and realises 'that in order to free herself from his spell she must regain the girdle he has snatched from her in passionate embrace' (anon. 1910: 14) is ripe for psychoanalytic interpretation. The very nature of myth, fairy tale and legend is that they function as a repository for the dilemmas of human thought and action. The music hall stories, however, were not presented with any intent other than to entertain and they were certainly not interpreted in any other way.

In the roles of the dancers, images of womanhood were presented which could be admired yet were not threatening, for they were so obviously otherwordly.[14] If roles such as Amazons had the potential for depicting powerful womanhood they were not perceived as such. The sight of a massed *corps* of Amazons in shining armour could have been chilling, in the way that the Queen and her Wilis in *Giselle* can be, but any possible power in these roles was subverted by the plot of the ballets in which they appeared to be totally ineffectual. Their potential to present a female collectivity was not realised; they were there for display, not meaningful action.

The hierarchical nature of any ballet company and the conventional narrative structure of the works have traditionally been based on a differentiation of roles between principals and other dancers. The ballerina sometimes appeared on programmes simply as '*Premiere Danseuse*' which established her as a separate entity even from the story of the ballet itself. In contemporary criticism, although words like 'charming' and 'vivacious' abound there is little sense of the real personality of the dancer emerging for her roles did not allow for individually expressive interpretation. Such a depersonalisation is inherent in the genre but was further emphasised by the fact that the powerfully expressive roles were played by the travesty performers, whose business was mime and dramatic action.

The fantasy world of the ballets, established by their supernatural subject matter, exotic locations and distant or mythological times was embodied in the stage persona of the ballerina. As a personification; representation of nature; picture of innocence and guilelessness or agent of morality, she was, in an unreal world, an even more unreal figure. The casting of other performers in character roles with particularly human traits acted as a foil to her but she remained quintessentially feminine in character, actions and looks.

The *corps*, even when in exotic or supernatural roles, were, by virtue of their *masse*, far less rarefied than the ballerina; they also, in their 'group' roles, acted as a foil to her individuality. As pointed out in Ch. 3, the dance vocabulary and aspects of staging differentiated the *premières danseuses* and the *corps de ballet;* this differentiation was endorsed by their respective roles and agency in the narrative. However, all dancers, whatever their role, served to please the eye and offered fantasy or the most pleasurable stories of reality. The subject matter of the ballets provided escapism; the outcome of the tales was inevitable, satisfying and there was nothing to disturb that satisfaction or make the audience uncomfortable. Woman as fairies, as jewels, as decoratively exotic, as essentially 'good' did not disturb the *status quo*; the composite world of the ballet effectively presented a 'Fairyland of Fair Women'.[15] The production and consumption of the music hall programme was entirely different from that of painting in that it evidently had to attract a large, paying audience in order to survive. Any 'virulent misogyny' (Dijkstra 1986: viii) would have disturbed the complacency of the audience by undermining their notions of Victorian and Edwardian womanhood. Thus, the images of women inscribed in the ballets were both commensurate with other forms of cultural discourse but also unique to the ballet itself.

NOTES

1. See Walkowitz (1992) for a claim that other aspects of music hall performance, particularly those by women, did challenge the *status quo* with regard to gender divisions in society.
2. The term 'narrative' is used here to describe the general story line. Licensing regulations prohibited narrative theatre in the music halls but the ballet, because it did not used the spoken word, was not classified as narrative theatre.
3. There are, of course, exceptions, such as a male Bluebird in *The Sleeping Beauty* (Petipa 1890) and Nijinsky's Rose in *Le Spectre de la Rose* (Fokine 1911). In these two examples, the 'femininity' of the roles is subverted by the bravura virtuosity of the dancing.
4. Although the New Woman was absent in painting she was much caricatured in sketches and cartoons of the period, particularly in the journal *Punch*. A few individual artists in the music hall did acknowledge suffrage issues in their acts (see Holledge 1981: 81).
5. Works which presented Amazons in the cast included *Dilara* (Empire 1887) and the Alhambra ballets *Antiope* (1888); *The Handy Man* (1900); *Femina* (1910) and *The Dance Dream* (1910).
6. See Warner (1985) for a discussion of such imagery. She points to how, during the nineteenth century, 'Britannia, the personification of the constitution, fades before Britannia as the might of Britain ... (this figure) ... achieves widest currency ... in the 1890s at the zenith of Victorians' imperial faith and enthusiasm' (Warner 1985: 48).
7. These agents of morality were not only spirits or goddesses but also more earthly creatures. An odalisque *(The Debutante*, Empire 1906); a gypsy queen (*Salandra*, Empire 1890) and young girls in several ballets (such as *The Girl I Left Behind Me*, Empire 1893, and *Sita* (Alhambra 1894) all display fidelity to their ideals and were epitomes of correct moral behaviour.
8. The 'evil' roles of Carabosse in *The Sleeping Beauty* (Petipa 1890) and Rothbart in *Swan Lake* (Ivanov/Petipa 1895) would appear to be much more malevolent creatures than those in the music hall ballets. However, such a statement must be tentative, for there are no extant 'original' works of the latter so comparison can only be made using the criticism of each period as a source. Also, interpretations of these roles in performance differ with each production.
9. See, for example, Harrison (1979), Casteras (1982) or Dijkstra (1986) for analyses of the *femme fatale* image in the visual arts.

10. In a few ballets the heroine was due to meet, before rescue, an unspecified but not deadly fate at the hands of a demon, pirates, brigands or a rajah (The Alhambra's *Nadia*, 1887; *Algeria*, 1887, *Zanetta*, 1890 and the Empire's *Cecile*, 1890). Such stories occurred during the early period of the music hall ballets. It could be tentatively speculated that this was a minor way in which the ballets reflected the growing emancipation of women in that they no longer needed rescuing so dramatically.

11. It would appear that when a 'love' scene was depicted it was acted out in mime. Guest (1958: 6l) relates how Genée mimed her love scenes with Santini in *The Milliner Duchess* (Empire 1903), a task she found distasteful due to the pervading smell of garlic on his breath.

12. As least one exception was the ballet *Roberto il Diavolo* (Empire 1909) in which the dancers were dead nuns, turned into nymphs, who tempt a young knight 'by the power of their wiles and seduction' (Empire programme note). However, the narrative of this ballet was based on a much earlier work, an opera of the same name produced in 1831. It was the ballet of the nuns in this opera to which the start of the Romantic movement in ballet is attributed (Koegler 1987: 348).

13. *The Sleeping Beauty* (Petipa 1890), for example, is a work which appears to be a superficial tale and yet, if perceived as an analogy of sexual awakening, it can reveal far more serious psychological issues.

14. An analysis of Genée's main roles at the Empire from 1897-1907 (Hockey 1983) reveals that out of the eighteen ballets in which she performed a major role, at least six of these were as personifications and two were dolls. Of a further six roles in which she played a 'real' woman, in four of these she either belonged to or married into the aristocracy. It could be said that such a world was equally unreal for the majority of the music hall audience. Although these ballets often transcended reality, when Genée was 'human' she also transcended the common mass of humanity.

15. 'The classical ballet: a fairyland of fair women' was the title of an article on the ballet in *The Play Pictorial* (Findon 1911: 75).

CHAPTER FIVE

Images and Imagination: Poetry, Fiction and the Eye of the Writer

So attractive was the glamour of the ballet that this became personified in the image of the dancers produced by the writing and fiction of the period. Some writers, however, were fascinated by the contradiction between this glamorous world and the more mundane reality behind the production of the ballets and this contrast became the subject matter of their work. Thus, in fiction, poetry and autobiography the stereotypical images of the dancers were either endorsed and perpetuated or their lack of authenticity was revealed.

The world of the music hall attracted young writers and artists, particularly during the 1890s.

> For the self-proclaimedly world weary and exhausted Decadents, it was the sheer vitality and colourfulness of working-class public life which drew them obsessively to music halls.
>
> Hennegan in Teich & Porter 1990: 197

As Sorell (1981: 302) says, these men 'were caught by this music-hall life as if it were a world apart, which in many ways it was.' The 'world apart' comprised not just the world of the working classes but also that of the stage itself.[1] Dijkstra comments in his analysis of the place of the stage performer in contemporary literature, that

> actresses were ubiquitous. They served as heroines whose prurient potential was outstanding since, being associated with the stage, they were a self evident part of the sinful underbelly of turn-of-the century culture.
>
> Dijkstra 1986: 120

Dancers, specifically the ballet girls, were doubly attractive, for they represented the forbidden territory on the other side of class boundaries and also the enticing world behind the stage curtain. 'The '90s poets wrote endlessly about dancers ... But they also enjoyed the dancers themselves and regularly fell in love with them' (Kermode 1962: 4).[2]

Verlaine, the French poet, made frequent visits to London and is reported to have said, 'I like to read Shakespear *(sic)* but I prefer to see a ballet' (Beckson 1977: 130). Verlaine encountered the social circle of the Rhymers Club, a group of poets who were particularly fascinated with the ballet girls. It was a member of this group, Arthur Symons, who wrote most evocatively about the ballet and most romantically about its performers.[3]

This Chapter examines the work of Symons and other writers from the perspective of an ordinary reader. The historian cannot, in one sense, be an 'ordinary' reader, for there is obviously a constant critical eye on all source material. An attempt can be made, however, to see through the eyes of a contemporary reader yet, at the same time, maintain the necessary distance in order to comment on the relationship between the source and the public reception of the source. In this respect, the written evidence examined in this Chapter is treated in the same manner as visual sources have been used throughout. That is, as there has been no attempt to evaluate the pictures or photographs as artefacts themselves, literature and poetry are here used to examine what kinds of image they presented to the reading public. They are not, therefore, subject to formal textual analysis but are used for cultural rather than literary readings.[4]

Painted angels

Arthur Symons was a poet, writer and critic and a central figure in the Rhymers Club. Symons himself recalls how he used to meet another of the members, Ernest Dowson, at a 'semi literary tavern near Leicester Square, chosen for its convenient position between two stage doors' (Beckson ed. 1977: 83). The stage doors were those of the Alhambra and the Empire and the tavern was The Crown, where 'it was the ballet girls' custom to meet The Rhymers ... after their performance and somewhat incongruously the group would include the Rev. Stewart Headlam.' (Fletcher 1960: 54). (The Rev. Headlam's campaign for elevating the status of ballet is discussed in the next Chapter. It is of interest that his work led him to mix with the dancers at the Crown.) Kermode notes that

> Symons and his friends would meet the Alhambra girls after the show and take them along to The Crown for a drink and a serious talk, serious not because of what Symons called the 'learned fury' of these 'maenads of decadence' but in a humbler way.
>
> Kermode 1962: 4

The terminology that Symons used to describe the dancers, 'maenads of decadence', indicates both the style and the sentiment of his writing on the music hall. He was concerned with impressionist literature, the aim of which, according to Stanford (1970: 111) was 'truth to the artistic eye rather than truth to reality'. Symons acknowledged the phenomenological nature of writing, 'an impressionist art ... (which)... owes its very existence to the eyes that see it' (116). To Symons, seeking and trying to record beauty and sensation, impression was more important than verisimilitude. As the ballet traded on the purveyance of beauty in order to elicit sensation, it is no wonder that it held such sway over him. On a personal rather than artistic level, Beckson (ed. 1977: 1), in his introduction to Symons' memoirs, notes that the music hall dancers 'provided Symons with a release from his strict Wesleyan upbringing'. Symons reveals his own fascination with the ballet in these memoirs. He contributed articles on the ballet to *The Star* and *The Sketch* and also wrote at least one highly evocative piece for his own short-lived magazine, *The Savoy*, a now-famed journal which was published monthly from

1896 and ran for eight editions only. Due to his literary profession and his personal enthusiasm, Symons was one of the few critics who was able to write about the ballet in a style that was, if overblown, at least unclichéd and with a content that was relatively informative. Compared with other critics of the time, his reviews and general writings on the ballet are as literary as his poems. Symons' general criticism has been drawn upon in previous chapters; it is the poems which appear in *London Nights* (1895) and his article in *The Savoy* (1896) which are considered here, for in these his obsession with the dancers and the resultant image he shares with his readers are most clearly revealed.

London Nights is an anthology which includes five poems about the ballet and/or the dancers, one poem which is most probably so, plus others which had for their title or their subject matter the name of a particular ballet girl.[5] In the introductory poem, 'Prologue', Symons sees the music hall as an allegory for his own life. (In an article written in 1898 entitled 'The World as Ballet' Symons similarly offers his reasons why 'how fitly then in its very essence, does the art of dancing symbolize life' [Symons 1925: 250].) 'To a Dancer' reflects the wish or the illusion that a performer's eyes are solely for the writer in the audience; he sees 'her eyes that gleam for me!' (1895: 5) A similar sentiment is expressed in 'On the Stage', wherein the writer believes that in the dancer's eyes he can 'know what memories, What memories and messages for me' (p.15). Even in 'At the Stage Door', as the lover awaits his ballet girl, he sees 'the smile of her heart to my heart, of her eyes to my eyes' (p.16).

The significance of the relationship between an artist's work and an artist's life is a problematic issue. What is of interest here is how the sentiments expressed in Symons' poetry are in accord with his perceptions of his real life experiences. He describes in his memoirs a visit to the Empire. During the ballet,

> suddenly I saw a beautiful girl whose face was strange to me. She was exotic, with passionate lips and eyes, magnetic. Then she ... that is you ... fixed her eyes on mine without surprise, without hesitation. As if drawn by some instinct, your eyes fixed on mine at every turn you made as you danced with the others.
>
> Symons in Beckson, ed. 1977: 160

It is difficult to comprehend how a dancer on stage, particularly one in movement, can so consistently spot one face in the sea of the audience. It must be noted, however, that Symons' autobiographical writings are as romantic, mystical and full of imagery as his poetry. Likewise, the same kind of relationship with the dancers, imagined or otherwise, appears in his critical writing: 'and in my mind's eye I look from face to face along two lines, resting, perhaps, on a particular oval, out of which two great, serious eyes smile strangely' ('A.S.' 1893: 301).

What is of interest is the general impression the reader would gain of the ballet girl. In the poems of which the above are an example, she is cast entirely in the role of an existing or potential lover, whose mind and heart are with the man in the audience. Whether on stage during the performance, or at the stage door afterwards, she exists only in relation to the man; she performs for him alone. This personalised, self-referential perception of the dancer by the writer is also found in accounts of backstage at the ballet. Bensusan, writing about behind the scenes at *Faust* (Empire 1895) describes how

> every few minutes half a dozen pretty girls would rush to their dressing rooms to change, leaving me heart-broken, while another contingent would arrive in fresh costume, as though to console me.
>
> 'S.L.B.' 1896a: 524

Scanlon & Kerridge (1988: 43-44) in their analysis of the uses of dance in late Romantic literature, note that: 'the forces ... (the dance) ... allows to surface are potentially uncontrollable ... the long opposition between Puritanism and pleasure recurs in all these literary uses of dance.' Similarly, the writer could control the Dionysian forces of the dance and the concomitant sensuality of the dancer by appropriating both not only through, but for, his own eyes.

In Symons' writings, particularly, the dancer is a woman of great sensuality, the pivot of the sensual world of the ballet. This world suited Symons' aesthetic; his attempts to record and heighten sensation. Jackson's (1931: 112–13) comment on the writer's romantic, quasi-mystical works was that: 'such poems are in many instances artificial to the extent that they are obviously the result of deliberately cultivated moods.' The ballet girl is the target of his moods and her sensual and sexual image is endorsed. Nevertheless, Symons was fully aware of the back-stage reality behind the on-stage fantasy:

> The little painted angels flit
> See, down the narrow staircase, where
> The pink legs flicker over it!
>
> Blonde, and bewigged, and winged with gold,
> The shining creatures of the air
> Troop sadly, shivering with cold.
>
> 'Behind the Scenes: Empire'
> Symons 1895: 21

As his article in *The Savoy* (1896: 75-83) reveals, it was this very illusion and artificiality which so fascinated Symons. His writing, whether fiction, poetry or journalism, perpetuates the glamour whilst acknowledging its artifice.

It was this very artifice which so attracted Symons to the dancers themselves but it was not the stars, the ballerinas, about which he wrote, but the ballet girls. For Symons,

> as they dance, under the changing lights, so human, so remote, so desirable, so evasive, coming and going like the sound of a thin heady music which marks the rhythm of their movements, like a kind of clinging drapery, they seem to sum up in themselves the appeal of everything in the world that is passing, and coloured, and to be enjoyed.
>
> Symons 1925: 249

As perhaps for so many men in the audience, these dancers were both human and remote, desirable but evasive. They represented the forbidden world of the stage, of sensuality, of sex and of an alien social class.[6]

In no other writer's work is the hothouse atmosphere of the ballet evoked so lovingly, or the infatuation of the writer with the dancers revealed so clearly, as in the poetry, memoirs and critical writing of Arthur Symons. Other poets also wrote about the ballet, but in more objective tones. 'J.M.B.' (who Guest 1992: 112 suggests might be J.M. Barrie) and Thomas Hardy both focussed on how the mass spectacle of the ballets obliterated the individuality of the dancers. As cited in Chapter 2, Hardy wrote,

> Though all alike in their tinsel livery
> And indistinguishable at a sweeping glance
> They muster, maybe
> As lives wide in irrelevance
> A world of her own has each one underneath
> Detached as a sword from its sheath.
> 'The Ballet'
> Hardy in Gibson (ed.) 1976: 492.

'J.M.B.'s poem, in which he describes the *corps* of angels in *Faust* (Alhambra 1895), opens

> A crystal stair, and in the air
> The angels hover round

and closes

> No more those angels deck the sky -
> Those angels hail from Peckham Rye,
> From Bow or Kentish Town
> 'J.M.B.' 1896: 524

It is not surprising that such a different image of the dancer should be constructed by writers whose literary aesthetic and personal involvement were so very different from Symons. Another writer who took a more detached, even cynical view of the dancer was Arnold Bennett. In his Journals for 1899, he describes the performance of a ballerina whom Guest (1992: 117) suggests was Cecilia Cerri at the Empire. Bennett uses terminology such as 'she hid herself in a labryinth of curves which was also a tremour of strange tints, a tantalizing veil, a mist of iridescent light' (Bennett 1971: 56). Such sensuous imagery does not extend to the dancer as person. As she takes her curtain call,

> what domination in her face, what assurance of supreme power. It was the face of one surfeited with adoration, cloyed with praise. While she was humouring us with her fatigued imperial smiles ...
> 1971: 56-57

It was as if, beguiled at first, Bennett then had to detach himself from the powerful and confident stage presence of the ballerina.

Such ambivalence is reflected in George Bernard Shaw's novel, *Immaturity* (1930) in which he describes a visit made by his hero to the Alhambra. Shaw was a frequent visitor to and often wrote on the ballet. His own opinions would appear to colour the description of the fictional ballet seen by his hero. (Holroyd [1988: 106] suggests that the dancer in *Immaturity* was, in fact, Pertoldi, a *danseuse* at the Alhambra. It is unclear as to whether Shaw ever had a relationship with Pertoldi, for although his notebooks for 1876 state 'inauguration during the year of the Terpsichorean episode', Holroyd claims that Shaw's relationships with women at this time 'appear to have been romances of the mind'.) Although the novel, which was actually written in 1879, predates the period of this study and, unlike the above extract from Arnold Bennett, is fictional rather than autobiographical, it similarly records how the seductive image of the dancer on stage is undermined by a condemnation of her personal qualities.

Smith, the hero of *Immaturity*, has fallen in love with the ballerina during the course of one performance. Again, the relationship is between the dancer and one man in the audience: 'at one moment he fancied he caught her eye, and that she was conscious of his presence' (Shaw 1930: 74). The next day, ashamed of his infatuation, he demolishes the object of his love by counting out the faults of her character which logically stem from her profession:

> In order to preserve her gymnastic skills she must pass hours every day in practice which has not one element of mental improvement in it. Therefore she must be utterly ignorant and narrow minded.
>
> 1930: 76

She also, without the disguise of her make up, must be 'coarse looking' and due to the length of her career, 'pretty old'. Finally, 'her profession is a guarantee of her low origin and indifferent character' (1930: 77). The hero later retracts his character assassination and in order to legitimise his infatuation, justifies to himself both dancer and dancing profession. A woman friend of his is less impressed with his protestations that 'dancing is a fine art':

> 'Nonsense!' said the dressmaker. 'It is a pretty thing for a girl to know, but not to get her living by, or to do before a crowd of people without being decently dressed. I'm sure no woman who respected herself would do such a thing.'
>
> Shaw 1930: 82

The internal debate the hero has with himself typifies the ambivalence with which the dancer was perceived, an ambivalence typified in Arthur Symon's real-life attitude (see Note 6). It is her physical appearance which is the locus of attention, but that appearance is censured. Further, her vacuity of mind is assumed. The dressmaker's comment also encapsulates another concern. The dancer is not decently dressed and, therefore, not respectable. (For a similar accusation, see

Chapter 6 on Laura Ormiston Chant's testimony for the London County Council Licensing Committee.) Thus, public attitudes to the dancer are expressed from the mouths of Shaw's characters.

One author who presented the world of the ballet both realistically and sympathetically was Compton Mackenzie. In his novel *Carnival* (1929) the heroine, Jenny, becomes a ballet girl at the Orient Palace of Varieties. This theatre was based on the Alhambra and Mackenzie's descriptions of the conditions, working life, habits and customs of the ballet and its participants appear to be authentic.[7] *Carnival*, and its sequel, *Figure of Eight* (1936) together present an evocative picture of the world of the ballet. In them, Mackenzie describes the ballet girls neither as glamorous nor as totally morally blameless but he is sympathetic to the harshness of their lives and not censorious of their inevitably thwarted aspirations. His description makes stark contrast with Symons' somewhat jolly, rose-tinted view of the community of dancers.

> The Orient stifled young life. The Corps de Ballet (*sic*) had the engulfing character of conventual vows. When a girl joined it, she cut herself off from the world ... in a few years she would inevitably be pale with the atmosphere, with grinding work and late hours. She would find it easy to buy cheap spirits in the canteen underneath the stage. She would stay in one line, it seemed for ever.
>
> Mackenzie 1929: 138-39

In *Carnival* the reaction of the heroine's aunt to the news that Jenny may go on the stage, again reflects the concern with moral respectability.

> 'A ballet-girl? Are you mad, Florence? Why, what a disgrace ... An actress? Better put her on the streets at once.'
>
> 1929: 76

Yet Mackenzie presents another view of the ballet girls from that expressed by the aunt. In view of the evidence presented in Chapter 6 it is one which would seem more accurate in relation to the actual lives of the great majority of dancers. He relates how the 'stage door johnnies' who 'often regarded the ladies of the ballet as easy prey' were misled in their perceptions, for the dancers

> were independent of masculine patronage ... They might desire applause over the footlights, but under the moon they were free from the necessity for favour. They had, with all its incidental humiliations, the self-respect which a great art confers.
>
> 1929: 141

Mackenzie continues with a description of how the appeal and apparent sensuality of the ballet girls on stage contrasted with their real selves at the stage door. It is this contrariety which is at the heart of the double image of the dancer, in fiction as in life.

Carnal lust: the dancer and pornography

Although some of the sources discussed in this Chapter refer to the general term 'dancers', the interest of the majority of writers is directed at the ballet girls. The one glaring exception to this is a novel, *Crissie* (anon. 1899b). This erotic, not to say pornographic, work gives a graphic account of the back-stage seductions of dancers, seductions in which they are portrayed as complicit. Interestingly, it is the only source found to date in which the moral image of a ballerina is not only tainted but positively destroyed.

The novel is set at the Pandora Palace of Varieties in Leicester Square. Its heroine, the ballerina Crissie Cazarotti, is known as the Pandora Prostitute. She is described thus:

> Lust, stark, carnal lust, was the predominant characteristic of her disposition, and for the gratification of this there was no depth of moral degradation to which she would not descend.
>
> anon. 1899b: 104

Unlike the fiction of Mackenzie, the novel lacks verisimilitude or any credibility as a portrayal of actual events. There appears to have been an attempt to give the publication some authentic status for, whilst no author is acknowledged, it is published by 'The Alhambra'. However, it is highly doubtful that these publishers were the Alhambra theatre. The text does not specify 'Alhambra Palace of Varieties' and, more significantly, it is very unlikely that the theatre management, who so zealously guarded the reputation of the venue and the performers, would have allowed such a scurrilous publication.

The moral image of the dancer is discussed in Chapter 6. Suffice to note here that, although the events and people in *Crissie* are fictional, there is clearly an attempt to locate the narrative in an actual venue, the Alhambra. The connection between the dancers in that venue and back-stage sexual activity is indisputable. It is the dancers of the music hall ballet who serve as the vehicle for the writer's pornographic imagination.[8]

Views of the audience

Two examples of other types of commentary on the ballet, a painting and a popular song, encapsulate the image of the dancer. The painting *The Alhambra* (1908) is by Frederick Spencer Gore.[9] A few rows of occupants of the front stalls are shown, looking up to the blur of colour which is the activity on stage. About three rows from the front, a man in a dinner suit holds binoculars up to the stage. The narrative inherent in this gesture epitomises the audience-performer relationship and the currency of that relationship, the dancer's body. A similar sentiment is expressed in a popular song, which also encapsulates many of the aspects of the dancers' image addressed in previous chapters.

> I'm a very strong admirer of the ballet and the play
>   But I haven't told the missus up to now!
> And to watch the fairies dancing I pass may (*sic*) an hour away,
>   But I haven't told the missus up to now!
> When I see their graceful attitudes with love I'm burning hot,
> And when the angels flap their wings, they mash me on the spot,
> And I feel as if I'd like to go at once and kiss the lot,
>   But I haven't told the missus up to now![10]
>
> Cornell 1887

Reference to the ballet in a popular song, a phenomenon barely conceivable today, testifies to its place in popular culture. In this song the man in the audience is depicted as *voyeur* and, as such, his interest is not in the dance itself but in the dancers. His interest is sexual. His feeling that he'd 'like to go and kiss the lot' suggests the dancers' accessibility and their amenability to his attentions. Fairies, angels, or otherwise, they are still women and kissable. His confession that he 'hasn't told the missus up to now' reveals the disreputable image of the ballet. Such a visit, in 1887, was not an outing for a married man. In keeping his *penchant* a secret from his wife, he separates his two worlds, his public and private morality. At the ballet he could indulge his fantasies, fantasies which were not only of time and place, natural and supernatural, but of the women who constituted that world. Similar sentiments are expressed in a song entitled *Oh, the Fairies*. Published in 1879 (but sung regularly at meetings of The Player's Theatre, London) it tells the tale of a 'fellow round town' who becomes infatuated with a dancer in the pantomime ballet:

> He sat in a trance
>   When he saw them dance
> As they hurdled around thro' the show;
>   And then his eye set
>   Upon a brunette
> Who was knocking them in the front row.
>
> When he saw her jump
>   His heart gave a thump
> And his senses went all ting-a-ling
>   Oh! yes you are right
>   He's there ev'ry night
> In the daytime you can hear him sing:
>
> (CHORUS)   Oh, the fairies, whoa, the fairies,
> Nothing but splendour and feminine gender,
> Oh, the fairies, whoa, the fairies,
> Oh, for a wing of a fairy queen.
>
> Words: T.S. Lonsdale, Music: W.G. Eaton,
in Gammond 1983: 52-53

Although the song relates to the ballet in pantomime, the notion of the man in the audience possessing the dancer on stage and some how bringing her 'down to earth' by dispossessing her of her wings, her symbol of 'otherness', endorses the notion of the potential sexual accessibility of the 'fairy' dancer.

In Chapters 3 and 4, I examined how the subject matter, roles, dancing and visual presentation of the ballets produced certain images of the performers. The predominant production value of the ballets was spectacle and both *premières danseuses* and *corps* were constituent features of that spectacle. In fiction, unlike in criticism generally, the writer could afford to explore the world of the dancer without confining himself to the actual stage esvent. It was, however, the happenings on the stage which determined how the writer perceived the dancers as women. The glamour, sumptuousness and sensuality of the ballets were attributed by Symons to the performers themselves, and his writings endorse the image of the dancer as sexual being. Mackenzie, writing for a popular market in a realist mode, and therefore totally at odds with Symons' aesthetic stance, refutes this image. 'J.M.B.' and Hardy, each in a single poem explore the contrast between the allure of the dancers as performers and the mundane reality of their personal lives. In Shaw's novel, as in Symons' memoirs, his hero encapsulates the dilemma of the thinking man in relation to the ballet and its executants. Seduced by both, the hero's intellect had to work on his emotion; sense had to be applied to sensibility. Fascination with all that was forbidden had to be tempered with reason, or the man himself would be demeaned. In popular song, the realities of the performers' lives, their age or marital status, their working conditions, the backstage hardship, all count for nought. The music hall context of the performance, the symbolic codes of the ballet itself and the instrument of the dancer's profession, her body, all conspired to locate the identity of the dancer as sexual.

The ballerina, isolated and idealised on stage, was not generally the subject of fiction or poetry except as the object of remote fantasising. Unsurprisingly, the *en travestie* performer does not feature in any of these sources. The ballet girls were of more interest to writers, either because of the sharper contrast between their personal and professional lives or because of their apparent personal accessibility. Therefore, both fictional and 'factual' writing compounded the contrasting images of ballerina and ballet girl which the ballets themselves constructed. These antithetical images are revealed even more tellingly in an examination of the morality of the ballets and the personal morality of the performers.

NOTES

1. See Fletcher (1960) for a discussion on the music hall as a Symbolist image of the unity of social class.
2. Sturgis (1995: 103) notes that although the poets Selwyn Image and Herbert Horne consorted with the Alhambra dancers at the stage door, their companion Ernest Dowson believed that their relationships were never actually sexual.
3. The Rhymers Club was 'a group of people that met regularly at the Cheshire Cheese in Fleet Street for two or three years, from 1891, to read poetry. Members and associates included Yeats ... (and) ... Arthur Symons. It published two collections of

verse, 1892 and 1894' (Drabble 1985: 824). See Stanford (1965) and Sturgis (1995) on the Club and Yeats (1955) for an 'inside account'.
4. Studies of the place of dance in literature include Priddin (1952) on French literature; Scanlon & Kerridge (1988) on the uses of dance in late Romantic literature, particularly the work of Yeats and Wilde, and Kinkead-Weekes (1992) on D.H. Lawrence and the dance. A detailed textual analysis of the symbolism of dance in the work of Symons and Yeats is undertaken by Fletcher (1960).
5. Poems which refer directly to the ballet are 'Prologue'; 'To a Dancer'; 'Nora on the Pavement'; 'On the Stage'; 'At the Stage Door' and 'Behind the Scenes: Empire'. In 'Renée' the exact context is unspecified but it would appear to be set at the stage door. Symons later changed a section in the anthology entitled 'Lilian' to 'Violet'. This was a reference to Violet Pigott, the first ballet girl with whom he had an affair (Beckson,ed. 1977: 261).
6. Symons' attitudes to the ballet would make an interesting topic for further discussion from a psychoanalytical perspective. Mixed with his fascination was also a sense of disgust, as evidenced by his memoirs of Violet Piggott (see above). He recalls an evening spent with her and her friends from the stage with 'horror, mixed with disgust' (Symons in Beckson, ed. 1977: 114). The bare flesh displayed on and off stage by the dancers, extolled in his poetry, eventually became to him 'the sign of degeneration'. The fictional dilemma of Shaw's hero, discussed later in this Chapter, is played out in real life in Symon's ambivalence.
7. For example, it is interesting to read Mackenzie's account (1929: 138) of conditions in the ballet girls' dressing room 'where the inspectors of the LCC presumably never penetrated' in conjunction with a letter written to the London County Council which described and complained about those very facilities (LCC 5 August 1911).
8. See Davis (1989) for 'The actress in Victorian pornography'.
9. An exhibition catalogue produced by the Arts Council of Great Britain 1955 lists eight paintings by Gore of the Alhambra and/or the ballet. See Amaya (1962) for an account of Gore's paintings of the Alhambra ballet. The painter Walter Sickert was interested in the music halls in general; see Baron (1973: Ch.III).
10. This song is also used by Davis (1991: 142) but for a different purpose.

CHAPTER SIX

Prejudicial to Public Morality: The Moral Image of the Dance and Dancer

'Decadent' is a term much applied to the *fin de siècle*, known also as the 'gay nineties' or 'naughty nineties'. The 'naughtiness' in this context applied not to the alleged vices of the working class but to the public flirtation with 'vice' engaged in by an intellectual, artistic and aristocratic elite. It was, perhaps, these social groupings breaking free from the moral constraints of the Victorian age. Prince Albert, consort to Victoria, died in 1861 and the longevity of her mourning and self-imposed seclusion contributed to the dampening of public spirit - at least, in its public manifestation. By the 1880s/90s this spirit surfaced, in certain social mileaux, in to one of excess, of the exotic, of so-called decadence. Decadence is specifically associated with certain movements in the visual and literary arts. In both its general and specific contexts it indicates a subversion of convention and morality, particularly sexual morality. Even the music hall has been described as decadent, which appears at odds with its fundamental political conservatism. Throughout its history music hall had been associated with prostitution, an association which appeared to be almost legitimised in the promenades of the larger palaces. For example, London's Oxford Music Hall, a more up-market West End hall, was regularly threatened with withdrawal of its licence for promoting prostitution during the 1870s.[1] In addition, the geographic location of the major theatres and halls in the sexual street market of London's West End and the common depiction of the 'actress' in pornographic literature, gave these venues an erotic ambiance. Such an ambiance was fostered by the acts themselves in which many of the songs, dialogue and repartee were based on innuendo, a device used as much by women performers as by men. At a time when the work of Sigmund Freud and Havelock Ellis was still unknown in Britain, any reference to sex and related matters was *risque*. This taint of sex, particularly in the context of Victorian morality, was one of the major attractions of the halls. If comedy and comic song provided titillating texts, women dancers, their movement and costumes tilted more tellingly at the windmills of Victorian morality. The ballet did not escape charges of immorality in two inter-related respects: in relation to the performances and to the personal lives of the performers. The attack on the ballets themselves came, most publicly, from the Ormiston Chant campaign.

One of the results of the late Victorian preoccupation with vice was a spate of morality campaigns. Laura Ormiston Chant, whose case against the Empire was discussed earlier, is presented in most sources as an interfering prude. Chant's actions, however, exemplify those of women reformers who were finding their own voices in order to challenge the moral imperatives constructed by men. These modern, 'progressive' (as they were called) women exposed the double standards inherent in these imperatives, calling for responsible sexual behaviour from both sexes. Chant's objections to the ballet can be seen in this light.

It was the fate of any woman who appeared on the stage to have her professional life and her personal morality conflated. The working class women who entered the performing arts fought much harder for their good name, though many found that the world of the theatre offered opportunities for fortuitous liaisons or marriage. However, the popular notion of the woman performer who *used* her career to find a wealthy husband or lover needs to be disentangled from the idea that, for many, their career *enabled* them to do so. In an era when marriage for women was the socially accepted norm, the number of women who chose not to marry but to continue their careers signifies the seriousness with which they treated their skills, their profession and the independence these allowed. Nevertheless, in the Victorian period particularly, when women led very far from public lives, the exposure of the dancer's body for such public scrutiny would have compounded the long-held association between immorality on and off stage.

Ever since Biblical times, dance in Western, Christian society was disapproved of for not only its pagan associations but also, in its public demonstration of the predominantly female body, its sexual connotations. Moral laxity was not only associated with the activity of dancing but also with the performers themselves. This generalised view, however, often made in dance historiography, is unsubstantiated when a closer examination is made of the contrasting images of the ballerinas and the ballet girls within the moral context of the music hall period.[2] In broad historical terms, the music hall ballet was rooted in the Victorian era and spanned the transitional Edwardian age, when old and new values merged or clashed and when extreme propriety met with questionable morality. Marriage was sanctified and prostitution was rife and for the man who frequented the promenades of the Alhambra and the Empire in search of female sexual services, full dinner dress was *de rigueur*. These polarisations were not unique to but were more pronounced in the Victorian and Edwardian age, for as Dijkstra (1986: 393) claims 'the cultural leaders of the years around 1900 much preferred the depiction of a simple world of dualistic absolutes'. These absolutes were manifest in two oppositional images of women, the Madonna and the Magdalene; opposites which were once seen as belonging to all women now characterised distinctions between women. The reasons for and manifestations of the polarisation of sexuality implicit in these and similar images are varied and complex, but this Chapter explores the particular relationship between these symbolic opposites and the representations of women in the music hall ballet.[3]

High kicks or high art: the moral image of the ballet

In the context of high Victorian society, it is hardly surprising that the ballets were a cause for moral consternation. Letters written to the London County Council (LCC)

Licensing Committee, who were responsible for the granting or withholding of licences for places of public entertainment, reveal the nature of public concern. The Rev. C. Copeland Smith of the 'West End Mission - Men's Social Department' complained about the costume and the actions in the ballet *L'amour* (Alhambra 1906). He suggested that it was 'the deliberate intention of the management to present a suggestive and sensual entertainment ... the whole tone and conception of the 'turn' is prejudicial to public morality' (LCC 17 September 1906).

This letter is of interest because, like Ormiston Chant, the writer blames not the executants of the ballets but the management who stage them. A similar sentiment is expressed in a letter signed by 'Comic Singer' who worked in the profession and, it can be surmised, performed at the Alhambra. The tone of the complaint can be gleaned from the following extract, even though some of the handwriting in the original letter is indecipherable.

> And who is responsible for the studied indecency of the costumes as exhibited in 'Enchantment' and 'Antiope'? ... the thing was introduced to please the ... men frequenters of the ... a class of men who use the place nightly.
> LCC 14 October 1889

Although the Inspectors' reports on the venues concerned themselves with matters of building regulations, fire exits, etc. it is evident that they were aware of other complaints. One report mentions that in the ballet *Oriella* (Alhambra 1891),

> some 80 - 100 persons took part in the performance. I saw nothing in the dancing that I considered suggestive or to which exception could be taken and the dresses or costumes were of the character usually provided in the ballet.
> LCC 5 December 1891

It is difficult to adjudicate the validity of these reports, for such a judgement depends on the moral perspective which is adopted. There were two campaigns, one against and one for the ballets, which reveal how the complexity of the debate is compounded by the possible motivations of the protagonists.

The social reformer Laura Ormiston Chant mounted a two-pronged attack on the Empire. Firstly, on the grounds that the promenade harboured prostitution and secondly, that the ballets on stage were indecent. She asserted that the two works seen by her, *The Girl I Left Behind Me* (1893) and *La Frolique* (1894),

> seemed to be for the express purpose of displaying the bodies of women to the utmost extent. There is not the least attempt to disguise that which common sense and common decency requires should be hidden.
> Chant in Donahue 1987: 58

Her main source of contention appeared to be the wearing of flesh coloured tights which gave the impression of no tights at all, short skirts, monks who transformed into scantily clad cavaliers and

> one central figure, as it were, in flesh coloured tights, who wears a light gauzy kind of dress and when she comes to the front of the stage it is as though the body of a naked woman were simply disguised with a film of lace.
>
> Chant in Donahue 1987: 58

Not only the costumes but also the actions of the ballet disturbed her.

> There is also a dancer who dances in black silk tights, with a black lace dress ... (who) ... gathers up all her clothing in the face of the man before whom she is dancing and stretches up her leg, and kicks him upon the crown of his head.
>
> Chant in Donahue 1987: 58

(The high kick which Chant describes indicates that she may be referring to the chahut, a variation of the can-can which appeared in the ballet *La Frolique*.)

The significant point about these accusations, like the dialectic of many Victorian reformers, is the recognition of a moral double standard:

> it is the motive at the back of it all, and the obvious suggestiveness which makes the thing evil ... the whole question would be solved if men, and not women, were at stake.
>
> Chant in anon. 1894: 3

It was not the prostitutes in the promenade or the performers on the stage to whom Chant directed her attack but to male manipulation of them, though implicit in her testimony is the assumption that these women could not be expected to know any better.

> If it should be said that these poor girls who act in the ballet and are thus shamelessly exposed, do not mind it, I say that a civilised community is not to take its standard of decency from those who to begin with are not in a position to hold the highest.
>
> Chant in Donahue 1987: 59

Chant's attacks are directed to the dominant patriarchal systems and attitudes. A speech she made ten years before the Empire campaign would seem to endorse this interpretation. Addressing the Annual Meeting of the Social Purity Alliance, she denounced the 'music halls and theatres, where every attraction woman possessed is pressed into that side which tends to evil and sorrow' (Chant 1883). In her publication *Why we attacked the Empire* (1895) she accuses the music hall directors and shareholders of exploitation for financial gain.

Chant's case against the ballet itself also needs to be seen in a contextual light. Although she stated in her testimony to the London County Council, in which she contests the renewal of the Empire's licence, 'I do not come before you as one who objects to dances or objects to theatres. I love these things, and because I love them I want other people to love them as well as I do' (Chant in Donahue 1987: 59) she was undoubtedly disturbed by what she saw on stage. In an era when women were clothed from head to foot, when ankles were erogenous zones, the sight of even a simulated bare leg would have been shocking. What is interesting to consider is how different sources have construed her motivation. She was ridiculed by her opponents for her 'Purity Cant Crusade' (Glover 1913: 143) and secondary sources continue to reinforce the 'do-gooder' image (for example, Pearsall 1983: 339-40). In almost none of the primary or secondary material on the Chant campaign is any recognition or endorsement given to her side of the debate. A revisionist reading of her statements, however, reveals that, even allowing for the complex motivations of the Victorian social purity campaigners, she had women's interests at heart. Her accusations were directed at the way dancers were presented in the ballets and, as such, could be seen as a defence of the women themselves.[4]

The level of opprobrium to Chant was such that the motivation of her attackers could be called into question, for the vehemence of this attack reflects as much on them as on their target. There were political interests invested in the music halls but, on reading accounts of the Chant campaign, a sense of outrage can be discerned which may be interpreted as a male response to female intervention in their world.[5] If women in the promenade were there to bring pleasure to men, then so were the women on stage. Any attack on the visual image presented by the latter interfered with the direct line of the gaze from male audience to female performer.

A social reformer who explicitly defended the dancers but, unlike Chant, also defended the ballets, was the Rev. Stewart Headlam. Headlam was an enlightened Church of England clergyman, a socialist and an unorthodox Christian whose enlightened attitudes are evident in his action of paying half the bail for Oscar Wilde, who went to Headlam's house immediately on his release from prison in 1897 (see Ralph 1984 on Headlam and Ellman 1988 on the Wilde case). Mentioned by Flitch (1912: 64) as the only writer to take the ballet seriously, he wrote frequently in its defence. In a long extract from an evening newspaper reprinted in *The Stage*, Headlam makes an impassioned case for the respectability of the ballet at the Alhambra.

> I am bold to assert that any candid person, looking round the crowded house any night will not dare to say that the ballets corrupt the men at all; on the contrary, they will see throughout a large proportion of the house, men and women healthily enjoying healthy, beautiful, artistic work.
>
> Headlam 1886: 17

This crusading Reverend came into conflict not only with the Church but with the Ormiston Chant campaign and also, in open critical warfare, with George Bernard Shaw. Shaw attacked Headlam and his Guild several times in his inimitably caustic manner.[6]

Headlam's pleas for the ballet to be considered as a legitimate art form give clear evidence of how it was perceived otherwise. His objectives for the Church and Stage Guild, which he formed in 1879, were not only to defend the theatre and music halls but also to break down prejudice against their practitioners.[7] In the context of the Church, Headlam had much prejudice to fight against, though this was not simply in relation to the suspected immorality of stage performers but a more complex concern about how men could potentially be led astray by sexual temptation. As Bettany relates, after Headlam had recognised two communicants as dancers, 'they implored him not to let other church attendants know how they made their living, because if the nature of their work were once known they would be cold-shouldered in the church' (Bettany 1926: 28).

Headlam's special interest was the ballet girls, an interest which caused the disapprobation of other Guild members.

> To some extent the limitation of his Guild was brought about by his special interest in ballet, and his desire to befriend those stage performers who were most exposed to attack - the dancers at the Empire and the Alhambra. Against no stage artist was the charge of immorality so lightly and recklessly urged.
> Bettany 1926: 103

Headlam defended the dancers against these charges of immorality but it is not clear whether or not he implicitly accepted them, and wished to save or rescue the dancers from possible falls from grace, a common aim of social reformers. Whatever his motivations, his defence of the ballet and of the dancers caused him to lose his parish and was one reason for the demise of the Church and Stage Guild. Actors and actresses who resigned in protest at the increasing number of dancers in the Guild were obviously anxious to protect the growing status of their own profession. The dancers not only lowered the social class level of membership but also, apparently, its moral tone. Headlam himself perceived that the 'respectable' members 'were disappointed because he did not carry on more of a religious mission among such chorus girls and members of the ballet as joined the Guild' (Bettany 1926: 103).

It is probable that the Rev. Headlam's special interest in the dancers as individuals was based on complex motivations but his passion for the ballet was sincere. His own stated aim was set out in the preface (1888) to his republication of Blasis' 1828 treatise:

> My chief object in producing this book is to enable the public to understand better than they do at present how difficult the art of dancing is, and so to induce them to appreciate more fully the Dancers and their work.

Perhaps, in order to raise the status of the ballet, Headlam had to improve the disreputable moral image of its performers. What his own words and actions do indicate is that it was an image firmly entrenched not only in the Church, as might be expected, but in the theatrical profession itself.

Sex and sewing: the moral image of the dancer

The inevitable problem when examining an issue such as 'immorality' is discerning what counted as immoral in the particular cultural climate, by whom and, when considering evidence, disentangling the different interpretations of events. A historian needs to consider the ideological, social and, in the following case, economic stance of the 'witnesses' making the testimony. Furthermore, undated primary testament referred to in secondary sources needs close examination when taken as evidence to ensure that the perception of a situation in one historic period is not ascribed to another.

An example of the above problems of historical research which is particularly pertinent to the question of the moral image of the dancer is as follows. The Alhambra possessed an underground canteen where the cast, who were not allowed out of the theatre between performances, went for refreshment. According to a contemporary writer named Ewing Ritchie, who was a temperance reformer, members of the audience were able to infiltrate the canteen. There, 'looking through a haze of tobacco smoke, you will see some forty or fifty ballet girls standing chatting or seated in company with their male admirers' (Ritchie, undated, in Scott 1977: 155).

In a telling comment which reveals how stage and private persona were conflated, Ritchie suggests how the glamour of the stage transformed the dancers.

> As a rule, the difference between her and other girls of the same rank of life is that she looks a little more shabby, and that her clothes are a trifle dirtier; but in the canteen she appears in her conventional dress as she is displayed on the stage with flashing eye and beauteous form.
> Ritchie in Scott 1977: 155

The result of this 'flashing eye' is, according to Ritchie, 'if she is virtuous she cannot be expected to remain so for long, as the Canteen is opened up for the convenience of herself and her admirers' (p. 155).

The management of the Alhambra responded to this and other attacks which suggested that they connived in facilitating contact between dancers and audience:

> There exists, despite all that has been said or written by ignorant or spiteful critics to the contrary, an exceedingly well-conducted Apartment, where, at a reduced Tariff, the whole of the Staff are accommodated with the refreshments which their frequently painful labours create a demand for. This snuggery is under the perpetual surveillance of the principal officers and, under certain modifications, open to visitors.
> Alhambra Handbook, quoted in Scott 1977: 155

Booth, who generally presented a more respectable version of events, noted that the man-about-town 'had the *entrée* to the "canteen" where he would have the privilege of drinking champagne in the company of the performers' (Booth 1929: 149).

Perhaps the most interesting perspective on the situation is revealed by a letter written to the London County Council Licensing Committee which is worth reproducing almost in full.

> I wish to draw your attention to a practice of quite recent growth at a West End music hall - the Alhambra - of the management taking or allowing

visitors from the front of the house to go behind the scenes and talk to the ladies of the ballet (in their stage costumes) which they - the ladies - strongly resent. In one case I know of, a young girl of sixteen – who had only been at the theatre a week - was spoken to by two men who came from a box in front who she was afraid not to speak to and who made her an improper proposal.

LCC 5 January 1899

The writer then requests an independent inquiry but asks the Committee: 'not to quote anything from this letter which would identify any particular girl as having made a complaint.'[8]

Thus, four interpretations are given of the same set of circumstances. There is innuendo present in Ritchie's statement that in the canteen the dancer, 'if she is virtuous, cannot be expected to remain so for long', but the management, anxious to protect the reputation of the theatre and its licence, defend their provision of a 'snuggery'. However, further investigation reveals that Ritchie's comments were made in his book originally published in 1857, a period before the ballet achieved independent status at the Alhambra. His interest in temperance reform would also have influenced his perception of the music halls. By the time Booth is writing, he is able to say that the opportunity for members of the male audience to mix with the dancers was 'a privilege'. The writer of the letter to the LCC who signed her/himself simply 'N.S. Parker' of Middle Temple Lane, E.C., may have been a relative or protector of the young girl or even the girl herself, using the disguise of the pseudonym Nosey Parker.

The historian need not adjudicate the accuracy of these statements for, in an example such as this, all four perspectives may contain an element of truth. What is of interest, however, is whose view was 'truth' for the times, whose perspective became reified in history and which reification was, and is, most potent in constructing the moral image of the dancer. Furthermore, the question is not solely one of which commentator presented the most accurate picture, for events need to be placed in their broader context. In this respect, Ritchie not only has on his side apparent historical precedent and what appeared to be common practice across the Channel at the Paris Opera but also the social circumstances of his time.[9] In the context of both mid- and late Victorian England, the sight of women mixing freely with men, individually unchaperoned and seemingly of their own volition, was bound to raise moral eyebrows and inevitable (if misconceived) connections were made between social intercourse and sexual intercourse.

The dancers' apparent sexual accessibility was directly linked to their profession. Ritchie's comment from 1857 (Scott 1977: 155) that 'there are those to whom the fact that a girl belongs to the ballet renders her additionally attractive' would still appear to be valid thirty years later. Grove, a stern critic, castigated the whole profession: 'The professional dancer is looked upon as one who has sadly misapplied talents which might have won reputation in some worthier path of life' (Grove 1895: 1).

In an interview with the dancers themselves ('M.L.C.' 1893: 24-25), they acknowledge that the 'young mashers ... like theatre ladies very much'. In response to the interviewer's question as to whether the attraction is mutual, the answer is, 'that depends, sometimes when they are nice.' This response is apparently given 'with a very superior air'. Furthermore, the writer stresses that

> most of the ladies have their young men, who seem to wait outside ... (the Rehearsal Club) ... until it pleases their charmers to come out ... and be escorted to their 'show' and who seem on the whole to be kept in a very wholesome, but no doubt pleasant, subjection.
> M.L.C. 1893: 25

Even allowing for its literary style, the interview presents a picture of what would appear to be a quite normal relationship between a working woman and her 'young man'.

Those writers of the 1880s onwards who were apologists for the ballet were anxious to stress not only the hard work involved in achieving the necessary skills but observed that the glamour of the ballet did not, in real life, embrace its executants. Willis notes with reference to the *corps de ballet* that 'in private life they were quiet and reserved and gave no hint of their profession in their appearance (Willis in Green, ed. 1986: 180). Hibbert similarly suggests that 'there is no more respectable type of a working woman than the trained dancer' (Hibbert 1916: 197) and Booth points out that 'not for the trained dancer is the little supper after the show; for her the champagne pops in vain, supper club and night club revelries have no meaning' (Booth 1929: 152). A similar sentiment is expressed later in an undated book (Howlett c. 1930s: 10) on the development of British ballet which cites W.S. Gilbert's Teasing Tom character who observes

> When he grew up he was lost to*tally*
> And married a girl in the *corps de bally*.

Howlett makes the following telling aside:

> Incidentally, if you meet someone who married in to the Alhambra *corps de ballet* you will probably find that the ex-ballet girl is a gentle and charming person of utmost respectability, which suggests either a miraculous conversion, or initial innocence.

If the above writers were biased because of their fascination with ballet, Charles Booth was not. His *Life and labour of the people of London* (1903) includes a relatively impartial account of the working conditions of the dancers.[10] He notes that those who were not 'skilful enough and fortunate enough to get into the *corps de ballet* of a house such as the Empire or Alhambra' and thus obtain full-time employment, could only take temporary engagements and

> at other times they go on tour in the country, live with their parents (who are usually of the working-class) or turn dressmakers and needle women, or may have recourse to less reputable modes of obtaining a livelihood. It is fair to add, however, that the appearance of the ballet girls as they leave the theatre

very much resembles that of any other body of young women leaving a respectable place of business.

Booth, C. 1903: 130

This account is worthy of examination. Like Willis, his last statement appears to be a conscious contradiction of received opinion rather than merely an observation (although one does wonder how dancers were expected to dress when off-stage.) His suggestion that the 'temporary' dancers 'may have recourse to less reputable modes of obtaining a livelihood' is not only speculative but, if it were true, points to the distinction between full-time dancers and those whose occupation was peripatetic. It is difficult to conceive how those in full-time employment would have found the time to engage regularly with other forms of paid employment, whatever its nature. It may be, however, that those with a less secure income, who joined the ballet as supernumeraries rather than trained dancers, did have to supplement their wages through what was, for the unskilled working class woman, one of the most accessible means of earning a living, prostitution. It is not this possibility which is under consideration, however, nor the fact that there is no evidence to verify or negate Booth's supposition, but it is clear that all dancers were implicated in the 'immoral' activities of some dancers. It is this generalisation which secondary sources perpetuate.

Secondary sources on the music hall ballet are rare and only brief mention is made in general dance history texts, if at all. Brevity entails generalisation and this can mislead by presenting only one view, one image. For example, Hanna's single reference to the music hall claims that 'many literary and artistic individuals had fixated on the dancers (the good time girls or prostitutes) of the 'decadent' music halls of the 1890s' (Hanna 1988: 130).

An image which may have little basis in fact can become reified over time or, if there is an element of truth in individual cases, the specificity can become generalised to embrace a whole phenomenon. Another example is Lansley who is quoted as saying that 'before ballet became a respectable art form in the 1930s, it existed only as 'acts' in the music halls, and ballet girls were regarded as high class prostitutes' (Lansley in English 1980: 18). This summary dismisses the ballet as an 'act', implicitly undermining the significance of the music hall in popular culture, and no other sources found to date have suggested that even if any of the ballet girls were prostitutes, they were 'high class'. Their profession may have accorded them some glamour but their social background and personal conditions of existence were anything but 'high class'.

Secondary sources can also distort the time span and thus apply the view of one era to another. Garafola (1989: 319) is guilty of this when she quotes a source from 1913 which suggested that the only difference between a guardsman (who had notorious reputations) and a ballet girl was that one sinned on two legs and the other on one. By applying this quotation to the 'ballet before Diaghilev' she would seem to be referring to the dancers of the music hall who preceded (and performed concurrently with) the Ballets Russes' appearance in London. However, her source ('I' 1913) is actually quoting a novel which was published in 1859.[11] The original target of the implication would have been the dancers of the late Romantic ballet. However, *if* the comment could be applied with accuracy to the performers of the 1850s or before, the evidence examined in this Chapter suggests that, contrary to Garafola's assertion, it was arguably no longer valid in relation to the music hall ballet from the 1880s onwards. Evidence to support this claim comes from the aforementioned writers such as Headlam, Hibbert and J.B. Booth but the most significant defenders of the dancers' morality are the dancers themselves.

A defence of the dancing profession was made by one of its practitioners, an itinerant stage dancer who trained partly in ballet but who was never a member of a house company. In her autobiography, she pleads,

> believe me, my readers, we are not nearly so 'immoral' as we are painted ... it may seem strange to some of my readers, yet it is a fact that many dancers and acrobats are quite respectable women; not only so, but many of them are straight laced and prudish.
>
> anon. 1913: 51

The fact that 'it may seem strange' to her readers that dancers were respectable very clearly indicates that the obverse image was the norm. The most useful source which supports this anonymous dancer is Phyllis Bedells whose comments on the *corps de ballet* at the Empire present a very different picture from the one painted by the unnamed Member of Parliament who 'in the course of a House of Commons speech, was reported to have said that the bulk of stage dancers led immoral lives' (Bettany 1926: l07). According to Bedells, the *corps* at the Empire comprised 'a lot of very sedate and almost narrow minded girls who had been in the same theatre for years and whose lives were of the strictest and simplest' (Bedells Mss.: 8). She adds, in the published version of her book, 'whatever was true at the front of the theatre, on our side of the curtain we had reached an extreme of rigid respectability' (Bedells 1954: 23).

The reaction of the *corps* to their costume makes an interesting comparison with Ormiston Chant's perception of ballet costume:

> I can remember an occasion when the *corps de ballet* were so shocked at being given dresses to wear without sleeves that they threatened to go on strike. If bare midriffs or bare arms were to be shown the girls were given flesh-coloured leotards to wear.
>
> Bedells 1954: 23

Similarly, Bedells recalls how appalled the dances were at the very short tutu worn by Lydia Kyasht. The anonymous *Confessions* (1913) defends the 'airy costume of the ballet dancer' as simply a uniform, a convention.

Bedells' picture of the *corps* and their attitudes is supported by her account of their backstage activities.

> At rehearsal times when they were not actually dancing they were more like a mothers' meeting, everyone doing crochet or knitting or sewing - not a bit like the ballet girl of fiction; in fact the whole tone and behaviour of everyone

> behind the curtain was in extreme contrast to conditions then existing at the front of the house.
>
> Bedells Mss.: 8

It might be that the composition of the *corps* and their moral attitudes had changed over time, for Bedells was with the Empire from 1907 to the demise of its house ballet in 1915. Her comment, quoted above, that 'we have reached an extreme of rigid respectability' suggests this might be the case.[12] Other evidence substantiates her account. Headlam discusses the response of the dancers to the aforementioned speech of the Member of Parliament:

> Our Alhambra and Empire girls were furious over it, and I was assured that the male relatives of more than one were prepared to lie in wait for the M.P. and take summary vengeance on him for the insult. There was talk of throwing him in the river.
>
> Headlam in Bettany 1926: 107

Another case where a male relative stepped in to defend the respectability of a dancer was over a gift sent by a member of the aristocracy to the daughter of Bertrand, who was ballet master at the Empire in 1884. The presentation of gifts from admirers, patrons or would-be patrons to actresses or dancers was a theatrical tradition though, as Bratton points out, by the music hall period it no longer signified the sexual possession of, and by, a rich admirer but 'the transaction it signifies is now between the woman and a new set of protectors, the managers and audience with whom she finds favour' (Bratton in Bratton, ed. 1986: 103). It appears to have been the traditional connotations which Bertrand had in mind when a diamond ring was left at the stage door, with an accompanying letter on coroneted notepaper:

> Dear Miss Bertrand - will you accept the enclosed little present as an appreciation of your artistic ability, by an admirer?
> Yours faithfully.

And the reply from the father was:

> My Lord
> Will you accept the enclosed 'present' back as an appreciation of your d.....d impertinence.
> From, Her Father.
>
> Glover 1913: 153-154

In both these cases the dancers do not speak for themselves, for female virtue was defended by male agency. Virtue not only reflected on the women who possessed it but on the men who possessed the women: husbands, fathers and brothers. In Phyllis Bedells' case, the absence of a father left the protective role to her mother.

> Then I received by first present of jewellery from an unknown admirer: it was a beautiful necklace ... My mother, even so early in my career, had insisted I should not accept presents from men ... I might be allowed to accept flowers, mother told me, but nothing else.
>
> Bedells 1954: 24

The citing of the above two examples are not for the purpose of illustrating the dancers' high moral ground, for two cases are an insufficient base from which to generalise. They do signify, however, that gifts were still offered, though there is no evidence, to date, to suggest that these were the precursors of patronage or sexual liaison as was apparently the case in earlier periods of dance history. However, in the context of one of the few professions where women were able to earn an independent living through their own skills, the gift, as a sign, 'remains powerful, enabling the patriarchy to perceive her wealth as the gift of men rather than the earning-power of women' (Bratton in Bratton, ed. 1986: l03).

Other contemporary evidence in which the dancers' self-perception may be ascertained through the voice of others is in relation to the distinction made between dancers of the ballet and the pantomime dancers and show girls. If you were to ask a ballet girl, says Booth, 'and to succeed in getting her to express her views, her opinion of the husky-throated, cigarette-smoking, jazzing little chorus girl is brutally frank' (Booth 1929:152). Similarly, the dancer, 'also sees in the "show girl" the incomprehensible creature of another world, who toils not neither does she spin' (Hibbert 1916: 198).

This distinction is also found in an oblique reference in Wagner (1899: 179). Discussing the pitfalls of the acting profession, he warns that 'actors of the lower order' do expect to 'have a good time' with the ladies of the ballet and show girls, and

> even the scene shifters and property men look forward to the pantomime season as a period during which they may play havoc among girls who do not stand on their moral dignity *but they draw the line at the corps de ballet*. (My italics)
>
> Wagner 1899: 179

The ballet dancers' contempt for the show girl or peripatetic dancer was based on matters of relative training, skills and the theatrical context of their work. Nevertheless, such evidence does contribute to the overall image of the ballet dancers, who took their profession seriously, setting themselves apart both artistically and morally from those who practised other dance forms in other venues.

The extent to which the occupation of 'dancer' connoted a morally suspect lifestyle depended not only on the dance genre, as above, but also on the dancer's position in the performing hierarchy. This is a distinction that sources fail to acknowledge although, even until recently, lax morals were far more likely to be associated with a chorus girl or musical theatre dancer than with a classical ballerina. From the Romantic period, certainly up until the end of the music hall ballet, there was a dichotomy between the perceived sexual virtue of the *premières danseuses* and that of the *corps de ballet*.

It would be expected that in their autobiographies, the *premières danseuses* would present themselves as beyond reproach. Kyasht (1978) appeared to enjoy the company of men and certainly acknowledged her admirers with pride rather than with bashfulness, but Kyasht, Bedells and Genée all appear to have led lives of the utmost respectability.[13] It is, in fact, this need for a respectable image which might very well have influenced Bedells' construction of her accounts of the morality of the dancers as a self-protective strategy. Other anecdotes confirm how the principal dancers guarded their reputation. Booth tells of La Belle Leonora, who appeared at the Alhambra from 1908 to 1910. When making her entrance as Eve in the ballet *Femina* (1910), she 'insisted on a corridor of curtains from her dressing room to the stage, and that all stage hands who should happen to cross her path should immediately turn their backs' (Booth 1929: 154).

Only in the context of the ballet itself was she prepared to display her 'realistic' Eve. Zanfretta gave up her dancing career at the Empire for *en travestie* roles after giving birth to her child because she and her husband considered ballet costume unsuitable for a wife and mother. The interviewer (referred to as 'Madame' in the article) of the Alhambra dancer, Vanda Adler, takes pains to let her readers know of the irreproachable character of her interviewee.

> Nothing could be like the traditional idea of the *première danseuse* than the appearance of the young girl who came in – no ornaments, no rouge ... and her delicate face and serious aspect would have led you to believe that Mdlle. Adler had spent all her life in a boudoir.
>
> 'L.H.A.' 1893: 374

Again, a few anecdotes and self-interested evidence from the dancers themselves do not make a weighty case for the moral image of the *première danseuse*. However, as charges of immorality were nearly always directed to 'ballet girls', a term never applied to the principals, it is by omission rather than inclusion that the image of the latter remained not only unsullied but positively enhanced.

Writers who seriously addressed the music hall ballet did so because of their interest in the art form. They tended, therefore, to be supporters rather than detractors, defenders rather than accusers. Nevertheless, their writing is of interest for, in stressing the hard work, blameless lives and ordinariness of the dancers, most specifically the *corps*, they provide unwitting testimony of the prevailing image. By refutation, they present the image itself. It is impossible to weigh the evidence in order to arrive at a conclusion for, with the lives of so many women under scrutiny over a period of thirty years, there cannot be one 'truth'. It is clear that there were substantially different readings of events, both simultaneously and over time. Whether the ballet girl knitted and crocheted backstage then met with her 'stage door johnny' after the performance; whether she was escorted home or whether 'shortly after eleven ... (she was)... at Charing Cross waiting for the Brixton bus' (Hibbert 1916: 197) is not in question. With so many women, each one possessing her own personal history, there are many 'truths'. What is evident, is how the social and artistic context of the music hall ballet has shaped the moral image of the dancers. The historical connotations attached to the dancing profession were compounded, in the music hall period, by the common practice of prostitution in society, with its concomitant perception of the sexual availability of a certain class or type or woman. This prostitution was manifest in the promenades of the Alhambra and the Empire. Furthermore, for women to venture out of the home into the world of the theatre, and therein demonstrate evident professional skills, was so at odds with patriarchal values that her motivation and her concomitant lifestyle could only be made comprehensible if construed as sexual. However, as this Chapter has demonstrated in relation to the ballet girl and the ballerina, the moral image of the dancer was not singular but binary.

The psyche of the era

Dance, as a form of cultural representation, both embodies and contributes to the complex construction of ideologies, including the politics of gender and sexual identity. The music hall ballets, and those who recorded them, produced differentiated images of women which were in accord with dominant notions of what constituted femininity in general and female sexuality in particular. Judgements made about the ballets were, more often than not, based on perceptions of the dancers rather than the dances. Even though dancers were often cast as artefacts, as personifications, as men or boys, there was no attempt to disguise their bodies; all representations of the dancer were not only identifiably human but also emphatically female. Three distinct representations of the 'female' emerge: those of the ballet girls, the ballerinas and the principal *en travestie* performers.

The ballet girls were the working classes, the 'rank and file' of the stage. Since skill was neither required nor developed, their career mobility within the company hierarchy was static. Even though their 'characters' were often supernatural or non-human, their dance vocabulary was mundane and earthbound. They moved as a homogeneous mass rather than as individuals and, whether dressed as females or in travesty, they served two main functions. The first, through obvious differences in movement vocabulary, technical skill and by the spatial patterning on stage, was to draw attention to the ballerina. The second, with their gorgeous costumes and mass movement, was to constitute the spectacle of the ballet. Like individual pigments of paint, they created a colour wash for the stage picture and that picture had to be, essentially, a pretty one. With their costumes, wigs and *maquillage* they created a fantasy world of feminine beauty and were there to attract and to please the eye of the beholder.

The ballerina, too, was there to please by her looks and feminine qualities. Within her stage image, however, there is a paradox. Her movement vocabulary, like her roles and her costumes, was other-worldly and she was set apart not only within the narrative but in relation to all the other characters on the stage. As such, she was remote, inaccessible; she did not belong to mere mortals. If a figure of romance, her liaisons were chaste, for her partners were women. She played, in the vast majority of ballets, characters that were essentially good and morally virtuous. Other facets of her performance, however, subvert this persona. The movement vocabulary of the *danse d'ecole* is designed to present the dancer's body in full-frontal exposure to the viewer. Her body, therefore, is always on display and her gaze is communicated not to the other performers but directly to the audience. Her lack of a credible male partner meant that there was no on-stage competition for her attention. Simultaneously distanced from her audience and yet accessible to them, it was her very chastity which eroticised her, a paradox which can also be found in the paintings of the period wherein the self-contained, self absorbed woman seems, nevertheless, voluptuously available. At the ballet, the male audience could be engaged from afar but the ballerina's image was unsullied by any suggestion of 'real' womanhood. This image was endorsed by the lack of any acknowledgement that the ballerina had a mind as well as a body. Unlike the actress who dealt with the spoken word, her art appeared to rely on practical and physical rather than cognitive and verbal skills. In this respect, neither the ballerina nor the ballet girl challenged the notion that women should be primarily decorative; their function was to display their bodies but not their minds.

The iconography of the ballet confirms the dual image of the ballet girls and the ballerina. Sketches of the former show scantily clad performers moving with an abandoned energy and gusto; in photographs they are posed solidly, with a direct eye out to the camera. Ballerinas are presented in static classical ballet poses but, particularly in photographs, with a body stance that is coquettish and a gaze that is coy. The *corps*, on stage or in their graphic image, are earthbound, human and accessible. The ballerina's image suggests that she might be, but who would dare to dream so?

The *en travestie* principal played a significant but ambiguous role on stage. She was eroticised by her costume and the sight of a woman dressed as a man would have had undoubted appeal to the audience. However, her mature age, her use of the body language of mime rather than dancing and, most significantly, her stage identity as a 'man', contributed to the fact that the *en travestie* lead was either written about with reverence for her acting skills, or not at all. Although central to the narrative of most of the ballets, the image of the travesty hero is faint and unplaced. With a predominant aesthetic of visual spectacle, the 'hero' of the narrative was virtually redundant. Besides which, whatever the private relationship of the audience to the travesty protagonist, there was understandably no public expression of how a man negotiated his relationship with his own image on stage.

The dreams of the audience, as revealed in 'fact' and in fiction, were similarly differentiated. The fantasies of writers were nearly all directed towards the ballet girl. (The one source which did eroticise a ballerina was pornographic and therefore out of the mainsteam of literary currency.) These sources were not numerous and often took the form of 'asides' in reviews or backstage accounts of the ballet. There are enough, however, to notice that the ballet girl, absent from history as a performer, is present in the writing of the period not as performer but as a woman. Her person is appropriated for the man in the audience; it is she whose eyes gleam intimately across the footlights (Symons 1895); she who breaks hearts ('S.L.B.' 1896a) and she who is kissable (Cornell 1887). The ballerina is admired but there is never any suggestion that she might be kissed.

Likewise, the personal moralities of the dancers off-stage were also perceived as contrary. 'Respectability' was not simply a prerogative of the upper and middle classes but it was the aim of most women, achieved through marriage and the maintenance of strict moral standards within marriage. Women who consorted with men unchaperoned, and who displayed their bodies to full public view on stage were far from respectable. Actresses and dancers had always been perceived with ambivalence but the strict moral code of the period, including the self-censorship of women themselves, made their place in society even more complex. Whilst their position in society was untenable, they themselves were desirable, though this seeming paradox is undoubtedly a case of cause and effect. However, although the ballet itself was implicated in the dubious moral behaviour associated with the venues and the West End of London generally, the ballerinas escaped implicit or explicit accusation. In this respect, they resisted the role of mistress and status of a male possession which accrued to their forebears of the Romantic period of the 1830s-1850s. There could be many reasons for this, not least of all the economic truth that principal dancers would not need to supplement their income by immoral earnings, or be kept by men, because of their greater earning capacities. The management of the theatres to whom the dancers were contracted, ever-anxious to keep, at least officially, a respectable 'house', would also be concerned to protect the reputation of their stars. There are other factors which may have influenced how the differing moralities of the principals and the ballets girls were perceived. The principals tended to be foreign and could not, unlike the *corps*, be associated with the British working classes. Their skills, dance roles, social class, nationality and their very place in the hierarchy of the ballet and their own investment in and responsibility to the profession all contributed to their immunity from overt, public charges of sexual accessibility. For the ballet girl, the historical connotations of her profession, her working class background, her nationality, age and the generalised but misconceived notion of her unmarried state all compounded the confusion over her sexual identity.

Whatever structural or social factors contributed to the dichotomous moral images of the dancers, they were in total accord with the dominant notions of female sexuality. The generally anodyne roles of the ballerina and the technically correct but passionless nature of her performances would have also served to construct a morally pure image. As such, she could be placed on a pedestal together with the rest of idealised womanhood. Her position there was maintained with the glue of male bonding, a phenomenon of the period evidenced in the Alhambra and the Empire's status as gentlemen's clubs for the upper class male and the *risqué* alternative for working class respectability.

The dichotomy of image which an analysis of the ballets and attendant commentary has revealed may not be particular to this period. It is, however, one that appears to be far more polarised in the music hall ballet. The binary distinction between the Madonna and Magdalene, the lily and the rose, the angel by the hearth and the whore in the street, had clear roots in the social class structure which sharpened its boundaries during the Victorian era. Also more pronounced were the separate worlds of public and private life and morality; the separation of the home and women in the home from public activity. In terms of both these polarities, the music hall ballet was uniquely designed to serve its age. The differing perceptions of dancers accommodated the need for the Victorian male psyche to categorise women as either chaste or impure. The moral behaviours attributed to women from different social classes are represented in the contrasting images of the music hall dancer. In order to sustain these norms the personal and professional lives of the working class dancers were mythologised. As women who not only earned an independent living but did so in a very public arena, their existence was justified and their image appropriated for the pleasure of men. This connection between the sexual appeal of the dancers on stage and their sexuality off stage, forms the complex and contingent basis of their overall image. The crucial site of that image is the female body. As I have argued elsewhere, however (Carter 1999) the body is not, as has been fashionable in scholarship to claim, just a surface upon which ideology is ascribed. The 'body' is a living, human subject with individual agency. A significant question which arises, therefore, is the role played by the dancers themselves in the construction of their own image.

The extent of the dancers' complicity in the construction of their sexual identity(ies) is a moot point and, as with debate on women's participation in any activities which are commercially designed to please men, the argument is complex. The ballet girls would have been fully aware of the titillating aspects of their performance. Yet, there is a paradox inherent in the juxtaposition of this consciousness and the dancers' pride in their art. The professional working ethos of the ballet would appear to over-ride if not preclude their endorsement of the erotic nature of their performance. Any conscious intention that an engagement with the men in the audience whilst on stage necessarily meant some kind of liaison off stage, is seemingly at odds with the evidence of the day-to-day working lives and personal circumstances of the dancers. It would appear that commentators on the ballet confused the demands of the dancers' public image, their willingness to 'play their role' in every sense, with their personal proclivities. As in Mackenzie's (1929) aphorism, the dancers may have desired applause over the footlights but under the moon, in the reality of the street, they were free from the imperative of having to seek favour. The problem lies in that whatever the dancers' personal perceptions of their activities, these did not necessarily accord with their public image, for the cultural meanings which accrue to the female body do battle with their personal motivation or intent. For the dancer, the meanings ascribed to her roles, her costume, to her very participation in an overt display of the female body for public consumption, would have had a resonance more potent during the Victorian period than in any other. One person who tried to reread the ballet from a woman's rather than a man's perspective was Laura Ormiston Chant. So much did she read against the grain of dominant social and artistic ideologies, that it was she who was considered warped, not the grain itself.

Dance, perhaps more than any other theatrical art, has the power to sexualise women. In the ballet of the music hall, the power of the body was controlled and any challenge to society's notions of gender which may have been presented by professional working women using their physical skills for their art, was deflected by the appropriation of the dancer's body by male writers. The dominant ideology which defined images of women in society coloured how the music hall ballets were described, the meanings ascribed to them and the criteria by which they were valued. Even within the sexual arena of the West End and the music hall itself, the sexuality presented on stage was constrained within the artifice of the ballets and nothing disturbed the *status quo*. Images of the music hall dancers were produced by or mediated through the kinetic and visual discourses of the ballet and its graphic representation; the 'factual' writings of journalism and history, and the fictive discourse of novels and poetry. In almost none of these did the ballet girls speak for themselves; they were unable to take possession of their own image. To fill this silence, we now hear the voice of Cara Tranders, a member of the *corps de ballet* at the Empire. The bones of her experience are historically verifiable; the muscle is constructed by historical speculation.

NOTES

1. The term 'prostitute' could have been used imprecisely, covering laxity of social behaviour between the sexes, temporary prostitution and sexual encounters which did not involve the exchange of money.
2. However, as argued in this Chapter, the reality often belied the myth. For example, Vita Sackville West (1983: 27), after relaying an anecdote about a rebuff Alexandre Dumas received from a ballet dancer, noted: 'it comes as a surprise to learn how very strict was the standard of conduct observed even by those professional dancers who had passed beyond the supervision of mother or parents. These ladies were of ferocious virtue.' Nevertheless, the stigma remained. Even in America, attitudes were not more progressive. Touring dancers in the 1880s and 1890s were 'condemned as absolutely outside the pale of normal American social intercourse' (Kendall 1979: 6).
3. Nead (1988: 6) discusses this dichotomy in relation to 'ways in which these categories were established and also the points at which they broke down and ambiguities reappeared'. She proposes that, from the 1870s, the demarcation between the 'respectable' woman and the 'immoral' woman began to be eroded as women started to display their dress and their bodies in ways that had previously coded the prostitute. However, as this study demonstrates, a different set of codes operated on the ballet stage. For other analyses of the polarisation of women's sexuality during the Victorian period, see Dijkstra (1986) on images of women in the visual arts and writing of the period. Millett (1971: 148-50) refers to the imagery of the lily and the rose in Victorian poetry and Bland (1981) considers the class connotations of the dichotomy.
4. Like many reformers, Chant endeavoured to: 'lead some of these girls who use the promenade of the Empire to a better life. I have had one or two of these girls to afternoon tea in my drawing room and have talked over this matter with them as to what this life is leading' (Chant in Donahue 1987: 57). A further example of Chant's sympathies with women is her insistence that they should be allowed to attend places of public entertainment on their own, if they so wished. The following is a transcript from Chant's evidence to the Select Committee which was investigating theatre licensing in 1892:

> Do you object to women going to places of entertainment alone?
> No; I think that women ought to be able to go into any assembly alone.
> Exactly on the same footing as men?
> Quite so.
> And not be interfered with so long as they conduct themselves with propriety?
> Yes.
>
> Reproduced in Cheshire 1974: 39

Trudgill (1976: 127-128) suggests that: 'Mrs. Chant, far from being a fanatical persecutor of defenceless outcasts, had been deeply involved for many years in welfare work to rescue them.' However, as Walkowitz (in Snitow *et al*, eds 1983: 419-39) also points out in a discussion of the complex motivation of social purity campaigners, those who aimed to 'protect' women actually reinforced patriarchal ideology by promoting the traditional values of domestic virtue. Chant could have been such a campaigner, for her advocacy was not only for women's suffrage but also for temperance and 'purity' (Donahue 1987: 152). In this respect, Chant would be an interesting case for further study.

5. Jones in Waites *et al*, eds (1982: 112) draws attention to the fact that reform movements tended to be associated with the liberal wing of politics whereas, because of their investments in the drink trade, it was in Tory interests to promote the music halls. The music hall became, from the 1870s to the 1900s, 'actively and self-consciously 'Tory'. Chant's campaign against the Empire was supported by the Labour bench of the London County Council and the Empire was defended by young Tories such as Winston Churchill and his fellow Sandhurst cadets.

6. Examples of Shaw's attacks on Headlam can be found in Laurence, 1981a: 163; 808-809; 929 and 1981b: 592. The vitriolic nature of these attacks, in which he accuses Headlam of starting a 'technicojargonautic fashion in ballet criticism' (1981a: 163) and the Guild of 'puerile gushes of enthusiasm about exploits that ought to be contemptuously criticised off the face of the earth' (1981b: 592) need to be considered in the light of Shaw's own appreciation of the ballet, but lack of expertise.

7. See Foulkes (1997) for a discussion of the relationships between Church and stage, including a chapter on Headlam and his Church and Stage Guild.

8. There is an interesting addendum to this complaint. A letter went from the London County Council (LCC) to an Inspector, requesting an investigation, but a handwritten note on the letter suggests that the matter was dealt with unofficially and no further action was taken. It would appear that the LCC was reluctant to interfere officially in such delicate matters. A similar complaint was made in the letter from the 'Comic Singer' who, acknowledging the fuss about behaviour in the promenade in the front of the theatre, pleaded 'let us have a little propriety at the back so decent girls can ... (*earn*?) ... their living without being annoyed by those at the back, or is the Alhambra too powerful to be interfered with! (LCC 14 October 1889). (*My italics as the original handwriting is illegible.*)

9. This canteen or apartment could be seen as the equivalent of the Green Room. The opening of the door of the Green Room to members of the audience began in the 1820s when it became fashionable for 'men about town' to adopt a singer, actress or dancer and become her patron. An engraving by Robert Cruikshank (Guest 1954 opp. p. 16) of the Green Room at the King's Theatre, London shows dancers surrounded by and in intimate conversation with the Regency dandies. Evidence of this supposed custom at the Paris Opera during the 1880s and 1890s can be seen in paintings by Jean Louis Forain (in Browse 1978: 90; 147 and 157 and Musée Marmottan 1978: 24; 60-

61 and 79) and Jean Beraud (Clarke & Crisp 1978: 87). The subject matter of these paintings is the ballet dancers and their wealthy admirers or patrons consorting in the wings and backstage. However, as Browse points out, these images are highly misleading for, with regards to Forain, 'he failed to recognise that once a dancer steps into the wings to await her entrance, she is highly committed and has neither the time nor the inclination to dally with suitors ... the pictures are, in essence, untrue' (1978: 36).

10. Booth (1903: 129) did include some personal comment in his survey noting, as a footnote on the music hall ballet, that 'it must be said that it is a long time since a Taglioni has made her appearance here'.

11. The original quotation from the novel, in which a young man at a dinner party ruminates on similarities between guardsmen (who were at the time notoriously promiscuous) and ballet girls, is as follows: 'They both lived by the strength of their legs, where also their wits if they do not altogether reside there, are principally developed ... wine, tobacco and the moon influence both alike; and admitting the one marked difference that does exist, it is, after all, pretty nearly the same thing to be coquetting and sinning on two legs as on the point of a toe' (Meredith [1859]; 1962: 363).

12. The eroticisation of the ballet girl seems to have been far more prevalent in the 1860s and 1870s than in Bedells time. For example, a fictional account was published c.1870 entitled *Intrigues and confessions of a ballet girl: disclosing startling and voluptuous scenes before and behind the curtain, under and upon the stage, in the light and the dark, by one who has had her share* (anon. c.1870). However, as claimed in this Chapter, such a reputation continued to be attached to the dancer whether it was deserved or not.

13. Several secondary sources (for example Clarke & Crisp 1981: 189) suggest that Genée gave the ballet profession a new respectability. However, no factual sources have been found which indicate that the *premières danseuses* of the music hall ballet before Genée were anything other than respectable. One exception to this is the novel *Crissie* (anon. 1899b) which is discussed in Chapter 5.

CHAPTER SEVEN

Cara's Tale

The reminiscences of Cara Tranders, ballet girl at the
Empire Palace of Varieties, 1892-1899[1]

It looms up, a large greyish shape with ill-defined edges. I like to think of it as a friendly whale in murky sea waters. Out of the dusky green of the fog, the omnibus that will take me to the Palace crawls to a stop. Like Jonah, I climb in. Its soft lights envelop me and the conductor greets me warmly, for he doesn't fear my travelling alone. He knows I am a dancer but he has seen my sharp eyes as I repel any potential threat to my reputation. Some people think, you know, that if you show your body to the public on stage you must be willing to show it to anyone in private. My aunt was horrified when mother told her I was hoping to be a dancer; she thought it was no better than going on the streets but mother told her what for and aunt changed her mind when she came to see me in our new show. Escorted by Uncle (for she would never have gone on her own) she was quite dazzled by the spectacle of it all, even though Uncle himself said that he couldn't tell which one was me, being so far from the stage and us all looking alike with our wigs and red and gold costumes and all holding the same long batons in our hands. Uncle was a bit quiet when we left the theatre and stopped going on about it was all 'bally nonsense'. I wouldn't tell Aunty, not even to spite her, but I believe he's been back to the ballet on more than one occasion since.

I sink into my seat, relishing the ride from Kentish Town up to Leicester Square when, trapped by my transport, I can do nothing. My body is exhausted, for we were at the theatre at eleven this morning for rehearsal of the new production. Finishing at two, I have time to get home to give mother her late lunch, for she's poorly now and since Dad ran off there's no one but me to look after her. What I will do when I meet that young chap of my dreams who'll want to whisk me away and look after me, I do not know. We seemed to move from mother looking after me to me looking after her without any stage in between. Perhaps my young man will take her in, too, because he'll be wealthy enough. Not too much out of our class, of course, because that would be unnatural, but he'll have just enough money for us to be 'comfortable', as they say. Till then, it seems I'm destined to be always tired, for I don't get the bus home after the show till gone eleven at night then it's up in the morning to tidy both mother and the rooms before I leave for the theatre.

Some girls are lucky; they don't have to come and go but can wait at the Rehearsal Club, started by that nice Lady Magenis for the likes of us to flop around during the afternoons when we've a few hours off. My wages aren't too bad, for I'm on twenty shillings a week now and if I can be promoted to the front row of the *corps* I can make thirty five, though by the time I've paid my Sick Club and other clubs that arise from time to time, my take-home's not special. Sometimes I get fined for being late which is a bit unfair because it's always such a rush and I can't help the traffic, especially in the pea-soupers. (Once, I was so worried about being late but they had to cancel the ballet, *Nisita* I think, because the fog in the theatre made it impossible to see the stage.) The scene painters earn three pounds, though. This doesn't seem fair either because they just slap on paint and no-one cares about where the edges are because the audience can't see that close anyway.

At least I'm lucky to have a job. We had a scare at the Empire only last year. That Mrs. Ormiston Chant nearly got us closed down for good, complaining as she did to the Council. She said the ballets were immoral and I said she was an interfering old busybody who should mind where she pokes her nose but some said she wasn't accusing us, just the management of promoting licentious shows. I don't know what licentious means, myself, but it doesn't sound like a compliment.

My friend Emily wrote to the Council appealing to them not to close the Empire, which was ever so brave of her. She's only in the middle row, like me, but she's become a bit of a star now. Fortunately, they did renew the Empire's licence and our jobs were saved. People get mixed up, of course, and confuse those 'ladies' of the night who ply their trade in the promenade at the front of the theatre, and us ladies of the ballet. We don't want to be tarred with the same immoral brush as them, though I must say, I do envy their elegance. Some say the men just enjoy the company of these women, but quite a lot goes on at the front there. Not just women but men, too, exchange their company for money.

Sometimes I wonder if it's worth being on this side of the curtain rather than out there in the promenade. Not seriously, of course, but I daydream a little when I suffer the conditions in which we have to work. Our dressing rooms are so cramped, and with a hundred and fifty of us in the big ballets, backstage is worse than Piccadilly Circus on Boat Race night. We have to fly down the stairs - all eighty of them, and stone as well - after each scene to get changed for the next one. We knock over anyone who gets in the way, especially those critic chaps who lurk around. They think we fancy them but we just give them nice smiles so they can write something good about us in the papers. They don't mean anything to us really - but we've got a job to do and all you can think of is getting to your room. There is that nice Mr. Guest, though, a real gentleman who said he'd write about us one day but we think he's mainly interested in the ballerinas. Still, all publicity helps.

It's off with one costume and on with the next, then running back up the stairs to make my next entry, panting hard but smiling. Hard, that is, panting and smiling. But we get used to it. We don't always get used to the rats, though they scarper and we just see their tails disappear. They don't like all the activity and, as you can imagine, twelve of us all cramped together in one little dressing room can be a very active occasion - elbows and legs everywhere. You're never sure whose tights you are putting on. We're not allowed out of the room during the break between the two nightly ballets when the other acts are on. It's less frantic then; we might knit or catch up with our sewing, but it's the smell we don't like. We can't help the sweat and the greasy make up, but there's no air and it's hot and sometimes you just hold your breath, so you're panting even more. But you have to keep smiling, because the management said so and we do what they say or we'll never make the front row. If I go to the back row before I go forward, I'll just die. The back row is for those who are beginners or those who are past it. Some of the girls' mums are in the back row. Quite companionable, being on the same stage as your mum, but you can see your future in hers if you're not careful. Madame Lanner, our ballet mistress, danced professionally until she was nearly fifty, so it can be a long career for those who are lucky, those who work hard and keep out of trouble.

Most of us are really careful to keep out of trouble. And we do work hard, even though it can be boring at times, especially towards the end of a six month run which is not unusual. Although we all think we can do more, most us know secretly that we're not trained to be able to display our skills. Mother sent me to Madame Aldavini's school first, then I went on to Madame Lanner's National Training School of Dancing in Tottenham Court Road, from where she gets most of the Empire girls. Not the principals of course - they come from abroad where the training's much better. That's why they star. Isn't fair, really. We are pretty well a world apart, as they don't have much to do with us and we wouldn't dare speak to them. But we watch them secretly, when we're framing their performance, and we talk about them after. Some of the girls can be really nasty. Jealousy, really, for that's all we are on the stage - a coloured frame around a pure white dancing picture. The ballerinas can go up and stay on their toes. I've tried, time and time again, but my legs won't let me do it. A skill, really. But they've got the muscles for it. Men don't see the muscles, though. I don't really know what they see. The ballerinas are a bit out of their class, being skilled and foreign and all that, but I suppose the men can dream.

Elly (we call her that behind her back, just to bring her down a bit; her name's really Elena Cornalba) wears a lovely gauzy dress in our current ballet, *Faust*. She doesn't do much else, mind. Got no 'character' to play but she does the proper steps. There's rumours that she's leaving and they're looking to Moscow for another star. That will be interesting. Management can't seem to find a permanent ballerina from Italy. Madame Zanfretta as Mephistopheles is as strong as ever; we know all her mime actions of course but could never do them as well as she can. I can imagine myself in that black costume with those grand arm gestures which tell the story. So dramatic.

My reverie comes to a jolting halt. I like having reveries as they sound foreign and glamorous - but it's time to get off the omnibus. Madame Lanner will be furious if we're late; she's like a big black beetle in her bombazine. She's good at her arrangements of us *corps de ballet*. Should be by now, for she's been with the Empire since 1887 they say. Her and Mr. Wilhelm work on most of the ballets together. For this *Faust* he's written the story (based on someone else's we think) so he worked more closely with her on each scene as well as designing the costumes as usual. We all know he's actually called William Pitcher and his dad is a ship builder, but he changed his name to sound more foreign because it helps in this business. You can't blame him. Sometimes when I'm standing there in yet another tableaux I dream up names I'd choose for myself. I fancy Cara Taglioni so I could keep the same initials, but there's already been one of those.

Costumes - I must get into mine. I fly off the bus and walk ever so quickly to the side street entrance of the Empire where I meet up with my friend Maria. Maria used to be with the Salvation Army but there wasn't much life there and she kept banging her tambourine in the wrong place (or so she told us, but we think there was a bit of hanky-panky with the collection box). So she came to us.

For tonight's ballet I'm a soldier in the first scene. We play quite a lot of soldiers. There aren't any proper men dancers except for the occasional foreigner but they're not much liked even when they're good, like that Monsieur Cecchetti who was with us a couple of years ago. Went on to become a teacher of sorts, I think. 'They're all the same' says my Uncle, 'one of those'. It took me a while to know who 'those' were and it isn't really fair because some of these gentlemen dancers were married. But you never know. The 'male' characters are nearly always played by women; *'en travestie'*, they call it. Nice to know a bit of French. We know that the audience like to look at our legs when we're dressed as soldiers and we have to keep our waists trim. But they can look at what they like. It's all part of the show to us. We march off after the first scene in *Faust*, being careful to listen to the stage manager's gong and keep in time and not rush, for we have a brisk break of one scene before the third, in which I'm a will-o'-the-wisp. It's the last scene that's the worst. We play angels, with lovely golden wigs, but we have to climb these very steep ladders backstage and perch on the top, sticking our heads through a hole in the backdrop, so our faces appear like 'angels in the sky'. We're terrified, because we're so high up and the ladders wobble and it's freezing cold up there, but we have to keep smiling. I imagine it must look good from the audience's point of view but we don't feel much like angels when we're up there, I can tell you. No wonder we get coughs and colds or worse, all this going from those damp and muggy dressing rooms up those cold stairs to the stage, then hot again under the lights. That's why the Sick Club is so important, to help us through those times when we're poorly.

Sometimes, as I said, the work does get a little boring, though we do two ballets a night. This *Faust* is quite different to the other recent one, *On Brighton Pier*, which has nice popular melodies and we had to learn to move a bicycle around on the stage to show how modern we were. Will Bishop used to make us laugh. He's not a 'real' dancer, of course, but he entertains us with his clog dancing and in *Brighton* he had a really clever masher dance - you know, showing off as a young man about town. The management like these different kinds of ballets - sometimes a really up-to-date work, or one celebrating our Empire; sometimes one from a fairy tale. Keeps everyone happy. The Alhambra is doing *Titania*, based on a Shakespeare play, but they're not as good as us. They say we just hold up the scenery which is a typical thing to come from an Alhambra girl. Admittedly, the movements we're given in all of the ballets are pretty much the same, and are not that difficult in themselves - but it's just the same at the Alhambra. We march a lot, and strike poses, drawing attention to the ballerina. The management always ask Madame Lanner to get a vision scene in, a 'transformation', as the audience love these. There'll be tinkly water music and the flimsy curtain at the back of the stage will be drawn back to reveal another tableaux, a 'transformed' picture within the picture of the stage. Clever, really. The best bits for us are when we waltz or galop as then you can really be carried away with the music and feel that you're really dancing. Not quite like the real ballet in that we're not on our toes but still an important part of the show. Often there are long periods when we do nothing at all, just stand in position. Sometimes I try to find faces in the audience but it is difficult to see them individually in that great sea of half darkness. My mind wanders then. I think about mother at home and feel the pity for her, all day in that room. That's why I try to get home in the afternoons but it makes my day such a squash. I always seem to feel tired. Sometimes I use those tableaux when the ballerina is doing her special solos to plan the next days' meals. Next door gave us some beef dripping, so we can have that with some bread tomorrow. Nice and nutritious.

Useful thinking time, these tableaux are, so long as I don't forget to move on the sixteenth beat after the big crash of the drums. (For *Faust* they've had an organ built and it's a lovely sound - sort of heavenly but majestic.) You don't often miss your cue, though. Even if your mind has wandered you sense it from the girls when its time to move as their breath and their muscles prepare. We've been working together so long we almost dance as one, especially when Mr. Wilhelm dresses different groups of us in colours that match. We must look like an artist's paint palette. Green's my favourite as it goes with my eyes. Not that anyone could see my eyes.

The important thing though, is to keep looking at the audience as if you can really see them. We musn't go too far with our character, of course (it's a bit difficult playing to the crowd as a daisy, anyway) but just sharing our joy of dancing and trying to look attractive. That's important because many of the people in the audience really do love the ballet. Others come just come for a night out, because the Empire means all that is 'home' to them, especially when they've been away in our colonies.

We know that some men also come to eye us up and some of the girls even walk out with men they've met at the stage door. Some even marry them, like that Jenny Pearl who used to be in the first row of the girls. She walked out with this farmer chap who fell in love with her right from first seeing her on stage. Took her off to Cornwall or somewhere remote but her tale ended badly. Some previous *beau* turned up and there was jealousy, we hear. The farmer shot her, dead. It was in the papers. You just can't be too careful with who you meet, can you?

I personally don't like to hang around with those johnnies - I'm in too much of a rush to catch the omnibus - but I don't blame those who do. Some of the dancers from the Alhambra used to go the Crown public house, just off Leicester Square, when they'd meet the young men who claimed they were poets. The girls used to try and explain how the ballets worked and how the steps were performed and they'd get really angry because the men didn't seem to take them seriously. These men belonged to some club - the Rhyming Club, or something. Violet Piggot had an affair with one of them called Arthur. He seemed very keen at first but some of these men don't seem to realise that you can't go to the public house in all your stage finery and in your real clothes, and close-up, you look rather different. What do they expect, a dancing will-o'-the-wisp in a pub? Arthur turned quite nasty, apparently, and dropped Violet pretty quickly. We hear these stories all the time, of course. At least this Arthur writes nicely about the ballet in the Star and the Sketch and stories come down to us girls about what he, and other writers, have said about the new ballets. They're nearly always complimentary, thank goodness. One critic said how much the dancing of the rank and file (that's us) had improved; that made us glow. Sometimes there are photographs and I was nearly in one of the *corps* photos once, but I didn't get chosen in the end. The girls have to pose for these in whatever position pleases the photographer, often with their arms bent up and their hands behind their heads. This doesn't appear anywhere in the ballet, of course, but the more worldly amongst us know that this position pushes up your bust, making you more attractive. The drawings on the covers of the Empire programmes don't look much like us in real life, either. You'd think we danced half naked, which is nonsense because we always have our fleshings over legs and arms, or that we all look the same when we're actually all shapes and sizes. But I suppose the management like to present a picture of us that will draw in the crowds. And if we don't get the crowds, there won't be the money to pay our wages, so we don't complain.

We do try to look attractive, those who can, that is. It's all part of showing off our skills. One critic said that so long as we had good looks talent goes for nothing. That made us cross but it is all part of the attraction of the ballets. For some girls, this is all they care about. Most of us, though, are proud of what we do. The ballet goes way back in to history, and we're part of that history. We get nearly two thousand people in on full nights (I shake a little when I think about it). Toffs; artists; soldiers on leave; men about town and ordinary people including, more and more, the women. No one knows what they think about the ballet. I imagine they get a different kind of pleasure in watching, perhaps imagining themselves as us, perhaps just enjoying all the colour and lights and movement and a night out. No one tells us what the women think.

What do I think? I think a lot. My body is nearly always exhausted, but I wouldn't do another job. It's wonderful, really, to be able to dance, to be part of such a wonderful artistic tradition. I know I'll never be a star, but that's all right. My job is secure, more or less, and the work is varied compared to the office, where so many young girls work nowadays. Some of the girls have tried out Miss Barfoot's typing school so they could gain a skill; being able to waltz beautifully with a fancy headdress on is certainly a skill but it doesn't get you far. But Miss Barfoot doesn't really like the less educated girls and that Rhoda Nunn was so strict she put them right off, with all her talk of women being able to lead their own lives independent of men. Many of us do anyway, but it's not through choice. And the stage is a million times better than the domestic. The ballet can take me out of my own domestic, out of the worry about home. When I'm dancing, I can dream, and sometimes my mind is empty as my body just takes over. But, I also think a lot. About my aching arms, holding this heavy pole at the exact right angle; about how late the 'bus will be in the fog; about how Cornalba can't get that crisp finish to her pirouettes; about what I would look like if I were out there in front like her and how that applause would be for me alone as I dazzled them with my spins and turns and jumps and balances. My legs would be strong as steel; my arms as light as gossamer. My smile would be confident, my gaze at the audience assured as I return theirs. I think about a man who will come along and look after me and mother. But he'll have to know the real me from the pretty picture he sees on stage. Yes, I think a lot. But nobody knows what I think. My thoughts won't go down in history. But the ballet will, and I'm proud to be a part of it.

NOTE

1. A close version of this tale was first published in *Rethinking dance history: a reader*, edited by Alexandra Carter, published by Routledge, London 2004.

Epilogue[1]

This study of the music hall ballet and its executants is mediated through my own selected critical perspectives which are neither innocent nor free from the interpretive imperative; nor are they a closure of the debate. The historian's drive for clear starting and finishing points, conclusions and completeness for certain periods or historical phenomena is no longer tenable. Nevertheless, in dance, the need of past historians and writers to create not only tidy packages of history, but also ones with social, artistic and moral credibility, has resulted in some periods of dance activity being rendered invisible. This is particularly so with the relationship of the music hall ballet to the claim for the 'birth' of 'English'[2] ballet.

The claim that English ballet started in the 1930s can be seen with hindsight to be part of the social and political thrust to stabilise and celebrate a national identity which culminated in the Festival of Britain in 1951. Not any old identity, however, but one which had cultural status. For artists and writers of the time, ballet's credibility rested on the aristocratic foundations of a Russian Imperial and an Italian heritage; it did not owe any allegiance to the indigenous music halls and commercial theatres which had been presenting ballet as a part of variety or pantomime during that ascribed 'blank' period in ballet history, the 1860s till the first decade of the twentieth century. The dominant notion that English ballet was established primarily with the Vic-Wells in the 1930s negates to the point of oblivion its preceding indigenous history. The music hall period, particularly from the 1880s onwards, was one of the most vibrant and popular contexts for ballet in the whole of its history. As such, it is viable for study in its own right and not just as a stepping-stone to the twentieth century. Nevertheless, the influence of this period on the development of ballet in England in the 1920s and '30s was far more significant than has been convenient to acknowledge. The influences of history sketch out not a line but a web, and the complexity of that web has been ignored in the fight for public recognition for ballet as an art form in England in the 1930s.

Our contemporary consciousness now allows us to question the stability of the notion of 'national identity'; we can ask, therefore, just what is 'English' about English ballet. It also acknowledges the significance of popular culture and the blurring of boundaries between the activities it embodies and so-called 'high' art. We can therefore revisit the past without such exclusive notions in place. Popular culture, including pantomime and the small as well as the large music hall venues can be accommodated in the web of influences on the development of ballet in England.[3] Of particular significance are the links between the ballet of the Alhambra and Empire palaces of varieties and the development of a so-called 'national' institution embodied in the Vic-Wells (later Sadlers Wells) theatre companies and school.

That the seeds of an English ballet were sown and quickly blossomed with the establishment of the Vic-Wells ballet by Ninette de Valois in the early 1930s permeates the primary source literature (for example, Haskell 1934, 1938 & 1950; Howlett c.1930s; Manchester 1946; Williamson 1946; Noble c.1949; Fisher 1954). Now accepted as 'fact', this claim is replicated in secondary sources. Percival, referring to the significance of Diaghilev's production of *The Sleeping Princess* in 1921, notes that 'no such thing as British ballet existed then' (1994: 5). Similarly, the critical view of the music hall ballet which Haskell exemplifies in his imagining that 'the Empire ballet was choreographically, musically and artistically negligible, just a form of light entertainment' (1934: 188) is perpetuated in Deborah Bull's assertion that 'at the beginning of the century, dance in Britain was in a sorry state, reduced to grabbing performances where it could between the variety acts in music halls'. It was de Valois who 'dragged ballet out of these artistic slums' (Bull 1998: 100). It is de Valois who is seen unequivocally as responsible for the establishment of the first English ballet company, though the decade she spent on the commercial circuit, including both large and small music halls, tends to be written out of early biographical accounts (for example. Williamson 1946) or noted apologetically (as in Fisher 1954).

Those with actual first-hand experience of the music hall ballets were both less damming of their quality and, significantly, more alert to their place in an English heritage. Perugini, writing in the mid 1930s, discussed how the Russians dominated the recent dance scene. He felt, however, that he was seeing ballet that was 'not English as we had seen it at its best at the Empire and Alhambra in the first quarter of this century' (1946: 272). Bedells, in a gentle dig, wished that 'the critics and balletomanes of today could have seen that production of *Coppélia* at the old Empire. They would know then that ballet in England was flourishing long before Diaghilev was heard of here' (1954: 15). Lawson (1964) suggests that a possible event for the dating of the start of British ballet could have been when Bedells took over from Kyasht at the Empire in 1914. Despite these views, the 1880s-1910s tend to be written out of histories and biographies of British ballet. In all the literature, however, whether primary or secondary, none of the writers are explicit about what precisely constitutes 'Englishness' in the context of an English ballet. By disentangling the concept, the slender threads which hold it together are exposed and it is possible to rupture the solidity of this ascribed discrete historical period in dance history.

What was this thing called 'English' ballet in the 1930s; what might constitute a national institution and what might be construed as the components of a national heritage which can be traced from the music hall era onwards?[4] These components might, arguably, be summarised as (i) activity and people who are ethnically indigenous (ii) repertoire (iii) production and technical style (iv) audiences and the performance context of the work. There is also, of course, a necessary self-consciousness of a national identity.

Ethnically indigenous

Haskell's claim in 1938 that 'there was never a trace of a native English ballet until the present day' (p. 32) is based on his characterisation of England as 'a consumer rather than a creator' of the ballet form, as opposed to the Russian ballet which 'absorbed foreign influences into the indigenous ballet which was part of the people' (p.33). This puzzling claim is more one of convenience than of historical accuracy, for an examination of any country's heritage will show a flux of imports and exports which interact, become assimilated, consolidate and change. And if the creators, in a literal sense, of the music hall ballets such as Katti Lanner and Carlo Coppi were of European descent, paradoxically, the 'mothers' of English ballet were an Irishwoman (Ninette de Valois) and a Pole (Marie Rambert). The concept of 'indigenous ballet' can be applied as much - or as little - to the music hall ballets as it can to any other period. Arguably, the most indigenous 'English' aspect of the so-called new 'English' ballet of the 1930s was the social and educational background or aspirations of the men who wrote about it.[5] This might be, perhaps, a significant if sub-conscious element in the ascription of the nomenclature.

On reading these writers' accounts of the formation of English ballet, one not only senses the subdued excitement about this 'new' period but that period is explicitly isolated from what has gone before. There is no sense that influences might have spilled over, to the extent that even when the contribution of artists such as Genée, Bedells and Cecchetti are recorded, their commercial history is elided.[6] But there cannot be a 'sweeping out' of the old in any historical transitions; if there is a broom it is in the hands of the writers who record the history. Many performers and teachers who were influential in the development of ballet in the 1920s and 1930s were deeply rooted in the traditions of the large music halls. These include Adeline Genée, about whom Bedells noted, 'much as the art in this country owes to the Russian ballet . . . I feel we owe still more to the influence of Adeline Genée' (Bedells in Genné 1995: 439). Bedells herself was hailed as the first English prima ballerina after succeeding Kyasht at the Empire. Edouard Espinoza worked briefly at both the Alhambra and Empire, as performer and creator; Lucia Cormani was choreographer and teacher at the Alhambra. All of these were instrumental in establishing the Association of Operatic Dancing (1920), later the Royal Academy of Dancing (1935), now the Royal Academy of Dance, and in the formation of a syllabus of training. Francesca Zanfretta, *première danseuse* and mime at the Empire for twelve years, taught de Valois and Ursula Moreton, who took Zanfretta's work in to the Sadlers Wells School. Her mime was written down and 'handed on in its complex and fascinating detail to the Vic-Wells Ballet and its successor companies' (Sorley Walker 1987: 65). Cavallazzi, who trained at the La Scala school and performed for many years at the Empire, passed on her knowledge of the Italian technique to Bedells. Less influentially, Madame Rosa, an ex-Alhambra dancer partly trained by Palladino, worked with de Valois in pantomime at the Lyceum for five years. International styles of dance - French, Danish, Italian - were embodied in these music hall performers and were passed on in to the 1920s, 1930s and beyond.

One of the props for the claim that an English ballet started in the 1930s was that the performers were English. Until Bedells, the music hall principals were mostly foreign, though the residential longevity of some might render them 'native'. However, the great majority of the other performers were English. As 'J.M.B.' (1896) describes in his poem on the *corps* who were cast as angels in the apotheosis scene from *Faust* (Empire 1905), they came from London suburbs such as Peckham Rye, Bow and Kentish Town. In this respect, although their social class background might have been different, the casts of the music hall ballets were no different in their Englishness than the later companies. Another claim is perhaps more tenable. Noble (c.1949: 13) notes that the Camargo Society 'played a most important part in establishing English ballet, for it encouraged new choreographers, designers, dancers and composers, put the spotlight on native capabilities'. Similarly, Manchester claimed that the Camargo Society season at the Savoy in 1932 'proved not only that the English could dance but they also possessed the creative ability to write, compose and choreograph their own ballets and present them in their own manner' (1946: 14). Implicit here is the notion that an English ballet rests not just on a company of native dancers but also on native artistic collaborators. Whilst the creative collaborators on those early ballets of the Vic Wells were British, so too were some of the key creators of the music hall ballets. Even Katti Lanner, ballet arranger at the Empire for twenty years, had her permanent home in London for over thirty years. If the majority of the music hall collaborators were European, however, it is important to question the significance of this criterion 'native creators' for a 'national' institution. After all, the Imperial Russian ballet owed its development and its golden age to two Frenchmen, Didelot and Petipa (the Russian Ivanov was initially written out of history). Perhaps it is more rewarding, in this quest for what constitutes national identity, to examine what was created - and for whom.

Repertoire

One of the recurrent claims for an English ballet in the 1930s was the national flavour of its early works. For example, Manchester describes *Façade* (Ashton 1931) as 'the first major English ballet; major ... because it was the first of the real English ballets, something truly national which no other country could have done in exactly the same way' (1946: 15). In this rather tautological statement, Manchester does not tease out just what is 'English' about the work. Haskell is a little more helpful in his claim for *The Rake's Progress* (de Valois 1935) as 'a truly English masterpiece - a truly national expression' because 'the new English dancer, lacking an inherited tradition, excels where she can hide her lack of self confidence behind a positive role ... she can best express herself through the medium of another character' (Haskell 1938: 163). In other words, 'English' works are those which privilege drama and character roles. Helpman (in Noble c.1949) again suggests that 'British choreography ... has ... a number of distinctive national features' without articulating them, though implicit in the rest of his chapter is the idea that these might be the influence of drama and painting which derived from Fokine and the Russian classical tradition, and an emphasis on the psychological import of the drama.[7] But an analysis of the music hall ballets reveals that, throughout their thirty-year history, there was a similar privileging of narrative and character. There may not have been the overt psychological dimension, for Freud was not, as yet, in public consciousness, but a psychological perspective is as much in the interpretation of a work as in its surface subject matter.

If works such as *Job* (de Valois 1931) have a literary source, so do many of the music hall ballets, such as *Don Juan* (Coppi 1892) and *Round the World* (Farren 1909). It could be claimed, in fact, that the subject matter of the ballets, with themes such as *Our Army and Navy* (Casati 1889) and *The Sports of England* (Lanner 1887) were more stridently and unashamedly English than anything that come afterwards.

None of the Alhambra or Empire ballets survive. Furthermore, several which were produced in these venues have been written out of the history of the works. These include *Giselle* (Bertrand 1884), *The Sleeping Beauty* (Leon Espinoza 1890) and *The Dancing Doll* (Lanner 1905). It cannot be argued, therefore, that the actual works of the music hall period have contributed directly to an English repertoire. What can be argued is that their influence continued through many facets of their production and technical style.

Production and technical style

Ninette de Valois' career in the commercial theatre between 1913 - 1923 is now well recorded (for example, de Valois 1959; Sorley Walker 1987). During this period, she 'had many an experience of the old fashioned type of English music hall, as well as the more opulent modern examples' (Sorley Walker 1987: 54-55). Although de Valois became dissatisfied with the artistic quality of the work, she took with her a supreme consciousness of the key characteristics of ballet in a commercial context which became the hallmark of her own repertoire. Although this influence has been acknowledged by de Valois and others in general terms, it has never been explicitly identified for, I would suggest, such a commercial heritage has not been one to dwell upon too overtly. Nevertheless, in the literature which records de Valois' achievements, it is her production values which are identified as her strength. As Robert Helpman said, her 'greatness was as a "choreographic producer", a form of blended talent that has enormously influenced the trend of British choreography' (in Noble c.1949: 29). Her production skills included the legibility of the narrative, the need in short-length works to speed through that narrative, the importance of characterisation, the necessity for a moral tale and general dramatic colour - all key characteristics of the music hall ballet. It could be argued that this production style was the historically dominant one but what de Valois undoubtedly learned from her experience in the commercial theatre was the need to entertain a popular audience.

It is also interesting to note that the production of ballets by indigenous artists such as Fred Farren, the character dancer who took over from Lanner at the Empire, and Will Bishop, an eccentric and clog dancer who became ballet master and producer at the Coliseum, brought a distinct English style to ballet in the 1880s and 1890s through the utilisation of their own theatrical expertise and dance vocabularies.

It would be erroneous to claim, however, that the features of the music hall ballet were distinctly English, for they were international. Although further research would need to be done, it is clear that even the Imperial ballet in pre-revolutionary Russia had a similar production style during the same period. Balanchine remembers how 'the third echelon of the *corps*, barely able to stand on point ... were called 'fountain girls' because they were always placed at the back, near the apparently ubiquitous scenic water' (Jowitt 1988: 243-44). Similarly, Jowitt notes how Petipa's mass dances emphasised changing colours and kaleidoscopic effects, just like Wilhelm's at the Empire. The production style of the music hall ballets was not unique and, therefore, cannot be dismissed as an aberrant 'blip' in dance history.

In the general deprecation of this period, an area which has been overlooked is that of its place in sustaining the presentation of the technical basis of the *danse d'école*, the classical ballet and mime, to English audiences. The Alhambra and the Empire presented ballerinas with an impeccable pedigree. Whether from Russia (for example, Kyasht) or Denmark (Genée) or, via a variety of international routes, from Italy (Palladino, Legnani), these dancers presented to English audiences a technical style rooted mainly in the system codified by Blasis. (Furthermore, it was Stuart Headlam, the moral advocate for the dance and dancers, who republished Blasis in 1888.) Although both venues used dancers for the *corps* from their associated training schools, there was little opportunity for the English dancer to receive an affordable and consistent, developmental training and there was no concept of an English 'school' of technical training, either in terms of an institution or a style. But even by the 1930s - 40s there was still no notion of a national 'style' of classical dancing, for as Haskell noted in 1950, 'British ballet has not yet a clearly defined British school behind it. Our dancers may be said for the most part to belong to the Russian school' (1950: 46). Such is the international cross-fertilisation of the *danse d'école* that the claim that the lack of an 'English' technical style was a contributory factor in the lack of an English ballet before the 1930s is a moot point. What distinguishes the music hall ballet as essentially English, yet distinct from the dominant notion of a national lineage, is the nature of its audiences and the context of its production.

Audiences and context

As we have seen, the large scale, professional music halls, with their bill of variety acts, developed from the self-made entertainment of working class public houses. The entrepreneurs who developed the palaces, the luxury music halls, did so with a view to expanding their clientele by appealing to a much broader range of social classes but they never lost their working class attraction. The origins of the palaces were undoubtedly indigenous and, to those men abroad, they became symbolic of 'home'. The context of the ballet was undoubtedly, self-consciously English. What does distinguish it from the subsequent period, however, was inadvertently suggested by the writer of the Sadlers Wells theatre notice in the press in 1930 who claimed that 'Lilian Baylis has cherished an ambition to establish, for the first time in theatrical history, a permanent ballet in a repertory theatre' (Fisher 1954: 13). Here is one of the main reasons why the music hall has been written out of history: the Alhambra and Empire were located in the centre of the world of popular entertainment, not the English repertory theatre.

As such, a large percentage of their audience was not one who went to see the Ballets Russes. Haskell conveniently claims that: 'the Empire public was certainly never Diaghilev's. From the first he created a fresh public of his own from the people who understood painting, followed concerts and loved the theatre' (Haskell 1934: 189). Haskell may have been right in general terms, though he forgets about the *fin de siécle* artists, writers and intellectuals who were deeply attached to the halls such as G.B. Shaw, Arthur Symons and Spencer Gore. Furthermore, the Ballets Russes performed on variety bills, so although a 'specialist' audience may have evolved over time the blanket nature of Haskell's claim is dubious. And Manchester, describing the Camargo season at the Savoy as 'an ambitious project of presenting ballet to a West End audience' (1946: 13) was clearly ignorant of history or just careless with words.

The complexity of the notion that there were two distinct audiences for the halls and for Diaghilev is compounded by Perugini's observation that, towards the end of the music hall period, there was a growth of a more discriminating and discerning audience for ballet who were more open to the Russians (Perugini 1925a). Apart from Guest (1992) no other writer has explored the connection between the 'instant success' of the Ballets Russes in London and the fact that there was already a receptive audience. In theatre scholarship, it is unfortunately in the area of audience composition and reaction where research is largely absent. As the web of tradition remains unexplored, so too does the web of audiences. That there were not two distinct audiences, but one which spanned the worlds of popular entertainment and the arts, is supported by Margaret Craske's memory that 'Ninette de Valois took me into a small company which played the music halls. It was divine! That was absolutely the most wonderful audience in the world. If they didn't like you they threw things ...' (Craske in Sorley Walker 1987: 25).

Not only were there not two distinct audiences but neither was there the total chronological dislocation which our books (and our dance consciousness) suggests. The first Ballets Russes appearance in London was in 1911; the last ballet productions at the Alhambra and the Empire were in 1912 and 1915 respectively. De Valois saw Genée and Bedells at the Empire in 1907 and entered the entertainment business in 1913, where she worked until the 1920s. Although it was not until the 1930s that her company was hailed as an impending national institution, she carried with her, in her own choreography and production values, that commercial experience, that fundamental notion of ballet as entertainment. But from the 1930s, it was in the guise and location of serious 'art'.

It is back to the 1930s that English ballet is conventionally dated; that is, when there was a drive for it to be taken seriously as an art form and not when audiences perceived it as entertainment. This implies a question of standards, for critics in the 1930s were dismissive of the music hall works due to their apparent lack of artistic integrity. Yet the standards of the early Sadlers Wells company were also perceived as shaky and some contemporary critics rejected the possibility of a high-quality indigenous company (see, for example, Howlett c.1930s: Ch. III).

Despite the claims of the writers of the period and most who came after, that the Vic/Sadlers Wells company was the first 'national' one, and therefore the start of English ballet, no writer actually articulates what those conceptions of 'national' or 'birth' comprise. Established by an Irish woman, strongly influenced by a cosmopolitan company based in France and led by a Russian, with a dance and mime technique which rested on the Italian school, the notion of 'Englishness' becomes destabilised. The young dancers in the Vic/Sadlers Wells ballet were British but so too were the *corps* of the Alhambra and the Empire; Markova was British but so was Bedells; de Valois' choreography was dramatic, colourful and based on narrative with a moral overtone - so too were the music hall ballets. The artists of the Alhambra and Empire - Genée, Bedells, Cavallazzi, Cormani, Espinoza and Zanfretta - not to mention those such as Cecchetti who gained performance experience there - were prime movers or significant influences on the development of British ballet. The situation can be over-simplified, but the history of British ballet has been over-simplified. Claims for both its birth and its national identity have rested on notions of 'art' and 'standards' rather than actual activity or people. Its history has been written as a lineage, with the line extending back to the Russian Imperial theatres. That line must now be seen to be one of many which form a complex web of activity, of influences and of practice. One of the more complex, and as yet unacknowledged, aspects of this web of history is that 'English' ballet's heritage rests not only on the social status of its audience (and its allegedly Imperial background), and the artistic standards of its repertoire; it also rests on the moral standing of its executants. Although, as argued throughout this book, the moral reputation of the ballerinas was impeccable, the ascribed reputation of the ballet girls was not, though this attitude was arguably changing towards the end of the music hall period. By the 1930s, however, there is nowhere near the same kind of implicit or explicit accusation - at least, not in published records - that the dancers who joined the Vic-Wells ballet, or Rambert's company, or the peripatetic dancers of the time, were anything other than 'respectable'. There are many reasons for this change of attitude: dancers worked in much smaller companies and therefore it was difficult to cast blanket aspersions; women of higher social class status became members of these companies and dancers such as Bedells had helped to construct a far more respectable image for the British dancer. Significantly, however, the ballets had changed and the times had changed. No longer were the bodies of women used for overt display, for 'playing to the crowd' over the footlights with pleasing smiles and seductive costumes. No longer were the promenades of the venues used for the soliciting of sex nor, by the 1930s, was the West End famed to the same degree as a market place for prostitution. Attitudes to women - and to their bodies - had changed profoundly, as had their own self-consciousness. The suffragette movement, the First World War, the 'flapper' of the 1920s, the expansion of women's employment and engagement in public life were some of the many social phenomena which rendered redundant the sexual categories of the late Victorian and early Edwardian age.

Much research remains to be done on the 'moral history' of the dancer but the links between women, dance and sexuality continue to fascinate the public.[8] Scholars are also fascinated by this axis, though much of the theoretical writing on dance and the body has broken free from any historical anchorage.[9] The music hall ballet has not only played a significant role in the web of English dance history but it has also provided a convincing case study for how dance - and the self and socially constructed image of the dancer - embodies the psyche of its age.

NOTES

1. This chapter is based, in part, on Carter 2003.
2. In most of the writing from the 1930s to the 1950s, the term 'English' is used but perhaps due to an expansion of national consciousness, the more recently used description is 'British'.
3. That web includes 'external' influences such as the Ballets Russes and Massine and, of course, the many other activities which paralleled those of de Valois such as Marie Rambert's school and company and the Camargo Society. Although pantomime was different from music hall/variety bills in that it contained spoken narrative, the ballet in pantomime was very similar. It often included a 'Grand Fairyland Ballet' and an obligatory transformation scene. The pantomimes also had their own *corps de ballet.*
4. I do not, of course, wish to claim the music hall period as the 'start' of English ballet but I use this period to smudge its lineage – if such a concept as 'lineage' is even tenable.
5. For example, Haskell was educated at Westminster and Cambridge, Buckle (writing later) at Marlborough and Oxford.
6. For example, Bedells' biography in Noble (c.1949), Cecchetti in Wilson (1974) or Koegler (1987).
7. As Sorley Walker notes, 'At the time *ballet d'action*, dramatic or *demi-caractère* ballet signified the peak of classical ballet. Not until the sensational vogue for Massine's symphonic ballets in the 'thirties were pure dancing works rated as highly. Not until after World War II were they considered rather more important in the Western world' (1987: 6).
8. For example, when Betty Boothroyd was appointed Speaker of the House, the press made much of her brief sojourn as a show dancer; likewise, the newscaster Angela Rippon's dancing appearance on the Morecambe and Wise show caused amazed jaws to drop. These are only small examples, and not drawn from the ballet world but they do indicate the resultant confusion when propriety meets dance.
9. See Carter (1999) for further discussion on feminist writing, ballet and the body.

Appendices

EXPLANATORY NOTES TO I AND II

1. All information is taken from the original programmes.
2. The lists presented in these Appendices do not indicate which works are revivals/reworkings of previous 'house' ballets. See Guest (1992) for these details, and information on producers, writers of the scenarios and number of weeks in repertoire.
3. The musical input is more complex than these listings suggest. Some ballets had pre-composed music, arranged in-house. Some had newly composed music and many ballets had a mixture of both.
4. In much of the primary source literature such as newspaper reviews of the ballets, it is often noted that 'costumes are by ....'. Unlike today, this tended to mean that the named person was the maker of the costumes, not the designers. Such was their skill of these executants that they were sometimes recognised in the curtain call. However, I have tried, where possible, to extrapolate the designers' names from the programmes.
5. Similarly, with credits such as 'scenery by ....' it is difficult to discern between those who designed the scenery and those who supervised the painting.
6. I have not included in these Appendices the many other collaborators on the ballets such as those working on scenarios, properties, stage effects and wigs (an important feature of the works). This is not to deny the importance of their contribution.

EXPLANATORY NOTES TO III AND IV

1. The categories of subject matter were arrived at by the following process. First, an impressionist account was gleaned from a wide range of source material; these impressions were then listed under recurring types of subject matter. Second, a formal process of analysis was undertaken in which each ballet was listed in the various categories. I was aware of manipulating these and was prepared to add new categories if necessary. The surprising outcome of this process was that no new categories were necessary, for the ballets followed a formula which changed in emphasis over time but remained generally consistent in the range of subject matter. In some cases theatre programmes were the only source of information but these do not always give a synopsis. In these cases, subject matter is surmised from the title of the work supported by the cast list and/or names of scenes and dances.

Notes on categories

Supernatural. 'Myth' denotes works which had themes based on Greek or Roman mythological characters though the well-known events of mythology were not presented. 'Fairy story' comprised works which were populated by fairies, demons, elves, 'queens' of the natural world, etc. 'Legend' also had a supernatural element but these works were rooted in tales of ordinary people.
Natural. These works were set predominantly in a natural or pastoral world.
International. With the exception of a few ballets which had a clear British setting, the great majority of dances were set in either a recognizable or unidentifiable international context. Ballets under this heading are those which are primarily concerned with depicting an international theme or event.
Historical. Similarly, with the exception of the topical works, most ballets were set in another time, either real or imaginary. Ballets listed under this category are those which dealt with a particular historical theme or event.
Topical. Works which appear under 'general' subject matter are those which featured a recent or current event or topical concern. A very large number of works had a patriotic flavour, but this listing includes those in which a patriotic and/or military theme is dominant.
Romance. Many ballets had some kind of romantic relationship between a man and a woman, though there were not as many as might be expected (see Ch. 4). Works included in this category are those where romance forms the dominant thread of the plot.
2. The ballets were complex and often dealt with several stories or sub themes. For example, *On Brighton Pier* (Empire 1894) was a topical work which included a supernatural vision scene, a contemporary romance and a military spectacle. Because of this complexity, these appendices are not intended to be read as statistical data but they serve to support statements about the recurrent nature of certain themes in the music hall ballets.
3. To date, the only list of ballets at the Alhambra and Empire appears in Guest (1992). The appendices here differ from Guest in the following instances.

ALHAMBRA BALLETS
In Guest but omitted here:
La Petit Bohemienne (1909). Although the dancer La Belle Leonora was in the cast so there was most likely a dance element, there was no *corps* and, in the programme, it was described as 'an episode'.
The Pool (1912). This was described in the programme as a 'wordless Mediaeval Idyll' and there were no dancers in the cast.

Not in Guest but included in Appendix 1:
On the Heath (1909). Described in the programme as a 'new revue divertissement', produced by Elise Clerc. The cast included the dancer Britta and a full *corps de ballet*.

EMPIRE BALLETS

In Guest but omitted here:

Hurly Burly (1885). Described in the programme as a 'grand Military Pantomime and Ballet' but the ballet was not arranged by an established choreographer and the work appears to be more pantomime than ballet. No details given of dancers or *corps*.

APPENDIX I

BALLETS AT THE ALHAMBRA 1884-1912: ARTISTIC COLLABORATORS

	Arranger/ Choreographer	*Composer/ Music Arranger*	*Costume design/ Execution*	*Scenery*
1884				
The Swans	Hansen	Jacobi	C.Wilhelm/Alias	C. Brew
Melusine	Hansen	Jacobi	Wilhelm/Bianchini/Alias	C. Brooke
1885				
Nina the Enchantress	Hansen	Jacobi	H.Sidney/Alias	T.E.Ryan
Le Bivouac	Hansen	Jacobi	L.Besche/Alias	T.E.Ryan
1886				
Cupid	Hansen	Jacobi	Besche/Alias	T.E.Ryan
Dresdina	Hansen	Jacobi	Besche/Alias	T.E.Ryan
The Seasons	Hansen	Jacobi	Besche/Alias	T.E.Ryan
1887				
Nadia	Hansen	Jacobi	Besche/Alias	Brew
Algeria	Hansen	Jacobi	Besche/Alias	H. Emden
Enchantment	Casati	Jacobi	Besche/Alias	H.Hicks/H. Watkin
1888				
Antiope	Casati	Jacobi	Wilhelm/Alias	T.E.Ryan
Ideala	Casati	Jacobi	Wilhelm/Alias	T.E.Ryan
Irene	Casati	Jacobi	de Lavigerie/Alias	T.E.Ryan
1889				
Our Army and Navy	Casati	Jacobi	Besche/Alias	T.E.Ryan
Astraea	Casati	Jacobi	Bianchini/Alias	T.E.Ryan
Asmodeus	Casati	Jacobi	Bianchini/Alias	T.E.Ryan
1890				
Zanetta	Casati	Jacobi	Besche/Alias	T.E.Ryan
Salandra	Casati	Jacobi	H.Grey/Alias	T.E.Ryan
The Sleeping Beauty	Leon Espinoza	Jacobi	M.Grey/H.Russell	T.E.Ryan
1891				
Oriella	Carlo Coppi	Jacobi	Bianchini/Russell	T.E.Ryan
Temptation	Coppi	Jacobi	Russell/Alias	T.E.Ryan
1892				
On the Ice	Coppi	Jacobi	Alias[1]	T.E.Ryan
Don Juan	Coppi	Jacobi	Russell/Alias	T.E.Ryan
Up the River	Henri Dewinne	Jacobi	Russell/Alias	T.E.Ryan
Aladdin	Coppi	Jacobi	Russell/Alias	B.Smith
1893				
Chicago	Emile Grédelue	Jacobi	Russell/Alias	T.E. Ryan
Fidelia	Grédelue	Jacobi	Russell/Alias	W. Perkins/ J.Harker/Ryan
Don Quixote	Casati	Jacobi	Russell/Alias	T.E. Ryan
1894				
Revolt of the Daughters	H. Agoust	Jacobi	Russell/Alias	T.E.Ryan

APPENDICES

	Arranger/ Choreographer	Composer/ Music Arranger	Costume design/ Execution	Scenery
Sita	Casati	Jacobi	Russell/Alias	T.E.Ryan
Ali Baba	Coppi	Jacobi	Russell/Alias	T.E.Ryan
1895				
Titania	Coppi	Jacobi	Russell/Alias	T.E.Ryan
The Gathering of the Blue Beard	Clans/ Coppi	Jacobi	Russell/Alias	T.E.Ryan
1896				
Donnybrook	Coppi	Jacobi	not specified (n.s.)	n.s.
Rip van Winkle	Coppi	Richard Planquette	Russell/Alias	T.E.Ryan
The Tzigane	Coppi	Jacobi	Russell/Alias	T.E.Ryan
1897				
Victoria and Merrie England	Coppi	Arthur Sullivan	Russell/Alias	T.E.Ryan
1898				
Beauty and the Beast	Coppi	Jacobi	Russell/Alias	T.E.Ryan
Jack Ashore	Giovanni Pratesi	George W.Byng	Russell/Alias	E.Banks
1899				
The Red Shoes	Pratesi	Raoul Mader/Byng	Russell/Alias	Schallud/ P.Howden
A Day Off	Pratesi	Byng	Russell/Alias	Howden
Napoli	Pratesi	Byng	Russell/Alias	Howden
1900				
Soldiers of the Queen (rev. 1901 as Soldiers of the King)	Charles Wilson	various	L.Edwards[2]	Howden
The Handy Man	Egidio Rossi	Byng	Russell/Alias	Howden
The Gay City	Lucia Cormani/ Fred Farren	Byng	Russell/Alias	Howden
1901				
Inspiration	Coppi	Byng	Comelli/Alias	T.E.Ryan
Gretna Green	Coppi	Byng	Comelli/Alias	Howden
Santa Claus	Coppi	Byng	Alias	
1902				
In Japan	Coppi	Louis Ganne	Comelli/Alias	Howden
Britannia's Realm	Coppi	Landon Ronald	Comelli/Alias	n.s.
The Devil's Forge	Cormani	Byng	Comelli/Alias	T.E.Ryan
Carmen	Cormani	Georges Bizet/Byng E.H. Ryan/ W.B.Spong	Comelli/Alias	Howden/
1904				
All the Year Round	Cormani/ Farren/ Giovanni Rosi	James M. Glover	Comelli/Alias	E.H.Ryan,/ T.E.Ryan/ B.Smith/ Spong/Howden

Title	Arranger/Choreographer	Composer/Music Arranger	Costume design/Execution	Scenery
Entente Cordiale	Alfredo Curti	Ronald	Comelli/Alias	E.H.Ryan/Howden/M.Menessier
1905				
My Lady Nicotine	Cormani	Byng	Comelli/Alias	E.H.Ryan/Howden
Le Rêve	n.s.	Byng	n.s.	n.s.
Lucertio	Rosi	de Anduaga/Byng	n.s.	n.s.
Parisiana	Curti	Glover	Comelli/Alias	E.H.Ryan/Howden/A.Menessier
1906				
L'amour	Curti	Francis Thomé	Comelli/Alias	E.H.Ryan
1907				
Queen of Spades	Curti	Mario Costa/Byng	Comelli/Alias	E.H.Ryan
Electra	Curti	Byng	Alias	E.H.Ryan
Les Cloche de Corneville	Curti	Planquette/Byng	Comelli/Alias	E.H.Ryan
1908				
Cupid Wins	Curti	Byng	Comelli/Alias	E.H.Ryan
Sal! Oh! My!	n.s.	Byng	n.s.	n.s.
The Two Flags	Curti	Byng	Comelli/Alias	E.H.Ryan
Paquita	Curti	Byng	Comelli	E.H.Ryan
Narcisse	Rosi	Byng	n.s.	n.s.
1909				
On the Square	Elise Clerc	Byng	Comelli/Alias	E.H.Ryan
On the Heath	Clerc	unknown	Comelli/Alias	E.H.Ryan
Psyche	Curti	Alfred Moul	Comelli/Alias	M.Amable
Our Flag	Curti	Byng	Comelli/Alias	E.H.Ryan
1910				
The Polar Star	Clerc	Byng	n.s.	n.s.
Femina	Curti	Byng/George Valverde	Comelli/Alias	E.H.Ryan, Amable
On the Sands	Clerc	Byng	Comelli/Alias	E.H.Ryan
1911				
The Mad Pierrot	Clerc	Byng	Comelli/Alias	E.H.Ryan
The Dance Dream	Alexandre Gorsky	various inc. Brahms/Glazunov	Comelli/Alias	E.H.Ryan, Amable
1830	Agoust/Clerc	Byng	Alias	E.H.Ryan
1912				
Carmen	Augustin Berger	Bizet/Byng	Alias	E.H.Ryan/J.Harker

1. Some programmes only note the name of Alias for 'Costumes'. This may have been an oversight or he/his wife might have designed as well as executed the costumes for these works.
2. Programme notes that 'uniforms' were designed by Edwards. No other information given.

APPENDIX II

BALLETS AT THE EMPIRE 1884-1915: ARTISTIC COLLABORATORS

	Arranger/ Choreographer	*Composer/ Music Arranger*	*Costume design/ Execution*	*Scenery*
1884				
Coppelia	A.Bertrand	Leo Delibes	A.Chasemore/ Miss Thompson	not specified (n.s.)
Giselle	Bertrand	Adolphe Adam	A.Chasemore/ Miss Thompson	Spong
1887				
Dilara	Katti Lanner	M.Hervé	C.Wilhelm/ Miss Fisher	H.Emden
The Sports of England	Lanner	Hervé	n.s./ Fisher/ Rouy & Felix	T.E.Ryan
1888				
Robert Macaire[1]	Martinetti			
Rose d'Amour	Lanner	Hervé	Wilhelm/Fisher, Mde.Auguste et Cie	n.s.
Diana	Lanner	Hervé	Wilhelm/Fisher/ Auguste	Emden/ Ryan
1889				
A Duel in the Snow	Lanner/Martinetti	Hervé	Choubrac/Landolff	Ryan Fisher
Cleopatra	Lanner	Hervé	Wilhelm/Landolff/ Fisher/ Auguste	Konski
The Paris Exhibition	Lanner	Hervé	Choubrac/ Wilhelm/ Landolff, Fisher/ Auguste	Ryan/ R. Caney/ Emden
A Dream of Wealth	Lanner	Leopold Wenzel	Wilhelm/Fisher/ Auguste/J.Harrison	Emden/ Ryan/ Konski
1890				
Cécile	Lanner	Wenzel	Wilhelm/Fisher/ Auguste	Ryan
Dolly	Lanner	Wenzel	Wilhelm/Fisher/ Auguste	Ryan/ E.G.Banks
1891				
Orfeo	Lanner	Wenzel	Wilhelm/Fisher/ Auguste	Telbin
By the Sea	Lanner	Wenzel	Wilhelm/Fisher/ Auguste	Ryan
Nisita	Lanner	Wenzel	Wilhelm/Fisher/ Auguste	Telbin
1892				
Versailles	Lanner	Wenzel	Wilhelm/Fisher/ Auguste	Ryan

	Arranger/ Choreographer	Composer/ Music Arranger	Costume design/ Execution	Scenery
Round the Town	Lanner	Wenzel	Wilhelm/Fisher/ Auguste/ M.Angel/ Harrison	Telbin B.Smith
1893				
Katrina	Lanner	Wenzel	Wilhelm/Fisher/ Auguste	K.Lautenschläger[2]
The Girl I Left Behind Me	Lanner	Wenzel	Wilhelm/Fisher/ Auguste/Angel	Ryan/Telbin Emden
1894				
La Frolique	Lanner	Ernest Ford	Wilhelm/Fisher, Auguste/Harrison	Ryan
On Brighton Pier	Lanner	Ford	Wilhelm/Fisher/ Auguste/Angel/ Redfern	Ryan
1895				
Faust	Lanner	M.Lutz,/Ford	Wilhelm/Fisher/ Auguste	Harker/ Glendenning Lautenschlager
1896				
La Danse	Lanner	Ford	Wilhelm/Fisher/ Auguste/ Harrison	Telbin
Monte Cristo	Lanner	Wenzel	Wilhelm/Fisher/	Telbin/ Harker
1897				
Under One Flag	Lanner	Wenzel	Wilhelm/Fisher/ Auguste/Angel	Telbin
1898				
The Press	Lanner	Wenzel	Wilhelm/Fisher/ Cooling & Laurence/ Hastings	Harker
Alaska	Lanner	Wenzel Auguste/ Hastings	Wilhelm/Fihser/	Harker
1899				
Round the Town Again	Lanner	Wenzel	Wilhelm/Fisher/ Auguste/Angel/ Cooling & Laurence/ Hastings	H.C.Craven/ Harker
1900				
Seaside	Lanner	Wenzel	Wilhelm/Hastings/ Angel	Harker
1901				
Les Papillions	Lanner	Wenzel	Wilhelm/Hastings/ Auguste/Angel	Harker
Old China	Lanner	Wenzel	Wilhelm/Hastings/ Angel	Harker

APPENDICES 155

	Arranger/ Choreographer	Composer/ Music Arranger	Costume design/ Execution	Scenery
1902				
Our Crown	Lanner	Wenzel	Wilhelm/Hastings/ Angel	Harker/ B.J.Simmons
1903				
The Milliner Duchess	Lanner	Wenzel	Wilhelm/Hastings	Harker
Vineland	Lanner	Wenzel	Wilhelm/Hastings/ Angel	Harker
1904				
High Jinks	Lanner	Wenzel	Wilhelm/Hastings/ Angel/Lawring & Co./P.Robinson	Harker
1905				
The Dancing Doll	Lanner	Josef Bayer/ Cuthbert Clarke	Wilhelm/Hastings/ Angel	Harker
The Bugle Call	Fred Farren/ Adeline Genée	Sidney Jones	Wilhelm/Hastings/	R.C.McCleery
1906				
Cinderella	Farren/ Alexander Genée	Jones	Wilhelm/Hastings/ Angel	n.s.
Coppelia	Alex. Genée	Leo Delibes/ C.J.M.Glaser	Wilhelm/Hastings/ Angel	Harker
Fête Galante	Farren	Glaser	Wilhelm/Hastings/ Angel	H.Craven
The Debutante	Lanner	Clarke,/ Glaser	Wilhelm/Hastings/ Angel	n.s.
1907				
Sir Roger de Coverley	Lanner	Osmond Carr	Wilhelm/Hastings/ Angel	n.s.
The Belle of the Ball	Farren/ Adeline Genée	Clarke	Wilhelm/Hastings/	Harker
1908				
The Dryad	Alex.Genée	Dora Bright	n.s.	n.s.
A Day in Paris	Farren/Alex. Genée	Clarke	Wilhelm/Hastings/ Angel	n.s.
Roberto il Diavolo	Alex.Genée	Giacomo Meyerbeer	Wilhelm/Hastings	McCleery
Round the World	Farren	Clarke	Wilhelm/Hastings/ Angel	n.s.
1910				
The Dancing Master	Farren	Clarke	Wilhelm/Hastings/ Angel	n.s.
The Faun	Farren	Bright	Wilhelm/Hastings/	Smith
1911				
Sylvia	Farren	Delibes/Clarke	Wilhelm/Hastings/ Angel	McCleery
New York	Farren	Clarke	Wilhelm/Hastings/ Angel	n.s.

	Arranger/ Choreographer	Composer/ Music Arranger	Costume design/ Execution	Scenery
1912				
The Water Nymph	Lydia Kyasht	Pouney (Pugni)/ Andrei Kadletz	Wilhelm/Hastings	McCleery
First Love	Kyasht	Mikhail Glinka/ Clarke	Wilhelm/Hastings	McCleery
1913				
The Reaper's Dream	Kyasht	Delibes/Piotr Tchaikovsky/ Clarke	Wilhelm/Hastings	Harker
Titania	Kyasht	Mendelssohn/ Clarke	Wilhelm/Hastings/ Angel	McCleery
1914				
Europe	Eduoard Espinoza	Guy Jones	Wilhelm/Hastings/ Angel	Smith
1915				
The Vine	Farren	Schumann/Grieg/ Debussy arr. Harvey Pinches	Wilhelm/Hastings	McCleery
1915				
Pastorale	A.H.Majilton	Pinches	Wilhelm/Hastings	McCleery

1. *Robert Macaire* was in repertoire for five weeks only; no information has been found as to its subject matter.
2. Notes as Royal Stage Mechanician to the King of Bavaria.

APPENDIX III

BALLETS AT THE ALHAMBRA 1884-1912: SUBJECT MATTER

	Super-natural	Natural	Inter-national	Historical	Topical General	Topical Patriotic	Romance
1884							
The Swans	x	x	Germany				
Melusine	x						
1885							
Nina the Enchantress	x						x
Le Bivouac						x	
1886							
Cupid	x	x					x
Dresdina	x						
The Seasons		x					
1887							
Nadia	x		Russia				x
Algeria			Algeria				
Enchantment	x						x
1888							
Antiope				Ancient Greece			
Ideala		x					
Irene	x						x
1889							
Our Army and Navy						x	
Astraea	x						
Asmodeus			Spain				
1890							
Zanetta			Austria				
Salandra			Bulgaria				x
The Sleeping Beauty	x						
1891							
Oriella	x		Japan				
Temptation	x		x				
1892							
On the Ice			Holland		x		x
Don Juan							x
Up the River					x		
Aladdin	x						
1893							
Chicago			USA		x		
Fidelia	x		Bavaria				
Don Quixote			Spain				
1894							
Revolt of the Daughters					x		x
Sita							x
Ali Baba	x						

DANCE AND DANCERS IN THE MUSIC HALL BALLET

	Super-natural	Natural	Inter-national	Historical	Topical General	Topical Patriotic	Romance
1895							
Titania	x	x					
The Gathering of the Clans			Scotland				
Blue Beard	x						
1896							
Donnybrook			Ireland				
Rip van Winkle	x						
The Tzigane			Hungary				
1897							
Victoria and Merrie England					x	x	
1898							
Beauty and the Beast	x						x
Jack Ashore				x			x
1899							
The Red Shoes	x						
A Day Off			France		x		
Napoli			Italy				
1900							
Soldiers of the Queen						x	
(rev. 1901 as Soldiers of the King)							
The Handy Man			Persia		x		
The Gay City			Paris		x		
1901							
Inspiration	x	x					
Gretna Green							x
Santa Claus	x						
1902							
In Japan			Japan				x
Britannia's Realm						x	
The Devil's Forge	x		Germany				
Carmen			Spain				x
1904							
All the Year Round						x	
Entente Cordiale						x	
1905							
My Lady Nicotine			various				
Le Rêve			Greece				x
Lucertio			Spain				
Parisiana			Paris	x	x		
1906							
L'amour		x	Assyria				
1907							
Queen of Spades					x		x
Electra[1]							
Les Cloche de Corneville	x	x	France	x			

	Supernatural	Natural	International	Historical	Topical General	Topical Patriotic	Romance
1908							
Cupid Wins							x
Sal! Oh! My!			x	x			
The Two Flags						x	
Paquita			Spain				x
Narcisse	x						
1909							
On the Square			New York				
On the Heath					x		
Psyche	x		Ancient Greece				
Our Flag						x	
1910							
The Polar Star	x						
Femina	x		various				
On the Sands					x		
1911							
The Mad Pierrot		x	France				
The Dance Dream	x		various				
1830			France	x			
1912							
Carmen			Spain				x

1. No reviews have been found and there is no indication on the programme of plot or characters. It did, however, use special electrical effects.

APPENDIX IV

BALLETS AT THE EMPIRE 1884-1915: SUBJECT MATTER

	Supernatural	Natural	International	Historical	Topical General	Topical Patriotic	Romance
1884							
Coppelia	x		Central Europe				x
Giselle	x		Bavaria				x
1887							
Dilara			The East				
The Sports of England					x		
1888							
Robert Macaire[1]							
Rose d'Amour		x	Hungary				
Diana	x		Ancient Greece				
1889							
A Duel in the Snow		Paris		x		x	
Cleopatra			Eygpt				
The Paris Exhibition		Paris		x			
A Dream of Wealth							x
1890							
Cécile			Paris/India	x			x
Dolly	x						
1891							
Orfeo	x		Ancient Greece				
By the Sea					x		
Nisita	x		Albania				
1892							
Versailles			France	x			x
Round the Town					x		
1893							
Katrina	x				x		x
The Girl I Left Behind Me							
1894							
La Frolique			France		x		
On Brighton Pier					x		
1895							
Faust	x		Central Europe				
1896							
La Danse							
Monte Cristo			France	x			
1897							
Under One Flag						x	
1898							
The Press					x		
Alaska			Alaska		x		
1899							
Round the Town Again					x		

APPENDICES

	Supernatural	Natural	International	Historical	Topical General	Topical Patriotic	Romance
1900							
Seaside					x		
1901							
Les Papillions		x					
Old China	x						
1902							
Our Crown						x	
1903							
The Milliner Duchess							x
Vineland		x	various				
1904							
High Jinks					x		
1905							
The Dancing Doll	x						
The Bugle Call			France	x			
1906							
Cinderella	x						
Coppelia		x	Central Europe				
Fête Galante			France				
The Debutante			Paris/the East				x
1907							
Sir Roger de Coverley				x			x
The Belle of the Ball					x		
1908							
The Dryad	x	x					x
A Day in Paris			Paris		x		
1909							
Roberto il Diavolo	x		Central Europe				
Round the World			various				
1910							
The Dancing Master		France	x				
The Faun	x	x	Italy				
Ship Ahoy						x	
1911							
Sylvia	x	x	Ancient Greece				x
New York		New York	x				
1912							
The Water Nymph	x	x					
First Love			Russia	x		x	
1913							
The Reaper's Dream		x					
Titania	x						
1914							
Europe					x		
1915							
The Vine		x					
1915							
Pastorale		x					x

1. *Robert Macaire* was in repertoire for five weeks only; no information has been found as to its subject matter.

Bibliography

'A.S.' 1893, 'At the Empire', *The Sketch*, 7 June p.301
— 1894a, 'The new ballet at the Alhambra', *The Sketch*, 3 October p.557
— 1894b, 'Notes from the music halls', *The Sketch*, 17 October p.624
— 1895, 'The new ballet at the Alhambra', *The Sketch*, 7 August p.77 *Alhambra Artists Engagement Book*, May 1898 - Dec. 1900, Theatre Museum Archives
Amaya, M. 1962, 'The dance in art 6: Spencer Gore at the ballet', *Dance and Dancer* March pp.30-31
anon. 1864 'Royal Alhambra Palace', *The Era*, 25 December p.16
— c.1870, *Intrigues and confessions of a ballet girl*, London: Rozez & Co.
— 1884a, 'Opening of the Empire theatre', *The Era*, 19 April p.11
— 1884b, 'The Alhambra', *The Times*, 23 December p.4
— 1887a, 'The Empire Palace', *The Era*, 24 December p.16
— 1887b, '*Nadia*', *Illustrated Sporting and Dramatic News*, 21 May p.266
— 1888, 'Our captious critic: at the Empire theatre', *Illustrated Sporting and Dramatic News*, 28 April p.198
— 1889, 'Empire theatre', *Daily Telegraph*, 27 September p.3
— 1891a, 'Empire theatre', *The Times*, 1 September p.6
— 1891b, 'The length of a petticoat: interviews with leading dancers', *Daily Graphic*, 14 February p.5
— 1893a, 'How ballets are made: an interview with Mme. Katti Lanner', *Westminster Budget*, 3 March pp. 14-15 (also reproduced in *Dance News* Vol.46: 6 June 1965 pp.10-11
— 1893b, '*Chicago* at the Alhambra', *The Sketch*, 5 April p.575
— 1894, 'Statement by Mrs. Chant', *Daily Telegraph*, 18 October p.3
— 1895a, '*Faust* at the Empire: a chat with Mde. Katti Lanner', *The Sketch*, 24 April p.694
— 1895b, 'Notes from the theatres', *The Sketch*, 25 December p.440
— 1896a, 'The new ballet at the Empire', *The Sketch*, 5 February p.71
— 1896b, '*Rip van Winkle* at the Alhambra', *The Sketch*, 12 August p.87
— 1897a, 'The art of movement: designing for the ballet', *Magazine of Art*, pp.162-164
— 1897b, 'Music', *Illustrated London News*, 29 May p.730
— 1898, '*Beauty and the Beast*', *The Sketch*, 12 January p.490
— 1899a, 'Our captious critic: the Empire', *Illustrated Sporting and Dramatic News*, 22 July p.808
— 1899b, *Crissie: a music hall sketch of today*, London: The Alhambra
— 1900, '*The Handy Man* at the Alhambra', *Illustrated London News*, 29 September p.439
— 1902a, Unreferenced source, 26 April, Theatre Museum, London
— 1902b, Unreferenced source, March, Theatre Museum, London
— 1903, '*The Devil's Forge* at the Alhambra', *The Sketch*, 14 January p.478
— 1904a, Unreferenced source, 3 September, Theatre Museum, London
— 1904b, 'New Alhambra ballet: fascination of the familiar', *Morning Advertiser*, 22 January p.4
— 1910, 'The Empire'. *The Stage*, 13 October p.14
— 1911, Photograph, '*Sylvia*', *The Sketch*, 12 July p.4 (Supplement)
— 1913, *Confessions of a dancing girl by Herself*, London: Heath, Cranton & Ouseley
— 1932, 'Empire memories', *Dancing Times*, June p.267

Anstey, F. 1890, 'London music halls', *Harpers New Monthly Magazine* December pp. 190-202

Arts Council of Great Britain 1955, *Spencer Frederick Gore 1878-1914*, Exhibition Catalogue

Bailey, P. (ed.), 1986, *Music hall: the business of pleasure*, Milton Keynes: Open University Press

Banes, S. 1998 *Dancing women: female bodies on stage*, London: Routledge

Barker, K.M.D. 1987, 'Dance and the emerging music hall in the provinces', *Dance Research*, Vol.2 Autumn pp. 33-42

Baron, W. 1973, *Sickert*, London: Phaidon Press

Beaumont, C. 1937, *Complete book of ballets* London: Putnam

— 1940, *The Diaghilev Ballet in London*, London: Putnam

Beckson, K. (ed.) 1977, *The memoirs of Arthur Symons: life and art in the 1890s*, Penn State University Press

Bedells, P. undated Mss. 'My dancing years' (published as *My dancing days* 1954) Royal Academy of Dance archives

— 1954, *My dancing days*, London: Phoenix

Beerbohm, M. 1906, 'A note on the ballet', *Saturday Review*, 19 May pp.614-615

Belfort, R. 1902, 'The Empire: an hour at London's smartest hall', *The Playgoer*, July p.236

Bennett, A. [1932], 1971, *Journals*, Harmondsworth: Penguin

Berger, J. 1972, *Ways of seeing*, London: Penguin/British Broadcasting Corporation

Bettany, F.G. 1926, *Stewart Headlam: a biography*, London: Edward Arnold

Bland, L. 1981, 'The domain of the sexual: a response', *Screen Education*, No. 39, Summer pp.56-67

Booth, C. 1902 & 1903, *Life and labour of the people of London*, London: Macmillan

Booth, J.B. 1929, *London town*, London: T. Werner Laurie

Booth, M.R. 1981, *Victorian spectacular theatre 1850-1910*, London: Routledge Kegan Paul

Borgnis, J. 1982, 'The forgotten ballerina: a portrait of Phyllis Bedells', *Dance and Dancers*, May pp.24-27

Bratton, J.S. (ed.) 1986, *Music hall: performance and style*, Milton Keynes: Open University Press

— 1987, 'King of the boys: music hall male impersonators', *Women's Review*, No. 20 June pp.12-14

Browse, L. 1978, *Forain, the painter*, London: Paul Elek

Bull, D. 1998, *Dancing away; a Covent Garden diary*, London: Methuen

Bulley, A. & Whitley, M. 1894, *Women's work*, London: Methuen

Carter, A. 1995, 'Blonde, bewigged and winged with gold: women in the music hall ballet', *Dance Research*, Vol. XIII: 2 pp.28-46

— 1996, 'Over the footlights and under the moon: images of dancers in the ballet at the Alhambra and Empire palaces of varieties 1884 – 1915', *Dance Research Journal*, Vol.28: 1 pp.7-18

— 1999, 'Dying swans or sitting ducks: a critical reflection on feminist gazes at ballet', *Performance Research*, Vol.4: 3 pp.91-98

— 2003, 'Webs of identity, webs of heritage', *Dance history on Shannon's shore*, Proceedings of the Society of Dance History Scholars 26th Annual Conference, Limerick. Pub USA : Society of Dance History Scholars

— (ed.) 2004, *Rethinking dance history: a reader*, London: Routledge

Casteras, S.P. 1982, *The substance or the shadow: images of Victorian womanhood*, New Haven: Yale Centre for British Art

Chant, L. Ormiston 1883, 'Speech at the Annual Meeting of the Social Purity Alliance', 13 June, *Tracts 1883-5*, British Library

— 1895, *Why we attacked the Empire*, London: Horace Marshall
Chazin-Bennahum, J. 2004, 'A longing for perfection' in Carter, A. *Rethinking dance history: a Reader*, London: Routledge
Cheshire, D.F. 1974, *Music hall in Britain*, Newton Abbot: David & Charles
Churchill, W. 1930, *My early life*, London: Thornton Butterworth
Clarke, M. & Crisp, C. 1978, *Ballet in art: from the Renaissance to the present*, London: Ash & Grant
— 1981, *The history of dance*, London: Orbis
Clarke, M. & Vaughan, D. (eds) 1977, *The encyclopedia of dance and ballet*, London: Pitman
Cochran, C.B. 1945, *Showman looks on*, London: J.M. Dent
Colls, R. (ed.) 1988, *Feminism and women's history: an introduction*, Leicester: University of Leicester Dept. of Education
Cornell, C. 1887, 'I haven't told the missus up to now', London: Francis Bros. & Day
Daly, A. 1987/8, 'Classical ballet: a discourse of difference', *Women and Performance* Vol. 3:2 pp. 57-66
— 1995, *Done into dance: Isadora Duncan in America*, Bloomington: Indiana University Press
Davis, T.C. 1989, 'The actress in Victorian pornography', *Theatre Journal*, Vol. 41 October
— 1991, *Actresses as working women: their social identity in Victorian culture*, London: Routledge
de Valois, N. 1959, *Come dance with me*, London: Hamish Hamilton
Dictionary of National Biography, London 1896 - 1970 Various volumes
Dijkstra, B. 1986, *Idols of perversity: fantasies of feminine evil in fin de siècle culture* Oxford: Oxford University Press
Disher, M. Willson 1938, *Winkles and champagne; comedies and tragedies of the music hall*, Bath: Cedric Chivers
Donahue, J. 1987, 'The Empire Theatre of Varieties licensing controversy of 1894: Testimony of Ormiston Chant before the Theatres and Music Halls Licensing Committee', *Nineteenth Century Theatre*, Vol.15 Summer pp.50-60
Drabble, M. 1985, *The Oxford Companion to English Literature*, Oxford: Oxford University Press
Dunn, J. 1990, *A Very Close Conspiracy: Vanessa Bell and Virginia Woolf*, London: Jonathan Cape
'E.F-S.' 1893, 'A chat with Signorina Legnani', *The Sketch*, 26 April p.761
Ellman, R. 1988, *Oscar Wilde*, London: Penguin
Empire Theatre, undated *List of productions and events 1887-1915*, (London: Royal Academy of Dance archives)
Empire Theatrical Souvenirs, 1906, February (Theatre Museum, London)
English, R. 1980, 'Alas alack: the representation of the ballerina', *New Dance*, No. 15 Summer pp.18-19
Englishwoman's Review (The): a journal of woman's work, London 1870 – 1910, Vols. 1-21
Espinoza, E. c.1946, *And then he danced*, London: Sampson Low, Marston
— 1947, 'A forgotten dancer: Emma Palladino', *Ballet*, Vol.3: 1 p.17
Findon, B.W. 1911, 'The classical ballet: a fairyland of fair women', *The Play Pictorial* Vol. XVIII June pp.74-75
Fisher, H. 1954, *The story of Sadlers Wells ballet*, London: A. & C. Black
Fletcher, I. 1960, 'Explorations and recoveries II: Symons, Yeats and the demonic dance' *London Magazine*, Vol. 7: 6 pp.46-60
Flitch, J.E.C. 1912, *Modern dancing and dancers*, London: Grant Richards

Fokine, M. 1914, *The Times*, 6 July
Fonteyn, M. 1980, *The magic of dance*, London: British Broadcasting Corporation
Foulkes, 1997, *Church and stage in Victorian England*, Cambridge; Cambridge University Press
Gadan, F. & Malliard, R. (eds) 1959, *A dictionary of modern ballet*, London: Methuen
Gammond, P. 1983, *The Good Old Days song book*, Essex: EMI Music Publishing
Garafola, L. 1985/1986, 'The travesty dancer in nineteenth century ballet', *Dance Research Journal*, Vol. 17:2/Vol.18:1 Fall/Spring pp.35-40
— 1989, *Diaghilev's Ballets Russes*, Oxford: Oxford University Press
Genné, B. 1995, 'Openly English: Phyllis Bedells and the birth of British ballet', *Dance Chronicle*, Vol. 18: 3 pp.437-451
Gibson, J. (ed.) 1976, *The complete poems of Thomas Hardy*, London: Macmillan
Glover, J. 1913, *Jimmy Glover and his friends*, London: Chatto & Windus
Golsworthy, A. 1902, 'At the Alhambra', *The Tatler*, 10 December p.410
Green, B. (ed.) 1986, *The last empires: a music hall companion*, London: Pavilion
Grove, L. 1895, *Badminton library of sports & pastimes: Dancing*, London: Longmans, Green
Groves dictionary of music and musicians, (1878, 1904, 1927, 1940, 1954) 1980, London: Macmillan
Guest I. 1954, *The romantic ballet in England*, London: Pitman
— 1958, *Adeline Genée: a lifetime of ballet under six reigns*, London: A. & C. Black
— 1959, 'The Alhambra ballet', *Dance Perspectives*, No.4 New York
— 1962, *The Empire ballet*, London: Society for Theatre Research
— 1992, *Ballet in Leicester Square*, London: Dance Books
Hanna, J.L. 1988, *Dance, sex and gender*, London: University of Chicago Press
Harrison, F. 1979, *The dark angel: aspects of Victorian sexuality*, London: Fontana
Haskell, A. 1934, *Balletomania*, London: Victor Gollancz
— 1938, *Ballet*, Harmondsworth: Pelican
— 1950, *Going to the ballet*, Harmondsworth: Penguin
— (ed.) 1957, *Ballet Annual*, Vol.11 London: A. & C. Black
— (ed.) 1960, *Ballet Annual*, Vol.14 London: A. & C. Black
— 1972, *Balletomane at large: an autobiography*, London: Heinemann
— & Richardson, P.J.S. (eds) 1932, *Who's who in dancing*, London: Dancing Times
Headlam, S. 1886, 'The moral ministry of the ballet', *The Stage*, 16 July pp.17-18
— 1888, (ed.) *The theory of theatrical dancing*, London: Frederick Verinder
Hibbert, H.G. 1916, *Fifty years of a Londoner's life*, London: Grant Richards
High, D. 1985, *1884-1984 The first 100 years: the story of the Empire, Leicester Square*, Surrey: David High
Hockey, S. (now Alexandra Carter) 1983, 'Adeline Genée: a choreochronicle', University of Surrey MA unpublished course work
Holledge, J. 1981, *Innocent flowers: women in the Edwardian theatre*, London: Virago
Holroyd, M. 1988, *Bernard Shaw Vol. I 1856-1896 The search for love*, London: Chatto & Windus
Houghton, W.E. 1957, *The Victorian frame of mind, 1830-1870*, New Haven: Yale University Press
Howard, D. 1970, *London theatres and music halls, 1850-1950*, London: Library Association
Howlett, J. undated (after 1935) *Talking of ballet*, London: Philip Allan
Hunt, B. (ed.) 1906, *Green Room book*, London: T. Sealey Clark
Husbands, C. 1996, *What is history teaching? Language, ideas and meaning in learning about the past*, Bucks: Open University Press

Hutcheon, L. 1989, *The politics of postmodernism*, London: Routledge
'I' 1913, 'The Russian ballet', *New Statesman*, 5 July pp.406-407
Image, S. 1901, 'Butterflies at the Empire', *Saturday Review*, 13 April pp.465-466
'J.M.B.' 1896, 'An earthly paradise', *The Sketch*, 1 January p.524
Jack-in-the-Box 1895, *Illustrated Bits*, Supplement 8 June (no page nos.)
Jackson, H. [1913] 1931, *The eighteen nineties: a review of art and ideas at the close of the nineteenth century*, London: Jonathan Cape
Jowitt, D. 1984, 'The return of drama - a post-modern strategy?' *Dance Theatre Journal*, Vol. 2: 2 pp.28-31
— 1988, *Time and the dancing image*, Berkeley: University of California Press
Kendall, E. 1979, *Where she danced*, New York: Alfred A. Knopf
Kermode, F. 1962, *Puzzles and epiphanies: essays and reviews 1958-61*, London: Routledge & Kegan Paul
Kift, D. 1996, *The Victorian music hall: culture, class and conflict*, Cambridge: Cambridge University Press
Kinkead-Weekes, M. 1992, 'D.H. Lawrence and the dance', *Dance Research*, Vol.X: 1 Spring pp.59-77
Kirstein, L. 1971, *Movement and metaphor: four centuries of ballet*, London: Pitman
Koegler, H. 1987, *Concise Oxford dictionary of ballet*, Oxford: Oxford University Press
Koritz, A. 1990, 'Moving violations: dance in the London music hall 1890-1910', *Theatre Journal*, December Vol.21 pp.419-431
Kraus, R. 1969, *History of the dance in art and education*, New Jersey: Prentice Hall
Kyasht, L. [1929], 1978, *Romantic Recollections*, London: Brentano
LCC/MIN/10,769, 14 October 1889, London Metropolitan Archives (formerly Greater London Records Office)
LCC/MIN/10,769, 5 December 1891, London Metropolitan Archives (formerly Greater London Records Office)
LCC/MIN/10,803, 10 October 1894, London Metropolitan Archives (formerly Greater London Records Office)
LCC/MIN/10,803, 13 October 1894, London Metropolitan Archives (formerly Greater London Records Office)
LCC/MIN/10,803, 15 October 1894, London Metropolitan Archives (formerly Greater London Records Office)
LCC/MIN/10,803, 16 October 1894, London Metropolitan Archives (formerly Greater London Records Office)
LCC/MIN/10,769 5 January 1899, London Metropolitan Archives (formerly Greater London Records Office)
LCC/MIN/10,770 17 September 1906, London Metropolitan Archives (formerly Greater London Records Office)
LCC/MIN/10,770 5 August 1911, London Metropolitan Archives (formerly Greater London Records Office)
LCC/MIN/10,770 6 January 1912, London Metropolitan Archives (formerly Greater London Records Office)
'L.H.A.' 1893, 'Mdlle. Vanda Adler', *The Sketch*,13 December p.374
Laurence, D.H. (ed.) 1981a, *Shaw's music*, Vol.I 1876-1890, London: Bodley Head
— 1981b, *Shaw's music*, Vol.II 1890-1893
— 1981c, *Shaw's music*, Vol.III 1893-1950
Lawson, J. 1964, *A history of ballet and its makers*, London: Dance Books
Leppington, C.H. d'E. 1891, 'The Gibeonites of the stage: work and wages, Behind the scenes', *National Review*, Vol.17 pp.245-261
Leslie, P. 1978, *A hard act to follow: a music hall review*, New York: Paddington Press

Lynham, D. 1947, *Ballet then and now*, London: Sylvan Press
'M.L.C.' 1893, *Westminster Budget*, 19 May pp.24-25
Macauley, R. [1923], 1986, *Told by an idiot*, London: Virago
MacDonald, N. 1977, 'Isadora re-examined: lesser known aspects of the great dancer's life 1877-1900' *Dance Magazine*, Vol. LI: 7 July pp.51-64
Mackenzie, C. [1912], 1929, *Carnival*, London: Martin Secker
— 1936, *Figure of Eight*, London: Cassell
Manchester, P.W. 1946, *Vic-Wells: a ballet progress*, London: Victor Gollancz
Maugham, W. S. 1934, *Liza of Lambeth*, London: Heinemann
'Max' 1898, 'Max, Mr. Archer and others', *Saturday Review*, 15 October pp.498-499
Mayhew, A. 1892, 'The building of the ballet', *The Idler*, August pp.61-69
Mayhew, H. 1862, 'London labour and the London poor', Vol.4 (reproduced in Quennell, P. (ed.) undated *London's Underworld*, London: Spring Books)
Meredith, G. (1859), 1962, *The ordeal of Richard Feveral*, London: J.M. Dent
Millett, K. 1971, *Sexual politics*, London: Sphere Books
'Monocle' 1894, 'Notes from the theatres', *The Sketch*, 30 May p.258
Morton, W.H. & Newton, H.C. 1905, *Sixty years stage service*, London: Gale and Polden
Musée Marmottan, Paris 1978, *Jean-Louis Forain*, Paris
Nead, L. 1988, *Myths of sexuality: representations of women in Victorian Britain*, Oxford: Basil Blackwell
Noble, P. c.1949, *British ballet*, London: Skelton Robinson
Palladino, E. 1891, Letter to the *Daily Telegraph*, 20 April
Pearsall, R. (1969), 1983, *The worm in the bud: the world of Victorian sexuality*, London: Penguin
Percival, J. 1994, 'The Sleeping Beauty', *Dance Now*, Vol.3:4 p.5
Perugini, M.E. 1915a, *The art of ballet*, London: Martin Secker
— 1915b, 'The story of the Alhambra', *Dancing Times*, February pp.166-169
— 1915c, 'The story of the Alhambra', *Dancing Times*, March pp.199-202
— 1915d, 'The story of the Alhambra', *Dancing Times*, May pp.273-276
— 1915e, 'The story of the Alhambra', *Dancing Times*, June pp.303-304
— 1925a, 'Where are we going?', *Dancing Times*, August pp.1171-1177
— 1925b, 'Where are we going?', *Dancing Times*, September pp.1245-1251
— 1925c, 'Where are we going?', *Dancing Times*, October pp.37-41
— [1935] 1946, *A pageant of the dance and ballet*, London: Jarrolds
Priddin, D. 1952, *The art of the dance in French literature*, London: A. & C. Black
Pritchard, J. 1995, 'The Empire in Manchester', *Dance Research*, Vol. XIII: 2 pp.11-27
Ralph, R. 1984, 'Stewart Headlam - the dancing priest', *About the house: the magazine of the Friends of Covent Garden*, Vol.7: 1 Xmas pp.56-61
Reyna, F. 1964, *Concise history of ballet*, London: Thames & Hudson
'S' 1898, 'How a ballet is designed: The Press, ballet at the Empire Theatre', *Magazine of Art*, Vol.22 pp. 371-377
'S.L.B.' 1896a, 'Behind the scenes II: The Empire', *The Sketch*, 1 January pp.523-524
— 1896b, '*The Tzigane* at the Alhambra', *The Sketch*, 23 December p.336
— 1899a, 'Mde. Cavallazzi bids goodbye to the Empire', *The Sketch*, 15 February p.173
— 1899b, 'Military display at the Alhambra', *The Sketch*, 20 December p.348
— 1901, 'The evolution of a dancer', *The Sketch*, 13 March p.318
Sackville West, V. [1930], 1983, *The Edwardians*, London: Virago
St. Johnston, R. 1906, *A history of dancing*, London: Simpkin Marshall
Scanlon, J. & Kerridge, R. 1988, 'Spontaneity and control: the uses of dance in late Romantic Literature', *Dance Research*, Vol.VI: 1 pp.30-44
Scott, H. 1977, *The early doors: origins of the music hall*, Yorkshire: EP Publishing

Shaw, B. 1930, *Immaturity*, London: Constable & Co.
— see Laurence, D.H. 1981a – c
Shires, L.M. 1992, *Rewriting the Victorians*, London: Routledge
Short, E. 1951, *60 years of theatre*, London: Eyre & Spottiswoode
Snitow, A., Stansell, C. & Thompson, S. (eds) 1983, *Powers of desire: the politics of sexuality*, New York: Monthly Review Press
Sorell, W. 1981, *Dance in its time*, New York: Anchor Press
Sorley Walker, K.S. 1947, 'Georges Jacobi and the Alhambra ballet', *Theatre Notebook*, Vol.1: 6 pp. 82-83
— 1987, *Ninette de Valois: idealist without illusions*, London: Hamilton
Stanford, D. 1965, *Poets of the 'nineties: a biographical anthology*, London: John Baker
— 1970, *Critics of the 'nineties*, London: John Baker
Stuart, C.D. & Park, A.J. 1895, *The variety stage: a history of the music halls from the earliest period to the present time*, London: T. Fisher Unwin
Sturgis, M. 1995, *Passionate attitudes: the English decadence of the 1890s*, London: Macmillan
Symons, A.J. 1895, *London nights*, London: Leonard Smithers
— 1896, 'At the Alhambra: impressions and sensations', *The Savoy*, No.5 September pp.75-83
— 1925, *Studies in seven arts*, New York: Dutton
'T.H.L.' 1893, 'A chat with a costumier: Wilhelm at home', *The Sketch*, 8 March pp.343-344
'T.W.R.' 1864, 'Theatrical types no. XI - the *corps de ballet*', *Illustrated Times*, 16 July p.43
Teich, M. & Porter, R. 1990, *Fin de siècle and its legacy*, Cambridge: Cambridge University Press
Tillett, S. 1982, *Victoria and Merrie England*, London: Sir Arthur Sullivan Society
Trudgill, E. 1976, *Madonnas and magdelenes: the origins and development of Victorian sexual attitudes*, London: Heinemann
Wagner, L. 1899, *How to get on the stage and how to succeed there*, London: Chatto & Windus
Waites, B, Bennett, T, Martin, G. (eds) 1982, *Popular culture: past and present*, London: Open University
Walkowitz, J.R. 1992, *City of dreadful delight*, Chicago: University of Chicago Press
Warner, M. 1985, *Monuments and maidens: the allegory of the female form*, London: Picador
Who was who 1897-1960, 1967, Vols. I - V London: A. & C. Black
Who was who in the theatre 1912-1976, 1978, Vols. 1-4 London: Pitman
Williamson, A. 1946, *Contemporary ballet*, London: Rockliff
— 1951, 'Sullivan's ballets', *Dancing Times*, April pp. 394-396; 400
Wilson, A. N. 2002, *The Victorians*, London: Hutchinson
Wilson, G.B.L. [1957, 1961], 1974, *A dictionary of ballet*, London: A. & C. Black
Wolff, J. 1981, *The social production of art*, London: Macmillan
Yeats, W.B. 1955, *Autobiographies*, London: Macmillan

SPECIALIST ARCHIVES AND COLLECTIONS

London Metropolitan Archives, 40 Northampton Road, London EC1R OHB
Mander and Mitchenson Theatre Collection, Jerwood Library of the Performing Arts, Trinity College of Music, King Charles Court, Old Royal Naval College, London, SE10 9JF
Public Record Office, Censuses of England and Wales, London, WC2
Royal Academy of Dance, 48 Vicarage Crescent, London, SW11 31T
Theatre Museum, 1E Tavistock Street, London, WC2E 7PA

Index

(References to illustrations are in **bold**)

actresses, number of 29
Alhambra Theatre 1
  ballet at 14
  ballet masters/mistresses 17-18
  ballets
    artistic collaborators 150-152
    subject matter 157-159
  Ballets Russes 15, 143
  becomes music hall 14
  closure 15
  designers 18
  dress rehearsal **73**
  musical directors 17-18
  programme covers **76-78**
  School of Dancing 35
Alias, Mons. & Mde. 18
Allan, Maud 87
Anstey, F. 9, 13-14, 22, 31, 52
arts, decadence in 107
Association of Operatic Dancing 139
audiences
  ballet 20-24
  English ballet 142-145

Baker, Josephine 1
ballet
  at Alhambra Theatre 14
  Arnold Bennett on 99-100
  audiences 20-24
  in British theatres 13-14
  commercial considerations 19-20
  costumes 12
  at Empire Theatre 15-16
  garden themes 83
  iconography 122
  international exoticism 85-86
  management 19-20
  moral image 108-112
  narrative 49-50
  New Woman, absence 88
  novels about 100-102
  personification 89-90
  poems about 96-99, 105 n.5
  popularity 12, 20-21
  Romantic era 12-13
  royal patronage 22
  social dances 53
  songs about 102-103
  subject matter, changes 12
  themes 81-82
    imperial 81, 87
    nature 83-85
    pastoral 83-84
    romance 90-93
    supernatural 82-83
    topical 86-89
  see also English ballet; music hall ballet
Ballet Annual 35
ballet companies, hierarchy 30-38
  corps 31
  danseurs 30
  danseuses 30
  principals 30
ballet dancers 30-38
  body shape 59-60
  costume 57, 58-59
  female, representations 121-123
  feminisation 59-63
  male 33, 34-35, 36, 64
  moral image 112-125, 144-145
  physical image 59-63
  as scenery 84
  training 33
  wages 41-43
  working conditions 43-46
ballet dancing
  as British women's career 30
  schools 39-40
  vocabulary 51, 53, 92
ballet masters/mistresses
  Alhambra Theatre 17-18
  Empire Theatre 17-18
ballet writers 5 n.2
ballets
  1830 152

Aladdin 32, 82, 150, 157
Alaska 82, 87, 154, 16
Algeria, 58, 94 n.10, 150, 157
Ali Baba and the Forty Thieves 82, 151, 157
All the Year Round 89, 151, 158
L'Amour 109, 152, 158
Antiope 64, 93 n.5, 150, 157
Asmodeus 150, 157
Astraea 70 n.13, 150, 157
Beauty and the Beast 151, 158
Belle of the Ball 155, 161
Le Bivouac 157
Bluebeard 88, 151, 158
Britannia's Realm 90, 151, 158
The Bugle Call 64, 155, 161
By the Sea 50, 58, 87, 153, 160
Carmen 64, 91, 151, 152, 158, 159
Cecile 94 n.10, 153, 160
Chicago 87, 150, 157
Chilperic 15
Cinderella 35, 36, 82, 155, 161
Cleopatra 88, 153, 160
Les Cloches de Corneville 152, 158
Coppélia 15, 40, 138, 153, 155, 160, 161
Cupid 150, 157
Cupid Wins 152, 159
The Dance Dream 93 n.5, 152, 159
The Dancing Doll 141, 155, 161
The Dancing Master 34, 54, 59, 85, 155, 161
La Danse 21, 154, 160
A Day Off 151, 158
A Day in Paris 36, 85, 155, 161
The Debutante 90, 93 n.7, 155, 161
The Devil's Forge 151, 158
Diana 35, 50, 83, 153, 160
Dilara 15, 70 n.10, 85, 93 n.5, 153, 160
Dolly 153, 160
Don Juan 91, 92, 141, 150, 157
Don Quixote 150, 157
Donnybrook 151, 158
A Dream of Wealth 153, 160
Dresdina 150, 157
The Dryad 31, 155, 161
The Duel in the Snow 41, 153, 160
Electra 152, 158
Enchantment 53, 64, 150, 157
Entente Cordiale 64, 81, 89, 90, 152, 158
Europe 156, 161
Excelsior 86
Façade 140
The Faun 83, 92, 155, 161
Faust 37, 66, 67, 70 n.12, 83, 98, 99, 140, 154, 160
Femina 61, 90, 93 n.5, 120, 152, 159
Fête Galante 83, 85, 155, 161
Fidelia 150, 157
First Love 156, 161
La Frolique 58, 61, 109, 110, 154, 160
The Gathering of the Clans 158
The Gay City 85, 151, 158
The Girl I Left Behind Me 58, 90, 93 n.7, 109, 154, 160
Giselle 1, 15, 32, 92, 141, 153, 160
Gretna Green 151, 158
The Handy Man 69 n.3, 93 n.5, 151, 158
High Jinks 88, 155, 161
Hurly Burly 149
Ideala 150, 157
In Japan 85, 151, 158
Inspiration 89, 151, 158
Irene 150, 157
Jack Ashore 151, 158
Job 141
Katrina 154, 160
Lucertio 152, 158
The Mad Pierrot 152, 159
Melusine 64, 150, 157
The Milliner Duchess 94 n.11, 155, 161
Monte Cristo 21, 154, 160
My Lady Nicotine 152, 158
Nadia 94 n.10, 150, 157
Napoli 151, 158
Narcisse 83, 152, 159
New York 155, 161
Nina the Enchantress 15, 150, 157
Nisita 153, 160
Old China 34, 69 n.6, 154, 161
On Brighton Pier 66, 87, 88, 148, 154, 160
On the Heath 88, 148, 152, 159
On the Ice 150, 157
On the Sands 87, 152, 159
On the Square 152, 159
Orfeo 70 n.18, 91, 153, 160

INDEX

Oriella 109, 150, 157
Our Army and Navy 69 n.8, 87, 141, 150, 157
Our Crown 87, 155, 161
Our Flag 87, 152, 159
Les Papillons 36, 84, 154, 161
Paquita 35, 152, 159
The Paris Exhibition 153, 160
Parisiana 71 n.22, 152, 158
Pastorale 156, 161
La Petite Bohémienne 148
Petrushka 70 n.11
The Polar Star 152, 159
The Pool 148
The Press 81, 87, 154, 160
Prince Igor 49
Psyche 83, 152, 159
Queen of Spades 152, 158
The Rake's Progress 140
The Reaper's Dream 84, 89, 156, 161
The Red Shoes 70 n.17, 151, 158
Le Rêve 152, 158
Revolt of the Daughters 150, 157
Rip van Winkle 151, 158
Robert Macaire 153, 160
Roberto il Diavolo 54, 94 n.12, 155, 161
Rose d'Amour 82, 83, 84, 153, 160
Round the Town 65, 154, 160
Round the Town Again 57, 154, 160
Round the World 87, 141, 155, 161
Sal! Oh! My! 1, 33, 87, 91, 152, 159
Salandra 85, 93 n.7, 150, 157
Santa Claus 151, 158
Seaside 154, 161
The Seasons 150, 157
Ship Ahoy 161
Sir Roger de Coverley 83, 155, 161
Sita 89, 93 n.7, 157
The Sleeping Beauty 32, 34, 93 nn. 3 and 7, 94 n.13, 141, 150, 157
The Sleeping Princess 15, 138
Soldiers of the King 87, 151, 158
Soldiers of the Queen 71 n.28, 87, 151, 158
Le Spectre de la Rose 93 n.3
The Sports of England 15, 65, 87, 88, 141, 153, 160
Swan Lake 32, 93 n.7
The Swans 64, 150, 157
La Sylphide 1
Sylvia 83, 155, 161
Temptation 150, 157
Titania 53, 67, **75**, **79**, 83, 84, 151, 156, 158, 161
The Two Flags 152, 159
The Tzigane 85, 151, 158
Under One Flag 58, 87, 154, 160
Up the River 150, 157
Versailles 83, 85, 153, 160
Victoria and Merrie England 22, 151, 158
The Vine 156, 161
Vineland 155, 161
The Water Nymph 83, 156, 161
Zanetta 94 n.10, 150, 157
Ballets Russes 14, 20, 23, 116, 143
    at Alhambra Theatre 15, 143
    at Empire Theatre 143
Banbury, Emily 43
Barker, K.M.D. 12
Barrie, J.M. 99, 139
Bedells, Phyllis 15, 17, 22, 24, 32, 37, 38, 40, 44, 60, 117-118, 118-119, 120, 138, 139
Beerbohm, M. 61, 67
Belfort, R. 20, 21
Bennett, Arnold 99-100
Bensusan, S.L. 18, 50, 52, 54, 60, 98
Beretta, Caterina 32
Berger, J. 52
Bertrand 15, 17
Bessone, Emma 32
Bettany, F.G. 112
Bishop, Will 20, 35, 36, 141
body shape, ballet dancers 59-60
Boer War (1899-1902) 11
Bolm, Adolphe 34
Booth, Charles, *Life and labour of the people of London* 115-116
Booth, J.B. 11, 21, 22, 23, 25, 40, 45, 60, 113, 119
Bournonville, August 16
Bratton, J.S. 67
Brianza, Carlotta 32
Bright, Dora 18
Bull, Deborah 138

Camargo Society 32, 140, 143
can-can 1, 49
Casati, Eugenio 14, 17
Casteras, Susan 90

Cavallazzi, Malvina 15, 23, 35, 64, 139
Cechetti, Enrico 34, 83
Cerri, Cecilia 99
Chant, Laura Ormiston 24-25, 57-58, 117
    morality campaigns 107-111, 125 n.4
    Why we attacked the Empire 110
choreographer, role of 16
Churchill, Winston 25
Clerc, Elise 14, 35, 88
Cochran, C.B. 36
Collier, Beatrice 35-36
Collier, Daisy 36
Collins, Cleo 38
Collins, Lottie 9
    'Ta-ra-ra-boom-de-ay' 1
Confessions 117
Copeland Smith, C., Rev. 109
Coppi, Carlo 14, 17, 20, 30, 39, 139
Cormani, Lucia 14, 139
corps de ballet 37-38, 46, 53-56
    functions 56
    morality 117-118
    movements 55-56
    pointe work 54-55
    shoes 53
    as spectacle 57
    vocabulary 54
costume
    ballet dancers 57, 58-59
    cross-dressing 65-66
    première danseuse 59
Covent Garden Theatre 13
Craske, Dorothy 35, 143
Crissie (novel) 102
cross-dressers 63-69
    costume 65-66
    eroticism 66-68
    and masculinity 68
    representations 122
Curti, Alfredo 14, 17

Daily Mail 81
dance
    history 4
    and ideology 121
    Italian technique 139
    moral prejudice against 26, 108
dancers *see* ballet dancers
Darwinism 11
Davis, T.C. 66, 67

de Valois, Ninette 3, 35, 39, 54, 139
    in commercial theatre 141, 143
    establishes Vic-Wells ballet 138
    production skills 141
decadence, in the arts 107
designers
    Alhambra Theatre 18
    Empire Theatre 18
Diaghilev, Sergei
    Ballets Russes 1, 32, 143
    The Sleeping Princess 15, 138
Didelot, Charles 140
Dijkstra, B. 84, 90, 95, 108
Dowson, Ernest 96
Duncan, Isadora 60

Edward VII 11
Edwardes, Hilda 36
Edwards, George 91
Ellis, Havelock 107
Empire Theatre 2
    ballet at 15-16
    ballet masters/mistresses 17-18
    ballets
        artistic collaborators 153-156
        subject matter 160-161
    Ballets Russes 143
    as club 21-22
    designers 18
    homosexuals, meeting place 22
    musical directors 17-18
    promenade 21-22, **73**
en pointe 51, 54-55
English ballet
    audiences 142-145
    identity issues 137, 139-140, 144
    indigenousness 138-140
    influences 137-138
    music hall origins 137-138, 142-143
    production 141-142
    repertoire 140-141
The Englishwomen's Review 29-30
The Era 15
eroticism, cross-dressing 66-68
Espinoza, Edouard 17, 34, 50, 139
Espinoza, Leon 17, 39

Farren, Fred 17, 27 n.12, 34, 35, 36, 141
feminisation, ballet dancers 59-63
Festival of Britain (1951) 139
Flitch, J.E.C. 12, 23, 32, 39, 53, 55

Fokine, Michel 17, 49, 50, 140
Folies Bergère 7
Freud, Sigmund 107
Fuller, Loïe 1, 49

Garafola, Lynn 20, 23, 49, 63, 67-68, 116-117
garden themes, ballet 83
Genée, Adeline 14, 15, 17, 18, 22, 23, 34, 64, 90, 120, 139
    career 31-32
    dressing room 43
    wages 41
Genée, Alexander 17, 31, 40
Gilbert, W.S. 115
Gissing, George, *The odd women* 88
Gore, Frederick Spencer 143
    The Alhambra 102
Grey, Lytton 91
Grove, L. 114
Guerrero 53
Guest, I. 42

Hanna, J.L. 116
Hansen, Joseph 13, 14
Hardy, Thomas, 'The Ballet' 37, 99
Haskell, A. 23, 138-139, 140, 142, 143
Headlam, Stewart, Rev. 38-39, 96
    campaign for ballet dancers 111-112, 118
Helpman, Robert 140, 141
Her Majesty's Theatre 12
Hibbert, H.G. 40-41, 42-43, 45, 115
Hill, Jennie 9, 82
historian, role of 3-4
Hitchens, H.J. 19
Holroyd, Michael 100
homosexuals, meeting place, Empire Theatre 22
Houghton, W.E., *The Victorian frame of mind* 10
Husbands, C. 3

iconography, ballet 122
identity issues, English ballet 137, 139-140, 144
ideology, and dance 121
Illustrated Sporting and Dramatic News 34
imperial themes, ballet 81, 87
International Academy of Dancing 40

Italy 32

Jackson, H. 98
Jacobi, Georges 14, 17-18, 19, 34, 86-87
Jowitt, D. 142

Kerridge, R. 98
King's Theatre (Her Majesty's) 1
Kyasht, Lydia 15, 17, 22, 24, 32, 34, 117, 120, 138
    illustration **75**
    wages 41
    workload 44-5

La Scala 32
Lanner, Katti 15, 16, 20, 38, 139, 140
Lauri, Charles 37
Lawson, J. 138
Lawton, Frank 36
Legnani, Pierina 32
Leno, Dan 82
Lloyd, Marie 9
    wages 41
Loftus, Marie 82
London County Council, entertainment licences 109, 110, 113-114

Mackenzie, Compton 5, 39-40, 43, 124
    Carnival 101
    Figure of eight 101
Manchester, People's Music Hall 13
Manchester, P.W. 140
Mapleson, Col 39
Martell, Flo 35, 64
masculinity, and cross-dressers 68
Mayhew, A. 18, 30, 44
mime 35, 49, 65
moral image
    ballet 108-112
    ballet dancers 112-125, 144-145
morality
    campaigns, and the music hall 107-112
    corps de ballet 117-118
    première danseuse 120
More, Unity 36, 37, 39
Moreton, Charles 8
Moreton, Ursula 35, 139
Mossetti, Carlotta 35
music hall
    acts 7

as allegory 97
British, French, compared 7-8
dance 12
and English ballet origins 137-138, 142-143
literary interest 95-96
meaning 7
and morality campaigns 107-112
origins 8, 24, 142
popularity 9-10
and prostitution 22, 24-25, 107, 109, 110, 121
reputation 24
music hall ballet 12-14
character roles 35-36
literary neglect 26
training 38-41
musical directors
Alhambra Theatre 17-18
Empire Theatre 17-18

National Training School of Dancing 39
nature themes, ballet 83-85
New Woman, absence from ballet themes 88
New York Metropolitan Opera House 35
Nijinsky, Vaslav 49
novels, about the ballet 100-102

Oh, the Fairies (song) 103
opera 13
Osmond, Lizzie 60
Oxford Music Hall (London) 107

Palladino, Emma 59, 69 n.4, 139
pantomime 13
Park, A.J. 8, 21
pastoral themes, ballet 83-84
Pavlova, Anna 32
Percival, J. 138
Perrot, Jules 12
personification, ballet 89-90
Pertoldi, Erminia 59, 100
Perugini, M.E. 12, 17, 18, 23, 25, 26, 30, 40, 42, 60, 138, 143
Petipa, Marius 13, 32, 140, 142
physical image, ballet dancers 59-63
pirouette 51
Pitcher, William *see* Wilhelm C.
Pitteri, Giovannina 59
poems, about the ballet 96-99, 105 n.5

première danseuse 50-53
costume 59
frontal stance 52
morality 120
pointe work 51
prostitution, and the music hall 22, 24-25, 107, 109, 110, 121

Rambert, Marie 3, 139
Reeve, Julia 90
Rhymers Club 96, 104 n.3
Ritchie, Ewing 11, 113, 114
romance themes, ballet 90-93
Rosa, Madame 139
Royal Academy of Dancing (Dance) 32, 139
Russian ballet *see* Ballets Russes
Russian Imperial Ballet 32

St Denis, Ruth 1
St Petersburg 32
Santini, Amadeo 34, 64, 91
The Savoy 96-97, 98
Scanlon, J. 98
scenery, ballet dancers as 84
schools, ballet dancing 39-40
Searle, Julia 35, 64
sexuality, women 4, 5, 124-125
Seymour, Kate 30
Shaw, George Bernard 34, 50, 51, 55, 59, 69 n.5, 111, 143
Immaturity 100
Shires, L.M. 2
The Sketch 32, 96
Slack, Edith 35, 90
Slater, Dundas 20
social dances, ballet 53
Social Purity Alliance 110
Somerset Maugham, W., *Lisa of Lambeth* 21
songs, about the ballet 102-103
Sorell, W. 11, 23, 95
The Stage 111
The Star 96
Storey, Fred 36
Strange, Frederick 14
Stuart, C.D. 8, 21
Sundberg, Paul 34, 91
wages 41-42
supernatural themes, ballet 82-83
Symons, Arthur 23, 54, 62, 65, 83, 143

poems, on the ballet 96-98
Rhymers Club 96
works
   'At the Stage Door' 97
   'Behind the Scenes: Empire' 46, 98
   London nights 97
   'On the Stage' 97
   'Prologue' 97
   'The World as Ballet' 97
   'To a Dancer' 97

Taglioni, Paul 16
Tiller Girls 12
Tilley, Vesta 9, 64
The Times 82
Tivoli Music Hall 9
Tranders, Cara 125
   reminiscences 129-135
travesty performers *see* cross-dressers

Vance, Alfred 13
vaudeville 7
Vaughan, Kate 30
Verlaine, Paul 95
Vic-Wells ballet 140
   foundation 137, 138
   see also Sadlers Wells

Victoria, Queen 10, 11
Victorianism, longevity 10-11
Vincenti, Vittorio de 34, 91
vocabulary
   ballet dancing 51, 53, 92
   corps de ballet 54
Volbert 64

wages, ballet dancers 41-43
Wagner, L. 119
Walls, Tom 36
Warner, M 90
Wenzel, Leopold 15, 18
Westminster Budget magazine 44
Wilde, Oscar 111
Wilhelm, C. (William Pitcher) 15, 18, 142
Wolff, Janet 16
women
   bodies, male appropriation 124-125
   employment opportunities 29-30
   and portrayal of virtue 90
   separate spheres 124
   sexuality 4, 5, 124-125
working conditions, ballet dancers 43-46

Zanfretta, Francesca 35, 37, 64, 66, 120, 139